THE ARCHITECTS OF AMERICA

THE ARCHITECTS OF AMERICA

HOW THE FREEMASONS DESIGNED THE REPUBLIC

RUSSELL CHARLES BLACKWELL

Algora Publishing
New York

Library of Congress Cataloging-in-Publication Data —

Blackwell, Russell.
    The architects of America: How the freemasons designed the republic / Russell
Charles Blackwell.
        p. cm.
    Includes bibliographical references and index.
    ISBN 978-0-87586-906-3 (soft cover: alk. paper)—ISBN 978-0-87586-907-0 (hbk.: alk.
paper)—ISBN 978-0-87586-908-7 (ebook: alk. paper) 1. Freemasonry—United States—
History. 2. Freemasonry—Symbolism 3. Freemasonry—Rituals. 4. Architecture—United
States—History. 5. United States—History. I. Title.
    HS517.B53 2012
    366'.10973—dc23

                            2012001686

Printed in the United States

ACKNOWLEDGEMENTS

A good few people have helped out with this idea, too numerous to mention. In particular, though, I would like to thank Duncan West, Levi Madeley and Maisie and Betsy for their support; Gill Caldecott, Mike Naylor, Mervyn Labweiler and Mum and Dad for proofreading an often incomprehensible manuscript; and Harry Blackwell for sorting out the illustrations.

ARCHITECTURE has its political Use; publick buildings being the Ornament of a Country; it establishes a Nation, draws people and Commerce; makes the People love their native Country which Passion is the Original of all great Actions in a Common-Wealth...Architecture aims at Eternity.

— Sir Christopher Wren, 1632–1723

Table of Contents

INTRODUCTION

Even the Philadelphia climate played a part at the beginning of July, 1776. On the first of the month — a Monday — a thunderstorm illuminated the skyline between four and six in the evening, investing the City with a dramatic touch, whilst on the Tuesday a low note was hit, as the inhabitants found themselves sheltering from showers of rain that lasted from the middle of the morning until two o'clock in the afternoon. On Wednesday, the third of July, however, change was in the air, for the weather started to take on a more reasonable hue. The climate became milder, with a clear sky, something that continued into the next day, Thursday the fourth, when temperatures rose to around seventy-six degrees Fahrenheit, and the wind moved from the north to the southwest as the day wore on.

Apart from serving as an example of how science was starting to tighten up its act during the eighteenth century, thanks for this little bit of knowledge should be given to two amateur meteorologists who noted it in the first place, Messrs. Phineas Pemberton and Thomas Jefferson. Pemberton was a local man, a member of a Quaker family prominent in Philadelphia since William Penn's day, who had kept records on the Pennsylvanian climate since 1748. Jefferson, by contrast, was in the City on business, namely the dissolution of America's connection to the British Empire, an event that, regardless of its magnitude, still didn't con-strain the future president from measuring the temperature twice a day with a thermometer carried around at all times for that exact purpose.

Indeed, science, or its conduct, had already played a pivotal role in the creation of the United States and would continue to play a part. Phineas Pemberton had long been a member of the American Philosophical Society, the Colonies' answer to the Royal Society, founded by Benjamin Franklin as far back as 1743. Franklin, the inventor of the lightning rod and bifocal spectacles, had long realized science could be harnessed for social improvement, and that, if applied correctly, it would provide not only a key but potentially *the* key to the future of America. In this he didn't necessarily have in mind research or application in its narrow sense, leading to new manufactures or sources of power, but more in its widest sense, in that rationalism and reason, when correctly calibrated, could transform the condition of the people themselves.

One essential component of the whole experiment was the relationship of the states to one another, and the collective whole. Reason demanded an element of equality be built in, to ensure as fair an apportionment of power, whilst logic called for a codified set of rights and responsibilities to ensure as perfect a Union as possible. This covered a whole range of innovations, though when it came to the states' territorial definitions, the British had already set in place the methodology by which they would be achieved: not only by surveyors armed with mathematics and measuring equipment, or for that matter politicians, administrators, or geographers, but also the idea that the union would be raised gradually, as circumstance demanded, to incorporate as much reason into the overall structure as possible.

Of course, one kind of inequality that couldn't be entirely rubbed out was the geographical character of each province. A few states were destined to be big, several small; some highly geometric, others irregular. Even bearing this in mind, one item absent from the above inventory was the idea of *planning*, for what few realised at the time was the existence of something else that made the thirteen provinces unique, insomuch as their relationship to one another already illustrated the touch of a deliberate hand. This silent design, inspired by symbolism millennia old, had first started to become evident during the days of the British, who, with a typically Anglo-Saxon cocktail of idealism and self-interest, had hammered a rough but specific, architectural shape onto North America as early as 1733. Even after England and America had parted company, this phenomenon would continue, a thread that runs through the whole history and geography of America, right up to the day the Republic was finally completed in 1959. It was to be a work of science, an example of what people could achieve in combination, and the signature of the men behind it. Stunning in its scope and ambition, this design was destined to leave its mark on and across America in a manner well familiar to men like Benjamin Franklin and George Washington, and for a purpose infinitely more far reaching than the political cartography of one particular country.

PART I. *FOUNDATIONS*

CHAPTER 1. "I Was Made a Freemason..."

> "He is to be a Lover of the Arts and Sciences, and to take
> all Opportunities of improving himself therein."
>
> — Part of a Charge to New Masons, circa 1734

I

"I was made a Freemason at the *Salutation Tavern*, Tavistock Street," scribbled Doctor William Stukeley, "with Mr. Collins and Capt. Rowe, who made the famous Diving Engine..." In this rather terse and uncharacteristically bald sentence, William Stukeley committed his personal experiences of the evening of 6th January, 1721 to his diary. As someone well known across England for floridly chronicling anything that caught his eye, it might be expected that this particular physician, well versed in the importance of good observation and reporting, could have drawn back the curtain on the ceremony that actually took place within the walls of the *Salutation* for the benefit of the future. This necessarily didn't mean the full works, just a whiff of detail, or a touch of drama perhaps; but this he failed to do, save for some supplementary commentary about the poor turnout at this particular Masonic assembly, for barely enough Masons had even bothered to turn out to induct the three newcomers, leading Stukeley to believe, quite wrongly, that he, Collins and Rowe were the first men in years to be "made a mason."

Regardless of the shortcomings of the Doctor's report, the above mixture of straightforward record and absurd conclusion does, however, illustrate something not only of the character of William Stukeley Esquire but also the life and times he lived in. Born on November 7th, 1687, in the town of Holbeach, close to England's east coast, Stukeley came to consciousness in an era when the power of subjectivity and superstition still hadn't buckled in the face of objectivity and science. Britain might be leading the World in terms of intellectual endeavor, but it was still a land of witch trials and religious persecution, a country of self proclaimed "freemen" toiling under an aristocratic and self-regarding polity. This particular mindset could affect anybody, even the Doctor's fellow Lincolnshire man, the great Isaac Newton, who, whilst publishing his seminal work on mechanics, *Principia*, during the year of Stukeley's birth, still found time to dabble in the occult, believing he, along with a few others, had been charged by God to decipher the Bible. Little wonder then that the intellectual chaos of the age was in turn to leave its mark on Stukeley himself, especially when the theories he expounded in his 1730s works *Stonehenge, a Temple Restored to the British Druids* and *Abury, a Temple of the British Druids* would eventually be viewed as ridiculous.

Battered as Stukeley was by competing belief systems, his eye for detail on the road to *Stonehenge* was at least sharpened by academic training considered conventional for the time. Whilst at grammar school, he started making topographical and architectural drawings, augmented with descriptions of historical artifacts and latterly plans of towns and buildings from across Britain, a collection that eventually saw the light of day as his 1724 book *Itinerarium Curiosum*. Going up to Corpus Christi College, Oxford, Stukeley initially studied medicine, and after graduation, he fine tuned his knowledge at Saint Thomas's Hospital, London, experience he used to good effect when he returned to Lincolnshire to practice in 1710. Possibly finding country life a little dull after the excitements of Oxford and the Capital, he was back in London by 1717, the year he was also elected a Fellow of the Royal Society. In 1719 he took his MD, and became a fellow of the Royal College of Physicians twelve months later.

Tending to the physical needs of humanity wasn't the end of Stuke-ley's intellectual odyssey, for the Lincolnshire man now turned his atten-tion to the spiritual, earning, within a decade of his Medical Degree, a doctorate in Theology, which in turn led to his ordination into the Angli-can Church. This was clearly a mind hell-bent on engorging information, so why was it that this particular theologian, archaeologist, but pre-em-inently scientist, heading off to the *Salutation* one freezing January night looking to be initiated into something expressing itself through the sym-bolism of physical labor? Whatever he may have thought lay ahead, it was unlikely the Freemasons were ever going to be of much use in his attempts to decipher Stonehenge, mapping the townscapes of England or analyzing some poor soul's cadaver; though conversely, it must have also crossed his mind, as he strode through chilly London, and eventually turned into Tavistock street, what on earth he, with his already great knowledge of science and scripture, could ever hope to offer *them*.

Naturally, an alternative method of shedding light onto why someone like William Stukeley desired to be "made a Freemason" is, of course, by looking at the other two men initiated that night. Regarding Collins, any attempt at understanding his motivation is, however, well near impossi-ble. Stukeley never committed any helpful references to Collins's identity to his diary, and neither is the man's background or achievements recog-nizable from existing records. This leaves the third man sitting outside the meeting at the *Salutation* to make up the shortfall, and this is Rowe, who thanks to his "Famous Diving Engine" has left behind an imprint on history, and like Stukeley, a scientific imprint to boot.

Rowe's Engine was basically a watertight iron barrel, with holes cut for arms and legs and a small window in front of the face. The idea was the "Engine" enabled the wearer, up to a certain depth, to perform salvage and, in the Captain's own words, "searching a ships bottom and stopping any leake at sea". Apart from epitomizing the go-ahead ethos prevalent in the early eighteenth century, the Diving Engine, if it worked, was of course invaluable to an ocean going nation like Great Britain. Keen to impress everyone, especially the Admiralty, Rowe naturally seized the opportunity, organizing trials during 1720 to show his invention off in the best possible light.

At first, the omens looked good, for the inventor's efforts resulted in a spectacular haul of thirty-three tons of silver being clawed from the hold of the East India Company wreck *Vansittart*. Such stunning success was, however, a false dawn. Despite further dives on shipwrecks, some dating back to the Armada, the "Diving Engine" failed to live up to its original promise, leaving a disillusioned Rowe no alternative but to publish a treatise called *A Demonstration of the Diving Engine* for the benefit and entertainment of a still thrilled and enthusiastic, but baffled, public.

Although neither Stukeley or Rowe could ever hope to match the effect of the great Isaac Newton, today both are remembered, alongside the author of *Principia*, more for their contributions to the enlightenment, the movement towards rationality and scientific progress that occurred during the late seventeenth and early eighteenth centuries. At this time, Britain — and indeed Europe and parts of North America — started to buzz with a new attitude towards science, in all its guises. New discoveries and rediscoveries were changing the way intelligent people looked at the world, which in turn would lead to a transformation of the global human experience in the centuries that followed.

This was the environment that Stukeley and Rowe found themselves in, a world dragging itself out of darkness and into light; a world that indeed demanded their participation. So much needed to be done, in so many areas, without the hindrance of seemingly pointless distractions; so it is all the more perplexing and still a mystery as to why these men, pushing hard at the frontiers of knowledge, on Salisbury Plain and beneath the sea, should be attracted to, and involve themselves in, a fraternal society celebrated for using terminology and symbolism drawn from the solidly mundane world of the building site.

Contrary to Stukeley's belief, however, he, Collins and Rowe weren't the only "enlightened" men being initiated into the Freemasons around this time. Throughout the 1720s, the Order was growing so rapidly in terms of members and Lodges that, some respects, it began to resemble a scaled down version of the nation of which it was a part. This frenetic growth was, of course, a trend that brought together some very strange bedfellows indeed. Take for example the Colonial Secretary and future Prime Minister Thomas Pelham — Holles, who was a "Brother", to "the father of modern boxing" James Figg, one of the most distinguished professional Pugilists and Swordsmen of the 1720s. It's also a fair bet both Pelham-Holles and Figg were familiar with another Masonic Brother, George Shelvocke, Captain of the privateer *Speedwell, who was, in reality,* an adventurer, pirate and author of the 1726 best seller *Voyage Around the World By way of the Great South Seas.* The publication of Shelvocke's experiences also illustrates how tight some Masonic relationships could become, in that it was yet another Mason, the Ludlow born map and globe maker John Senex, who published *Voyage Around the World.*

Outwardly, these Englishmen didn't have much in common. In a deeper sense however, they are a clear illustration of how the early Masonic Order was able to attract people from across the board, a pattern borne out by research into the wider membership of the time. These investigations have been carried out primarily by one historian, W. J. Williams, who has cross-referenced entries in Grand Lodge Minute Books covering 1723 to 1739 with the British *Dictionary of National Biography,* the publication listing these individuals who have made a contribution to the life of the nation worthy of its attention. According to Williams, Freemasons of the period warranting entry into the *Dictionary* include the following:

> Twenty-eight of noble birth;
> Eighteen painters, sculptors and engravers;
> Seventeen authors, poets and dramatists,
> Fifteen clergy and ministers,
> Fifteen scientists, antiquarians, etc;
> Fourteen physicians and surgeons;
> Twelve actors, musicians, singers etc;
> Six architects;
> Five printers and publishers;
> Four lawyers;
> Three men of fashion, dilettantes etc; and two public servants of high standing[1].

The importance of Stukeley, Rowe and Williams is that they all, in their own way, draw attention to an underlying strength of this particular fraternity; its ability to attract members from a far larger constituency than other societies sprouting up all over George I's London. Without doubt, something that appealed to Pirates, Mapmakers, Dukes and the

---

1 Cited by Bernard E Jones in *The Freemasons' Guide and Compendium*, London, 1952.

inventor of the "Famous Diving Engine" was inevitably destined to over-shadow any competition, and in time expand its geographical influence. Combined with the novel and revolutionary idea that men of all races and religions were welcome to join, there was nothing to stop the Masonic Order becoming a national, and then international phenomenon.

Even so, the story that began with the founding of the Grand Lodge of England on June 24th 1717 can also be looked upon as a mere change of direction for the Fraternity, rather than a completely fresh start, for it only signaled the creation of the first Masonic *authority* in the World, Far from being something completely new, the Freemasons had already chalked up a tradition several centuries old by 1717, and this story, with a far longer pedigree, had unfolded with a cast of characters whose lives and circumstances were a universe away from the Surgeons, Actors and Sculptors *et al* of King George I's England.

II

Arguments abound about the beginnings of the Masons. At one extreme, some have suggested modern Freemasonry represents the continuance of a tradition whose roots lie with the architects and builders of Egypt's Pyramids. Such ideas, in the absence of hard evidence, do however, fall into the same trap as William Stukeley's works on Stonehenge, in that they again merge fiction with contemporary fact, and are all but useless unless as a measurement of the writers ignorance. It goes without saying that relying on such farfetched opinions, it would be just as credible to view the Freemasons as heirs to the builders of the Parthenon or the Great Wall of China.

A far more popular — and probable — idea has the Masonic Order as a last link in a chain starting with the methodology and symbolism of a fraternal society belonging to medieval Scottish[2] or English stonecutters and artisans. The idea of such a fraternity emerging during the middle ages isn't so farfetched, for contrary to popular belief, Britain during the Middle Ages wasn't a country where "everyone knew their place and there was a place for everyone." Even in the twelfth and thirteenth centuries economic insecurity was a fact of life for a sizeable percentage of the

---

2 See Stevenson's *The Origins of Freemasonry* and Hammill's *The Craft*

British people, a state of affairs the progress of which can indeed be inferred from the rise of guilds, and other fraternal organizations founded to protect the interests of particular trades, around this time.

It was perfectly understandable therefore for men engaged in the raising of buildings to want their own proto-labor union so to speak. For such men, collective protection for them and their trade from economic fluctuations, never mind the caprices of the Church or the Monarchy, was not only logical, but absolutely vital. No one was going to come to their aid if they fell to sickness or unemployment, unless they looked out for one another, and the only proper way to do that was to form a fraternity of their own.

For this "union", whose *raison d'être* was working in stone, the foundation date — symbolically — has to lie with the Norman Conquest of 1066. The invasion of William the Conqueror, and with him great numbers of Norman churchmen and skilled operatives, led to an astonishing change in the quantity and quality of native construction. England was to be completely rebuilt, and compared with the preceding and architecturally stagnant Saxon era, the post-conquest period was — and still is — unparalleled in the sheer number of new buildings erected, not only in Britain but also in any similar period in any other European country.

Starting with Saxon places of worship, many of these were flattened and then completely rebuilt, augmented over time with new Norman churches and cathedrals, although the "Gothic" era, lasting from the eleventh to the sixteenth centuries, was also remarkable for other forms of building activity in stone. Castles, bridges and other structures rose over the English landscape in unprecedented numbers, a movement qualitative too, for the Normans imported a standard of workmanship that had not been seen in Britain since the time of the Romans. These changes were, and are, too numerous to list here, but a single example, the masonry joint, makes the point well. During the eleventh century, the joint was often poorly made in Britain as well as Northern France; but during the following century, the quality of this simple but essential element in construction underwent a radical change for the better, on both sides of the English Channel.

Improvements in the science of turning out a decent masonry joint in twelfth century Britain was not, however, matched by a corresponding increase in literacy. The people of England remained overwhelmingly ignorant of the written word, due in part to the non-invention of print, but largely because of its relative pointlessness to a people only ever one step ahead of starvation. Of course, there were some, even at this time, who didn't have the constant worry of where their next meal was coming from and who could spend their hours mastering the art of reading and writing. Officials going about the King's business were obviously one such select group, although another, with their eyes and ears better attuned to everyday matters, were the clergy, and in particular monks, from whose accounts the most detailed picture of medieval life — and the role masons played in it — can often be found.

A glimpse of this world can be gleaned from the writings of one monk in particular, Gervase of Canterbury, who wrote of the fire that destroyed the Cathedral in that city, and its subsequent reconstruction. Amongst his narrative, *On the Burning and repair of the Church at Canterbury* Gervase commented liberally, sometimes positively, and sometimes not, on the masons engaged in the rebuilding. One whom he saw in an approving light was a certain William, a native of the French town of Sens, who had been appointed by the ecclesiastical authorities to oversee the repair. "A craftsman most skilful in wood and Stone", Gervase enthused about the Frenchman, and an asset "on account of his lively genius and good reputation".

With hindsight, and not a little irony, the Monk might have added William of Sens was "a craftsman most skilful" in another area as well: persuasion. Church authorities were initially of the mind that the Cathedral could be restored to its original condition. Sens, however, thought differently, and brandishing his professional status, impressed on them that nothing short of complete reconstruction was necessary, a point of view they grudgingly accepted. Whilst this anecdote may or may not indicate something of the character of William of Sens, it highlights another dynamic within the relationship between the medieval builder and his employer, and that was the craftsman's ability to sell total reconstruction to the Clergymen of Canterbury was not only testament to his powers of diplomacy — or salesmanship — but also illustrates the influence skilled masons often had over their literate, but architecturally ignorant patrons.

Once the grumbling of the Church had subsided, William of Sens commenced work, although his role differed fundamentally from modern day practice. Throughout the rebuilding, the Frenchman would have employed both a mastery of both architectural theory and the construction trade, in sharp contrast to today, where, to a degree, architects and builders work separately. As a consequence, the skills needed by a Master Mason of the Middle Ages were several: to be designer, engineer and manager all at once, at a time when formal education or training in those trades was non-existent. For William of Sens and his colleagues, learning only took place through experience, and knowledge an accumulation of practice through trial and error.

Sens' presence was vital at every stage of the Cathedral's rebuilding. It would be he who shouldered responsibility for drawing up the preliminary plans, skills that required understanding of both geometry and drafting techniques. At the same time, he would not only be called upon to organize the logistics of obtaining and transporting building materials to the site, as well as constructing machinery, such as lifts, hoists and scaffolding, but also to supervise the preparatory work: to see the area to be built on cleared of encumbrances such as rocks, trees, or, in this case, the ruins of the original cathedral.

Clearance always had to meet the standards of his critical eye, for his next objective was to lay out a plan of the new cathedral on site, using cord and a series of wooden pegs. The usual practice was the one peg marked the position of a corner, and then cord was run at right angles to other pegs, to indicate the future site of walls and so on. Geometrical shapes — such as floor patterns or a series of pillars — were positioned in a similar fashion.

Heavy involvement in the preparation didn't mean Sens could sit back as Canterbury's new Cathedral began to take shape. Once construction was underway, this particular master mason's continued presence was essential in ensuring the quality and speed of work progressed to his satisfaction. Management called for observation, inspection and direction, although William would have devoted some time to the artistic details of the building too. For large features — a window for example — a full-scale drawing was made, using compass and square, on plaster floor surfaces[3]. These designs were then used as models for the wooden templates or "moulds" defining and regulating the work of the stonecutters.

Sens drew up his plans and issued his instructions from the temporary residence and workshop the Masons had on site, the Lodge. Like so many innovations of the time, the idea of the Lodge was again a Norman import, for early English records often refer to it via its French spelling, *Loge*[4]. Apart from planning and direction the Lodge was also where the highest ranking workmen dressed stone, kept their tools in order, took their meals, and spent some of their rest time. Due to its vital role, this building was often the first structure built on site, although quality of construction varied greatly due to the length of time the main objective took to complete. For jobs that lasted a short time, Lodges made of wood, and covered with thatch would suffice; but for works that might continue for years, or an entire lifetime — the erection of a Cathedral for example — something more substantial, potentially even of stone, was built.

A solidly built Lodge didn't mean Master Masons lived in luxury compared to their lower ranking colleagues. The Medieval Catholic Church wasn't in the habit of paying good money for men to lounge about, and by modern standards the Lodge they subsidized was Spartan and unhygienic. Even so, notwithstanding the lodge's limitations and privations, it was here, in relative privacy, that the crucial decisions about raising buildings like the new Canterbury Cathedral were made, away from the intrusions and interference of the laborers and clergy[5].

---

3   York Minster has a surviving example of one of these plaster 'tracing floors'
4   Jones, *The Freemasons' Guide*
5   Supplementing slightly more salubrious living conditions were higher than average wages. Quality workmanship was of paramount importance here, although there were other reasons playing a part as well. For example, among the final accounts for the construction of Westminster Abbey during 1259 is an entry for the purchase of two hundred weight of reeds to cover a wall. The idea was to provide protection against frost damage and water penetration during the winter, although it also illustrates a further characteristic of the

Another character William of Sens was keen on keeping out of his Lodge was the phony mason, the cowboy builder of the age. Gervase of Canterbury commented bitterly on how one such imposter, a chancer by the name of Hugh de Goldclif, had provided "treacherous advice" which led to carved work "unnecessary, trifling and beyond measure, costly"[6], to the Church. To put it bluntly, the problem faced by Gervase and Sens was basically one of scale. Whilst a village church was repairable by one or more of the locals, whose reputations were public knowledge, the same approach couldn't be applied to masons employed on far larger projects, where skilled labor would be drawn in from across a far larger area. For a contractor like Sens, something was therefore needed to show workmen possessed necessary skills, in the absence of something as abstract as a certificate. Apart from time wasting tests, the most obvious method of establishing a standard, or membership, was by a commonly agreed set of signs, words or symbols, shrouded in secrecy to exclude the unskilled and the crooked; and it was these secret signs that provided the builders of the new Canterbury Cathedral and a thousand other structures with some of their security, a tradition, or at least a symbolic variant of such a tradition, that still lives on in the "secret" modes of identification amongst modern day Freemasons.

III

Collectively, Canterbury Cathedral, and other buildings raised in the medieval era celebrate these men and their skills. Individually though, very little remains, for although Sens, Crump, the renegade de Goldclif plus a handful of others are, thanks to Monks like Gervase, known by name, the identity of most Master Masons is circumstantial. Illiteracy meant there was no *Dictionary of National Biography* or an equivalent during the Middle Ages, consigning the overwhelming majority of Cathedral

---

medieval trade: it was basically seasonal. Another reason for good remuneration was it constituted a form of 'danger money'. The building trade throughout the ages has never been a particularly safe industry to work in, an aspect that was probably even more important seven hundred years ago. Fatality or serious injury was a common fate for many masons. William of Sens himself, whilst conducting an inspection of the vaulted roof of Lincoln Cathedral, was to suffer a crippling fall when scaffolding beneath him collapsed.

6 Hislop, *Medieval Masons*, p.9

and Church builders to permanent anonymity, except in one particular way.

For stonemasons of all ages — and places — have scratched or cut a permanent record into the stones they worked on, marks illustrating the Medieval Masons individuality. Usually nothing more than a collection of scratches in a distinctive pattern, it is unlikely these carvings were solely for the sake of vanity, for such marks had practical applications apart from identifying the man responsible. One idea is they indicated a section of work — a door or wall for instance — was completed to the mason's satisfaction whilst another is they were cut for purely operational reasons, to define the direction a stone should be laid for example.

Varying degrees of validity can be attached to all of the above, especially a mark being the "signature" of a specific individual. It stands to reason a qualified Mason had his own individual pattern of scratches, simply because of the likelihood that not only was he illiterate, but so was the person he answered to. There are certain marks a man with a mason's axe or hammer and chisel will instinctively make, and such are the marks that are repeated again and again in buildings erected during the "Gothic" period.

What is interesting about these marks is their simplicity, which can be explained by the demands and technology of a medieval building site: they tend to be extremely easily executed — in fact, made in a few seconds by the application of very simple tools. We find the same marks or types of mark used in many places, with infinite variations to please the fancy of the individual mason. Curves are comparatively rare, neither the tools of the mason nor the material on which he worked favoring the easy or natural production of a curved mark, and in a quantitive sense, there are probably a hundred straight marks for every curved one.

Most of the marks are extremely obvious and many of them originated with two lines forming a cross. From these simple "cross" figures, a multitude of variants could be developed, enough for each individual mason in England to have his own specific mark. In one way only do these marks differ from their modern counterparts, and that is where they are positioned within the finished building. During the middle ages, marks were generally put on the face of the stone near one of the edges, so that they remained exposed when the stone was built into the wall. Today however, masons marks are applied to indicate ultimate position, and are consequently covered up when the wall is finished.

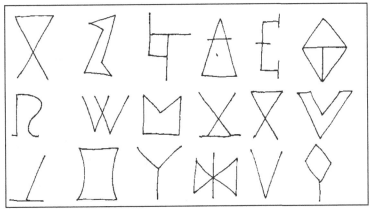

Fig. 1: A sample of Masons' Marks from the Middle Ages (Source: Malcolm Hislop, Medieval Masons)

Stone cutting provided lucrative, if back breaking, work for a sizeable number of men in Britain between the Eleventh to the Fifteenth Centuries. But in the years and decades that followed — the Sixteenth — the stonemasons trade started to wither, a trend from which it never properly recovered. The causes of decline were numerous, although the decision of King Henry VIII to axe the Roman Catholic Church, removing it from its leading role in England, over the issue of his divorce, was hugely significant. Schism led to collapse in the demand for the construction of religious buildings, and, in the case of the monasteries, which were dissolved by Henry in 1540, demolition was the usual fate.

Innovations used at the raising of Henry's new palace, Hampton Court, illustrate another threat to the stonemason's world: the use of brick. Although an idea as old as civilization itself, brick spent the Middle Ages on the sidelines, so to speak. From the sixteenth century onwards however, it bounced back to challenge, and ultimately dominate stone as the material of choice for builders, a supremacy lasting until today, an era of concrete, steel and glass. For the masons, alternative work couldn't be procured by building new castles or other fortifications to defend the Realm either. The strong English state forged under Henry and his daughter Elizabeth I was fearless in the face of domestic trouble, whilst at sea the Royal Navy proved it was quite capable of seeing off any external menace.

The aforementioned do not approach — or even attempt — an exhaustive list of the challenges facing stonemasons as the sixteenth century wore on: there were other, more subtle and numerous causes, too. But whatever those reasons were, and whether they accelerated or delayed the "operative" masons' fall, what is certain is that by 1600 the great medieval construction era known as the "Gothic", symbolized by the castles and cathedrals that still dot the English landscape, was over.

Against this backdrop, the operative's fraternity should, in theory, have followed the trade into eclipse; and that might have been the end of the story. But during the seventeenth century, the moribund society — or a symbolic successor to it — began to gain popularity amongst men of a completely different cut from the "operatives" that had gone before. These "speculative"[7] Masons were, on the whole, well off, educated, and with a healthy curiosity about the world, characteristics that were destined to become crucial to the direction the fraternity would take over the next two centuries.

Indeed, there was undoubtedly a measure of serendipity in the way the symbolic variant of the "operatives" fraternity came into contact with — and successfully absorbed — such men. Seventeenth century Britain was a place where radical ideas in all spheres of human experience began to flourish, and as the pace of scientific experimentation, exploration, imperialism and trade started to gather speed, the number of distinguished men becoming Freemasons increased proportionately. Examples abound, from the length and breadth of Britain, although possibly the earliest — and best — illustration of this "new" Mason was Elias Ashmole.

Hailing from the Staffordshire town of Lichfield, Elias Ashmole was born in modest circumstances. As a sign of the times however, a poor background was not powerful enough to prevent him from following a highly successful career in the law, or marrying the much older — and wealthier — Lady Mainwaring. One of the consequences of sharing

---

7 The modern English equivalent would be 'theoretical'

Mainwaring's wealth was that, from a relatively young age, Ashmole was free to concentrate much of his time and energy on interests outside of work. He rose to be an author of some note, penning *Theatrum Chemicum Britannicum* during 1652, *The Way to Bliss* six years later, as well as works on the Order of the Garter, the antiquities of Windsor and a biography of the Elizabethan spy and alchemist, Doctor John Dee[8].

Like William Stukeley seventy years in the future, Ashmole was also an inveterate hoarder. Over time he amassed large collections of coins, manuscripts, archaeological and astrological specimens, items that, in 1675, formed the basis of the first public museum in Britain, the Ashmolean in Oxford. To be fair, by today's standards Ashmole, like Stukeley, was no scientist; but rather an accumulator of knowledge, which in the right hands could be properly classified to provide the basic building materials for the conduct of modern science.

With regard to the Freemasons, a surviving handwritten note states Ashmole was initiated into a Lodge in Warrington, Cheshire during 1646. Like Stukeley, Collins and Rowe, his reasons for doing this are again a mystery, though in hindsight it is highly unlikely that he wished to undergo the experience of cutting stone, or anything else practical for that matter. It goes without saying that for men of leisure like Ashmole, whilst the attractions of belonging to the Order may have been several, manual labor wasn't one of them. So what could they be? Perhaps the search for an answer lies in the state of society Freemasonry was being born into, for, alongside the scientific progress mentioned above, it should also be remembered that England in 1646 was a nation marked by division, and this wasn't only in terms of wealth and poverty.

Religious intolerance had reached such an impasse that some people thought it better to leave for the wilds of North America than stay put. Perhaps they were the lucky ones, for a general prejudice against those who worshipped in a different way — primarily Roman Catholics — was to mark British history, all the way up to the monarchy, for the rest of the century, and into the decades beyond. There was also the question of who was actually in charge of running the country. Ashmole's Masonic affiliation started halfway through a civil war that was to see the king

---

8 *Masonic Quarterly*, issue 11, October, 2004, *Elias Ashmole: Masonic Icon*

beheaded within three years, Oliver Cromwell's military dictatorship by 1653, and the return of the king's son to the throne seven year later. Throw economic turmoil into the mix as well, and It was hardly surprising that Elias Ashmole and friends suddenly began to show an eagerness to come together in a "club" that — for an evening at least — banished the aforesaid divisions.

Another possible inspiration for Ashmole and his contemporaries was a fascination with the symbolism of the "operatives" fraternity, especially its overarching emphasis on building. A select group employing construction imagery in its terminology and metaphors was naturally going to be extremely adaptable, and throughout the seventeenth century the Order was gradually colonized by the kind of men who could make maximum use of that adaptability. Whether it was in a theoretical, spiritual or practical sense, the symbolism and imagery of the construction site could be applied to the "improvement" of almost anything: be it a person, town, or even something bigger:

> Building and all practical processes comprised at one time considerable "speculative work," what would now mostly be called "theory." The theory of constructional design and the theory of the strength and behavior of building materials were "speculations" and were the province of the master craftsmen. The application of the science of geometry was "speculation"; in a very real sense, such work was practical, but if it did not call for the use of a workman's tools it could not be practical, in the old time language; it was just speculative.

> The learned men who would come into freemasonry in the sixteen hundreds would meet practical men skilled in the use of the stone worker's tools — the masons and operative freemasons. Some of these operatives would be men of education, men of the architect and surveyor type, men who backed up their practice with theory, users of pencils and fine instruments; the newcomers would mentally dub them "speculatives." With the passing of many generations the word "speculative" acquired a new meaning. As the accepted masons built up or acquired knowledge of their symbolic Craft they fell back on their favorite word, however inadequate it was, there being none other apt enough to their purpose, and distinguished themselves from stonemasons by calling themselves "speculative masons" or "speculatives". Generally, "speculative" still means theory, contemplation; but when it is used to connote morality, philosophy, esoteric doctrines or principals it means freemasonry[9].

---

9 Jones, *The Freemasons' Guide*, p.192

The use of symbolism and imagery wasn't however, an invention attributable to the Freemasons. The medieval Catholic Church often put its message across through symbolism, which was, of course, a far more effective medium in a largely illiterate society. The Reformation emphasized a more straightforward Christianity, thus putting a temporary stop to this habit, although as a method of imparting information it bounced back towards the end of the sixteenth century and ironically, it was the Anglican Church, the principal beneficiary of the split with Rome, which was the first to renew the use of symbolism as an illustrative medium.

The effectiveness of symbolism and imagery was so powerful that during the following century its use in interpreting scripture became common — along with allegory — not only with other Protestant denominations, such as the Puritans, but with other organizations too. Fraternal Orders certainly picked up the idea, and it is highly likely the "speculative" Masonic Order saw the advantages of both symbolism and allegory, and adopted them into its ceremonies and rituals around this time.

IV

Having men like Elias Ashmole become Freemasons was all very nice, but to hold its own, and indeed prosper, the Order needed to grow, both geographically and numerically. Had this been a time and place bereft of competing societies, growth should have been relatively straightforward; but it was the lot of the Speculative Masonic Order to emerge in an environment and era home to an enormous number of fraternities and clubs of all kinds. London in the late seventeenth and early eighteenth centuries swarmed with taverns, coffee and chocolate houses, a reflection not only of the free time enjoyed by the citizenry, but also the role the City was beginning to assume in respect of international trade.

The consumption of coffee, first imported from the Ottoman Empire during Cromwell's time, not only symbolized this era, but also provided the raw material for the retailing phenomenon forever characterizing restoration London: the coffee house. Described by one contemporary detractor as "black, thick, nasty bitter tasting, nauseous puddle water"[10], the new beverage was an instant hit with London's *hoi polloi*, although

---

10 Waller, *1700: Scenes from London Life*, p.195

not everyone shared in the general enthusiasm, for coffee — and especially the establishments in which it was imbibed — had incurred the displeasure of the newly restored King Charles II.

Otherwise affable and (in contrast to his Puritan predecessors) relaxed about public entertainments, Charles saw in the coffee house phenomenon a potential breeding ground for plots against the still fragile monarchy. Even as the Crown firmly re-embedded itself during the sixteen seventies and eighties did royal paranoia not fade, for the struggle against coffee and its purveyors outlived Charles, and continued during the reign of his brother, James II. Perhaps Charles and James even had a point; for one side effect of the latter's ouster in the Glorious Revolution of 1688 was the end of the Crown's disapproval of coffee and where it was consumed. Freedom to trade kick-started an astonishing growth in numbers of such hostelries, and within twelve years of the Revolution, London alone[11] boasted an estimated total in excess of two thousand coffee houses.

Inevitably, competition for custom was stiff, and proprietors naturally looked for ways to ensure their establishments stood out. One well used tactic was to appeal to people following a particular profession. Over time, *The Grecian* in Devereux Court became home to members of the aforementioned Royal Society, the elite grouping of some of the finest minds in the country. Across in Pall-Mall, meanwhile, the political issues of the time loomed large in conversation within the *St. James*, and the *Cocoa Tree*, respective haunts of the Whig and Tory factions in Parliament and William III's Court. Occupations as disparate as lawyers, slavers and the military had their coffee houses of choice; although the most famous of all were those engaged in maritime activities, which congregated at *Edward Lloyd's* in Abchurch Lane. Lloyd's angle was to supplement his coffee sales with the practice of holding auctions of ship's cargoes, a business sideline that — via *Lloyd's List* — would one day evolve into the insurance giant Lloyd's of London.

In such a hothouse atmosphere, a myriad of societies and clubs were born. Some were political and religious in nature, a reflection of the uncertainties of the time; whilst others burst into life for fraternal, scien-

---

11 Waller, p.196

tific, mystic, economic or merely social reasons. Men — and women — belonged to one or several simultaneously; some were deliberately temporary, whilst others aimed for a more long term existence. Membership could be open, or restricted on the grounds of sex, religious affiliation, income or one of a thousand other reasons. Fraternal societies rose and fell, bloomed and withered at an astonishing rate, and the odds against one particular society — a relative late comer — ascending above the rest were high enough. The belief that, within a few decades, that same fraternity could expand across Britain, Ireland and be successfully exported to North America and Europe was extreme to say the least.

However, even in these early formative days, Official Freemasonry enjoyed two advantages that made a crucial difference to its future. The first of these was the relatively "open" criteria for membership. All that was required from an aspiring member was to be male, aged over twenty-one, of good character, and hold a belief in a "Supreme Being", qualifications meaning a large percentage of the male population were theoretically eligible. The second reason was that membership rapidly became a "fad" amongst Englishmen during the early eighteenth century, regardless of whether they lived in London or frequented its coffee houses, a craze before long spreading to men of other nationalities.

All of this activity was, inevitably, also noticed by "outsiders": the general public. Contemporary periodicals and newspapers occasionally referred to the Order, often sarcastically, inferring not only were Masons and their Lodges already spread the length and breadth of Britain, but familiar enough to the population at large — or at least those who read the press of the time — not to warrant a lengthy explanation. "They had some secret Intimation of each other like the Free-Masons," was how Sir Richard Steele referred to them in a 1709 essay in *The Tatler*, whilst a year later he derided certain types he thought secretive as having their "Signs and Tokens like Free-Masons"[12]. Steele's comments were reinforced by *A Letter from a Clergy-man in London*, a pamphlet published in 1710 by an individual named Baldwin, who referred to the Freemasons in the following way:

---

12 Steele's comments were made in issues 26 and 166 of *The Tatler*, for the periods 7-9 June, 1709 and 29 April–2 May 1710 respectively. Both are cited by Hammill in *The Craft*, p.39

> The Word, Mark, or Token of a certain Company called the Free Masons, which is well known to every Member of that Sage Society, but kept a mighty Secret from all the World besides[13].

For all their nosiness, Steele and Baldwin failed, however, to see the big picture, for the Masons and their Order were still in the same disorganized state that had characterized the fraternity back in Elias Ashmole's day. Men were being initiated into something that lacked any sort of administration, either at a local or national level, where all that existed was a picture of isolated Lodges and fraternities of Freemasons scattered across Britain, with no allegiance to anyone but themselves. Some common ground existed in these small groups adhered, in their own individual way, to a symbolic interpretation of the rituals and methodology of the operative stone cutters fraternity that had withered away over a century earlier. Such commonality was however, the sum total of what held the fraternity together, even into the second decade of the eighteenth century.

Change was in the air, however. On 24th of June 1717, four Masonic lodges met at the Apple-Tree Tavern in Charles Street, Covent Garden, to found the first Masonic authority in the World, the Grand Lodge of England. The idea at the time was the Grand Lodge would assume a superior role in relation to ordinary Lodges, acting as the final word on all matters pertaining to the Fraternity, and indeed, the Grand Lodge of England has, from June 24th 1717[14] to today, acted as the "Government" of the Masonic Order in England and Wales: administering, arbitrating and presiding over every possible aspect of the Fraternity, from registration of individual members to the Order's relations with society in general.

Of course, like any government, many functions only emerged over time and changing circumstances. Back in 1717 therefore, it was the organization of the new institution that was the sole concern of the Brethren meeting at the *Apple Tree* and the *Goose and Gridiron*. These events that were captured for posterity years later by Doctor James Anderson, author of the Masonic rule book, *The Constitutions of the Free-Masons*, who included them in the preamble of the 1738 edition:

---

13 Baldwin's comments are cited in *The Freemasons' Guide*

14 This is Saint John the Baptist's day, one of the patron saints of the Mason's. The other being St John the Evangelist, whose Saints day is 27th December.

A.D. 1716, the few *Lodges* at *London*...thought fit to cement under a *Grand Master* as the Center of Union and Harmony, *viz.* The *Lodges* that met,

1. At the *Goose* and *Gridiron* Ale-house in *St Paul's Church-Yard.*
2. At the *Crown* Ale-house in *Parker's-Lane* near *Drury-Lane.*
3. At the *Apple Tree* Tavern in *Charles-Street, Covent-Garden.*
4. At the *Rummer* and *Grapes* Tavern at *Channel-Row*, Westminster.

They and some old Brothers met at the said *Apple-Tree*, and having put into the chair the *oldes Master* Mason (now the *Master* of a *Lodge*) they constituted themselves a GRAND LODGE pro Tempore in *Due Form*, and forthwith revived the Quarterly *Communication* of the *Officers* of Lodges (call'd the GRAND LODGE) resolv'd to hold the *Annual* ASSEMBLY *and feast*, and then to chuse a GRAND MASTER from among themselves, till they should have the Honour of a *Noble Brother* at their Head.

Accordingly

On *St John Baptist's* Day, in the 3rd year of King GEORGE I., A.D. 1717, the ASSEMBLY and *Feast* of the *Free and accepted Masons* was held at the fore-said *Goose and Gridiron* Ale-house.[15]

Whilst the above signaled a shift towards greater organization, much of what took place at the *Goose and Gridiron* must be consigned to the realm of speculation. Te reason for this is that even though it is generally accepted Anderson presented the world with an essentially correct version of events, there is, also the possibility the agenda covered far more than has ever been stated. For instance, one area obviously open to speculation was whether the "brethren" present saw the new formal structure as applying to just the four Lodges listed, or as the precursor to an organization that today claims a membership of five million men around the World. This subject, by its very nature, *must* have arisen around the dinner table following the Assembly, and various opinions made as to what that future might actually be, and doubtlessly, some individuals — erring on the side of caution — would have insisted the future of Official Masonry lay solely in maturing into a London-wide fraternity.

At the other end of the scale, others — possibly fortified by the food and drink on offer — potentially, and loudly, interpreted the events of the day as the birth of a new, worldwide Order. Even so, whatever was

---

15   There is no evidence the Quarterly Communication existed prior to 1717, or for that matter many of the other characteristics of the 'new' fraternity, representing some kind of misunderstanding on Anderson's part. See Bullock's *Revolutionary Brotherhood*, p.15

discussed with regards to the future, Anderson has been silent on the matter, no doubt due in part to his own non-attendance at either the *Apple Tree* or the *Goose and Gridiron*. Even using the inexact tool of inference doesn't help much. Take, for instance, the social circumstances surrounding the foundation of the Grand Lodge of England. They didn't lend much credence to the "worldwide fraternity" scenario, for probably no more than two hundred "good men and true" were present at the *Apple Tree* back in 1717, whilst the "jurisdiction" of the Grand Lodge of England extended over four Lodges, scattered across a mere three square miles, or less than two thirds of contemporary London[16].

As the sun set on the *Goose and Gridiron* that warm June day, there was nothing to say the Freemasons would ever go global, for all existing evidence suggests something modest was the eventual aim. Nevertheless, from the inauspicious beginnings chronicled by Anderson, the Order, and the World, were about to undergo massive change, and undoubtedly amongst conversations held nearly three hundred years ago at least some of these changes were discussed. Drunken Plans were laid, extravagant possibilities weighed and technical difficulties assessed, although it would be stretching credulity to believe many of these Masons present realized their capability in concert, and the nature of the truly awesome edifice they would one day erect.

---

16   Bernard E Jones, *The Freemasons' Guide*

CHAPTER 2. "TO BE SEEN AT THE ROYAL-EXCHANGE EVERY DAY..."

> 'Now *Masonry* flourish'd in Harmony, Reputation and
> Numbers; many Noble-men and Gentlemen of the first
> Rank desir'd t be admitted into the *Fraternity*, besides other
> Learned Men, Merchants, Clergymen, and Tradesmen, who
> found a *Lodge* to be a safe and pleasant Relaxation from
> Intense Study or the Hurry of Business, without Politicks or
> Party.'
>
> — Anderson's *Constitutions*, 1723

I

From 1717 onwards, the Grand Lodge of England began to assert its authority over Masonic Lodges apart from the original four, and naturally, this growth started in London and its environs and then spread further afield. Within a decade, over seventy such Lodges in England and Wales accepted the Grand Lodge's jurisdiction[17], a measure of not only how widespread the old, casual fraternity had been, but also testament to the burgeoning popularity of the new, formalized Order. Expansion across Britain certainly found favor with the leaders of the Society, for it emphasized the effectiveness of their movement and its attractiveness to newcomers, though they were still acutely aware there were still challenges to be addressed, primarily the need to codify procedures for the

---

17 Hammill, *The Craft*, pp.43–44

management of the organization, and particularly the regulation of new additions.

The Grand Lodge found the answer to the latter difficulty through the employment of a straightforward, but simple instrument. From 1721, "unofficial" Lodges aspiring to come within the orbit of the "Official" Fraternity were suddenly required to procure from London a charter or warrant before they could open for business. Whilst this "new entrants" regulation naturally had the effect of tightly defining the limits of the Grand Lodges' influence, its adoption didn't signal the end of the new fraternity's administrative inventiveness. Too many managerial aspects still required a definitive protocol, resulting in, two years later, the publication of a far more comprehensive rulebook, Doctor James Anderson's *The Constitutions of the Free-Masons*.[18]

The efforts that had gone into the writing and adoption of the *Constitutions*, was not only a clear illustration of how seriously the Grand Lodge took governance of the Fraternity, but also an indication that the men at the top — the scientists, clergymen and nobles etc; — had ordained that the Masonic Order in England was to be a professionally run outfit unlike anything that had gone before. Even so, expansion and tighter governance weren't the only changes the Order was about to undertake, and by the year 1721, the Grand Lodge of England was on the verge of taking steps that were to further distance "official" Freemasonry from its unorganized predecessor: the rewriting of much of the Masonic ritual and the establishment of the Order overseas.

After five or six hundred years as an operative fraternity plus a century as a speculative Order peculiar to the island of Great Britain and parts of France, from around 1720 onwards the movement began to metamorphose into a global phenomenon. In countries "Western" enough in character — primarily Europe and the settled regions of North America — the decades following the foundation of the Grand Lodge began to witness the arrival of "official" Freemasonry from the British Isles, and following the pattern in England, the fraternity overseas quickly took root.

---

18   There were two early editions of Andersons' Constitutions, 1723 and 1738, the latter including the description of the founding of the Grand Lodge quoted in chapter I.

This isn't to say that the Grand Lodge of England operated a deliberate policy of exporting Masonry to other countries; rather, it was recognition of the interdependence already characterizing the relationships between western nations. By 1720 London was already the world city where merchants, diplomats or people with a thousand or more different reasons turning up on a daily basis, primed for exposure to the capital's curiosities and novelties. Conversely, as the world's greatest port, sailors, emigrants, a pirate like George Shelvocke, or even Jacob Rowe, eager to repeat his success with the *Vansitartt*, were well positioned when it came to exporting a certain British institution where ever they went.

So successful indeed was the transplant to foreign soil to be that within fifty years of the foundation at the *Goose and Gridiron*, newly initiated international brethren rapidly began to resemble a veritable *Who's Who* of the age. Amongst others, Voltaire, Mozart and Goethe were signed up in Europe, whilst across the Atlantic the Order had already attracted the likes of George Washington and Benjamin Franklin to its ranks. It would be fair to say that during the middle decades of the eighteenth century international Freemasonry was on the march, and the speed of its progress can be measured by the establishment of national Grand Lodges around the World. For by 1749 — only thirty two years after the initial foundation — the Grand Lodge of England had its equivalents in Ireland, France, Italy, Germany, the North American Colonies, Austria, Denmark and French Canada[19].

Logistically, it would have stretched the Grand Lodge of England to breaking point to attempt "direct rule" over such a huge area. The first half of the eighteenth century wasn't a time of effective communications, and disadvantages due to distance were compounded by the possible displeasure of foreign governments, who could, on occasion, view their citizens' involvement in something taking orders direct from London with suspicion. National and provincial Grand Lodges were therefore brought into existence, and although theoretically independent, a measure of continuity was maintained in that they looked to England for guidance on matters of ritual and protocol. This "federal" system has endured and matured over the ensuing quarter of a millennium, and to-

---

19 Knight, *The Brotherhood*

day, official Freemasonry operates as a worldwide institution, albeit one whose Anglo-Saxon origins are still recognizable due to a marked concentration of members and Lodges in countries that have, at one time or another, fallen under the influence of the British.

Another vital change affecting the fraternity was at the opposite end of the spectrum from globalization: the rewriting of the ritual that underpinned the entire edifice. To put it simply, ritual — whatever its purpose, origin or form — is definable as "a proscribed order of performing rites"[20] and whilst the use of this medium is carried on, in one form or another, within every society and nation in the world, its usage has tended to be a characteristic of cultures where written and recorded information were (or are) either non-existent or only employed in a primitive way. In such societies, unaccustomed to modern media, the conducting of ceremonial in a specific manner naturally has a far more central role with regard to the preservation and transmission of information from one generation — or group — to another.

Oral techniques, such as rhyme, allegory and storytelling, occasionally bolstered by mime and dance, are essential to the effectiveness of successful ritual, for if properly applied, they enhance the chances of the "message" tucked away inside surviving over a far longer period, and in greater detail, in the same way that in modern consumer societies song lyrics and advertising catchphrases embed themselves in the sub-consciousness. Inevitably therefore, ritual is recognizable as an educational tool that may appear more attuned to the needs of people living in highly traditional cultures, though whilst such concepts may appear quaint to people of the "West", it is also a proven fact that many universally known statements defining the Christian milieu — the Lord's Prayer for example — owe their long-term survival to being transmitted in a ritual manner.

Although ritual has undoubtedly been an integral part of the British oral tradition since human beings first arrived on the island, the ceremonials of the Freemasons are a relatively recent phenomenon. The scant manuscript evidence that survives hints that Masonic ritual evolved during the middle ages for the reasons outlined in chapter 1, where the medi-

20 *Concise Oxford Dictionary*

eval builders developed forms of words and imagery amongst themselves as a set of instructions for fellow members of the fraternity. Certainly, the subject matter of early Masonic catechisms — an alloy of building terminology and Biblical imagery — neatly summarized the Masons' immediate environment: the building terms being drawn from the trade, whilst the imagery originated in the only book familiar to working men in a highly illiterate, but deeply religious country.

Bearing in mind the ceremonial developed this way, for a trade that endured a disastrous contraction by 1600, it is remarkable that it survived for over a century after the "operatives" eclipse, for material surviving from the turn of the eighteenth century again suggests the Fraternity was still adhering to the basics of the medieval ritual. Whilst this situation might suffice for a motley collection of small independent lodges across Britain, it couldn't for something far larger. The Grand Lodge was again aiming at change, this time to its rituals; but it again stretches the imagination to believe that many masons of the time realized how fundamental and radically different this was to be.

II

Up to 1717, the progress of the ritual had been slow and erratic. Variations abounded, depending on location and dialect, and the fact that individual lodges owed allegiance to themselves alone. It was therefore understandable that once the Grand Lodge appeared, some attempt would be made towards a definitive version, not only because "change" was starting to become emblematic, but because a stated aim of the Grand Lodge was, of course, to bring together men of all races and creeds under one roof. A recalibrated ritual was therefore absolutely essential, for without it the fostering of fraternal relations between men of differing London Lodges, never mind the meeting of Masons in or from foreign lands would have been impossible.

What was surprising however was how long, and to what degree "standardization" was to take. The "rewrite" was far from a mere synthesis of already existing ceremonial, in that "new" ritual often had an extremely tenuous connection to the Bible and building trade amalgam dominating before. Undoubtedly, part of the reason for this can be laid at the door of the frenetic popularity the Order enjoyed after 1717, in that the huge array of interests and occupations absorbed by the fraternity impacted on, and permeated much of the language and phraseology, to the point where "new" ceremonial was completely different when compared with the former.

It is also noticeable how long these changes took to complete, for the alterations, and their successful imposition on Lodges worldwide, was doubtlessly one of the major tasks the Grand Lodge had set itself. All in all, transformation of the ceremonial formally ended in 1816, a full ninety nine years after the inaugural meeting at the *Goose and Gridiron*. Naturally, such an awesome task conducted over more or less a century was the work of many hands. Like the medieval masons however, the identity of many of these men are, and will probably remain, anonymous. Even so, like Sens, a few names do come to the fore, especially in the early period, and this small number includes a London map maker and publisher by the name of John Senex, and more significantly, one of Britain's leading scientists of the day, John Theophilus Desaguliers.

Being smuggled across the English Channel in a wine cask wasn't the most salubrious way to enter Britain, but this event marked the start in life for Desaguliers. His unorthodox travelling arrangements came courtesy of the French King, Louis XIV, who, in 1685 had revoked the Edict of Nantes, which for nearly a century had enshrined in law religious liberty and legal status for France's protestant minority. Forced to flee from potential persecution, Desaguliers' father, a Huguenot clergyman, settled in London, where he awaited his two year old son John's rather more clandestine arrival in the capital. Refugee status didn't have lasting effects on the family however, for Desaguliers senior rapidly found his feet in his new adopted home, becoming the chaplain of a French Huguenot church in London. Here, he instructed his son in the classical languages, which the younger man put to great use later at Christ Church, Oxford, where he studied experimental philosophy.

Sometime around 1713, Desaguliers junior left Oxford for London, where he soon became the first public lecturer on science in Europe. This was a hugely popular enterprise, and the former cask incarcerate soon found himself the toast of the city; indeed, so much, that the adopted

Englishman was called to give lectures on science to the King, George I, and his court. With such powerful backers, it was inevitable that in time Desaguliers gravitated to the circle around Sir Isaac Newton, eventually becoming his assistant. Membership of the Royal Society soon followed, and the measure of how influential he became can be seen in the fact that, in three specific years — 1734, 1736 and 1741 — he received the Society's highest award, the Copley Medal.

Like Jacob Rowe, Desaguliers was also an inventor, his third Copley medal being awarded for his discoveries regarding the properties of Electricity. Other inventions included improvements to Thomas Savery's steam engine, a method for heating liquid boilers with steam rather than fire, and, of far greater significance, the planetarium. Desaguliers greatest contribution to enlightenment science was, however, *A Course of Experimental Philosophy*, Volume I of which was published in 1734. This huge work was concerned with theoretical and practical mechanics, and an explanation of the basics of Newtonian physics, followed up in turn by Volume II, ten years later. By this time, 1744, the polymath was however, a shadow of his former self. Now leading the life of a clergyman, he had fallen out with his patron, the Duke of Chandos, and was confined to to the upstairs of the Bedford Coffee House, suffering from gout, in circumstances, according to one contemporary poet, somewhat straitened:

> How poor, neglected Desaguliers fell;
> How he who taught two gracious kings to view
> All Boyle ennobled and all Bacon knew,
> Died in a cell without a friend to save,
> Without a Guinea, and without a grave[21]

Desaguliers died on the 29th February, 1744, one of the leading scientific minds of the age. It is all the more mysterious therefore why he should involve himself — and indeed lead — an organization that exhibited itself to the World via the symbolism of the building site. Grand Master in 1719, and Deputy Grand Master throughout much of the 1720's, he was also a zealous collector of Masonic manuscripts, and the guiding brain behind Anderson's *Constitutions*. This was a man determined to mould the Fraternity in his own image, again treading the same path as Stukeley and Newton, in combining the esoteric with the scientific.

---

21 Cawthorn: 'The Vanity of Human Enjoyments'

So why should the Masons, who already boasted great writers — like for example, Jonathan Swift — turn to Desaguliers the scientist and Senex the map maker to rewrite their rituals? Certainly, someone had to do it, for apart from providing common and contemporary ground for Freemasons, there was also, potentially, a further reason for change: security. Amongst the huge influx of new brethren there were some who saw membership as a means of easy enrichment, primarily through publication of the "secrets" of the Fraternity. By constantly altering the ritual, even over the huge timescale of ninety nine years, the scientist and cartographer minimized the damage such publications could wreak, although ironically, it is through these "exposures" that today the degree of change to the ritual can best be measured.

For, by an inscrutable irony, and in the same way that *The Tatler* and *A Letter from a Clergy-man in London* illustrate how geographically widespread the pre-1717 fraternity was across England, the only documented changes to the ritual were again due to the fascination of the general public. The "New" Masonic Fraternity was already viewed with suspicion, and had to endure, on occasion, its ritual and ceremonials published for all to see. Such disclosures sometimes took the form of books, although as a general rule it was in the newspapers and periodicals of the era that the public's curiosity was indulged, starting with the appearance of *A Mason's Examination* in the London broadsheet *The Flying-Post* during 1723[22].

Even though the readership of the *Flying-Post* were likely to be disappointed, in that *A Mason's Examination* was merely a collection of ritual fragments, a precedent had been created. From 1723 onwards, the public's insatiable hunger for "Masonic Secrets" meant "exposures" became a regular occurrence in the press, not only in Britain, but Europe and America too. Each exposure in turn claimed to throw some much needed light into the workings of the Fraternity, although the one-sided nature of these revelations meant there has never been a tried and tested method of verifying their authenticity. Skepticism is therefore called for when assessing the potential historical value of such material, although in the absence of any official record or explanation, and by careful comparison

22 Hammill in *The Craft* gives the edition as 11–13 April, 1723

with modern ritual, there is a strong possibility that their origins do lie with individuals who were, at one time or another, members of, or at least familiar with, the Masonic fraternity.

Of all of these exposures, arguably the best — in measuring the degree of change to the ritual — was neither *A Mason's Examination* nor the last, William Morgan's 1826 *Illustrations of Masonry*, but *Masonry Dissected*, which was first published in London during 1730. Claimed by the author to be a comprehensive description of the three degrees of Freemasonry at the time[23], *Dissected* was the idea of one Samuel Pritchard, an individual of whom it can be said was a "peculiarity" of Freemasonry, the reason for which is that exhaustive searches have failed to turn up any evidence of "Pritchard" ever existing, never mind belonging to the Fraternity in the years up to 1730. Of course, considering the risks faced by this particular author, there was never anything to stop him using a pseudonym, a common occurrence in English literature, especially — as in "Pritchard's" Case — someone who wanted to avoid the wrath of his former Masonic brethren.

The mystery surrounding "Pritchard's" identity is compounded by speculation about his publication of *Dissected* in the first place. Pritchard claimed at the time his reason was to allay the public's fears about the movement, though this corny attempt at justification does, however, conveniently ignore the fact *Masonry Dissected* earned a fortune, the book making Pritchard a wealthy man. *Masonry Dissected* even became the publishing best seller of the time: running through three editions in eleven days, reprinted in two newspapers, separately published in Scotland, Ireland, Europe and America, and passed through an immense number of editions on average one every three years in England alone — well into the nineteenth century[24].

Despite Pritchard's motivations, the significance of his actions weren't recognized until long after his death. For over time, in the face of a comprehensively different "official" ritual, *Masonry Dissected* gradually emerged as the yardstick to measure how fundamental eighteenth century changes actually were. What immediately catches the eye is

---

23 Entered Apprentice and Fellow Craft.
24 Jones, *The Freemasons' Guide*

the sheer volume of "new" material compared with the old. Pritchard's book claimed to be a comprehensive account, running to a mere twenty-two pages. By contrast, *The Perfect Ceremonies of Craft Masonry*, a book of "modern" ritual published in 1926, runs to two hundred and forty five pages — with a similar number of words per page — or put another way, roughly eleven times the size of *Masonry Dissected*. This huge difference in wordage is compounded in that *The Perfect Ceremonies* only describes the rituals of Craft Masonry[25], and doesn't even tell the full picture of "modern" Masonic ceremonial: that there are additional rituals for allied Masonic degrees, such as the Royal Arch.

Naturally, such a massive overhaul heralded radical change in the language of the ritual too. The English of *The Perfect Ceremonies* is decidedly more "Georgian" than that of *Masonry Dissected*, employing words and phrases reminiscent of Doctor Johnson and John Locke. By contrast, *Masonry Dissected* fails to convey the feel of the eighteenth century in that the gravity and consistency of the ritual is far more sporadic. Considering the kind of men drawn to Freemasonry at the time, this isn't surprising; but what is intriguing is that "new" ritual is littered with examples that these same men deliberately inserted references to contemporary scientific and intellectual thinking. These additions not only covered the almost obligatory Architecture and geometry, but other popular "Enlightenment" subjects too, like astronomy, mathematics, history and geography.

Alterations and additions to the volume, wording and phraseology of post-*Masonry Dissected* ritual were paralleled by a change of focus in the overarching imagery as well. Taking one specific element — construction — the building terminology was not only retained, but indeed bolstered and refined. For instance, the ritual now, for the first time, stated the order in which the first two cornerstones of a Masonic building should be laid: "North East", followed by "South East", the Northern and Southern limits of the said structure: two "Grand Parallel Lines" running East — West, as well as, in the *Perfect Ceremonies of the Supreme Order of the Holy Royal Arch*[26], a description of the entrance on the Eastern side.

25 The basic three degrees, Entered Apprentice, Fellow Craft and Master Mason.

26 Published in London, 1907

The above three examples represent a fraction of "new" construction features and detail; there were many other innovations defining further aspects of the building, such as interior fixtures and the roof. Paradoxically, however, these new characteristics didn't amount to a comprehensive list of stages or dimensions, or even anything remotely approaching such a list. "New" ritual — or at least those parts of it referring to construction — was riddled with gaps and omissions, which would have rendered the raising of a physical building based on its precepts virtually impossible.

Take, for instance, two of the examples already mentioned, the cornerstones and the North and South sides of the building. Whilst the order in which the eastern cornerstones should be laid was clearly defined, no mention was made in the Masons' ritual of western cornerstones at all. Likewise, the detailed description of the North and South of the building, "bound north and south by two grand parallel lines" contrasted sharply with the absence of a stab at defining the Eastern and Western sides of the structure, although the "Royal Arch" ritual, written separately from the mid 1730s onwards, went some way to answering this question, for the Eastern side at least.

So why were there so many omissions in the new construction rituals of the Masons? It is inconceivable that the men rewriting the rituals post — *Masonry Dissected*, with nearly a century to get it right, left out any mention of the Western side and its cornerstones accidentally. Too much care and attention, by too many people, suggests there had to be a *deliberate* reason why these features, and other aspects of the building, weren't included.

Of course, there has to a logical reason behind these omissions, and superficially, one possibility is that the men rewriting the rituals left out much of the "construction" terminology to retain a balance. An assumption can be made that they had the full picture at their disposal, but consciously chose to select singular examples to get their message across. If this is so, then it suggests the "speculative" fraternity were again inspired by practices common to both medieval stonecutters and contemporary architects like Sir Christopher Wren. Both were adept at putting together, in stone and on paper, singular examples of features appearing more than once in their buildings, and it is plausible that the men rewriting the Masonic ritual were as equally skilled at employing the same technique.

A second potential cause behind the "gaps" is that they refer to aspects of the structure that couldn't measure up to the writers desire to imbue their "building" plan with as much geometry as possible. Certainly, many of the features defined are highly geometric in their relationship to one another; and whilst this may reflect a straightforward attempt by the ritualists to emulate contemporary architectural science, it also suggests the "building" contained additional features that couldn't be explained away in a geometrical manner. If this is so, then it is strongly suggestive of something else: that the construction wasn't purely a product of the ritualists' imagination, and that it did indeed have a physical basis, or, at a bare minimum, co-existed with a physical background.

There is however a third, far more radical explanation for the patchy specification: it referred to something *already in the process* of being built. Here, the ritual, far from a blueprint, is more of a simple description of work already completed; a historical record. This argument would explain why, of all of the exterior features that could have been included, only the eastern cornerstones, the Northern and Southern boundaries and, from 1735 onwards, the "Royal Arch" were in place — they were the sum total of the sections of the building that already existed. Ditto the failure to mention the sequence of laying out the "Western" cornerstones. Had the ceremonial been some kind of specification, then their inclusion would again have been almost obligatory. Absence therefore suggests not only were they non-existent at the time of writing, but the men penning the new ceremonial were not even prepared to hazard a guess as to the eventual sequence in which they would be laid.

To summarize, the rewritten "construction" element in Masonic ritual could therefore be a collection of singular examples, a geometrical specification or even a historical record. It may be any one of these possibilities in isolation, a combination of two or maybe all three of them, whilst it is also conceivable it is none of them at all. The difficulty of identifying a definitive answer highlights the essential problem raised by the Masonic ritual devoted to building: what kind of edifice was it describing? Was the building physical, in the way the operative masons would understand it, or a symbolic design, more in tune with the ideas of speculative masons' like Ashmole and Stukeley? Or could the ritual refer to some kind of unrealized ideal? The confusing combination of detail and omission, theory and guesswork, science and supernatural raises question after question, although of all the possible explanations, there is one thing that cannot be disputed: "the building" celebrated in Masonic ceremonial referred to a standard Masonic Lodge, itself a symbolic interpretation of the structure at the heart of modern Freemasonry: King Solomon's Temple.

III

The building of the Temple of Solomon is, of course, the great construction story of the Bible. Unlike the Tower of Babel, which symbolizes human arrogance culminating in failure, the Temple story by contrast represents the ideal, in that it was a construction worthy of being called "The House of the Lord". As an "ideal" structure, it is highly improbable the Old Testament story actually refers to a building made from stone, wood or clay: it is more likely a metaphor for the establishment of an edifice symbolizing perfection, whether in a spiritual, physical or temporal sense. Underpinning this argument, the archaeological evidence — or more importantly the lack of it — strongly suggests no such building was ever built, although detailed histories covering the Temple's construction are described in two books of the Bible, *Kings* and *Chronicles*. Both accounts are essentially similar, which is why only one — from *Kings* — is summarized below, a selection aimed at highlighting specific aspects of the building:

> And it came to pass in the four hundred and eightieth year after the children of Israel were come out of the land of Egypt, in the fourth year of Solomon's reign over Israel, in the month Zif, which *is* the second month, that he began to build the house of the LORD... And the house which King Solomon built for the LORD, the length thereof *was* threescore cubits, and the breadth thereof twenty *cubits*, and the height thereof thirty cubits...And the porch before the temple of the house, twenty cubits *was* the length thereof, according to the breadth of the house; *and* ten cubits *was* the breadth thereof before the house... And the house, when it was in building, was built of stone made ready before it was brought thither: so that there was neither hammer *nor* axe nor any tool of iron heard in the house, while it was in building... So he built the house, and finished it...In

the fourth year was the foundation of the house of the LORD laid in the month Zif...And in the eleventh year, in the month Bul, which is the eighth month, was the house finished throughout all the parts thereof, and according to all the fashion of it. So was he seven years in building it.[27]

— 1 Kings 6

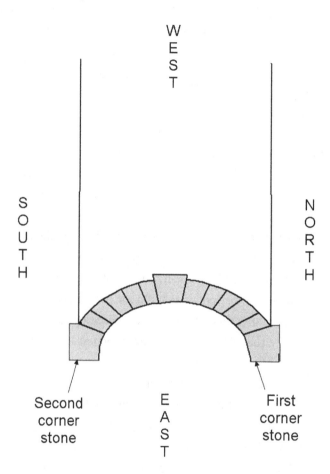

Fig. 2: The external aspects of a Masonic Temple according to "new" ritual. The "Two Grand Parallel Lines" are drawn from the *Explanation of the First Degree Tracing Board*, "The North East Corner of the Building" from the First degree, and the "South East Part" from the second. These features were incorporated into the ritual between 1730 and 1760. The Arch comes from the Royal Arch degree, whose rituals were written from 1734 onwards. Note how a relatively well defined East contrasts with a complete failure to describe the Western side of the structure.

---

27 This quotation comes from the King James Bible, the version that King James I ordered to be used throughout the United Kingdom. All Biblical quotes will come from the KJV, on the grounds that it was this Bible that the Masonic ritual writers of the 1730s drew their inspiration from. Italics and spelling mistakes are as in the original.

It is therefore easy to see why a fraternity whose rituals revolved around construction adopted the Temple to play such an important part in its imagery. Aiming for the ideal was absolutely essential, especially in an era when Biblical stories were still being taken literally, not least by many of those men joining the Order. Even so, what is curious was the provenance of the relationship of King Solomon's Temple and its place within Masonic ritual. For back in 1730, Pritchard's *Masonry Dissected* had only made scattered references to the Temple, and significantly, it was only with the advent of the "new" ceremonial that the building was elevated to an absolutely central role in Masonic lore.

Superficially, the change of focus at this time made sense. Anyone could see the Temple story neatly combined the two strands constant throughout the known history of the Masonic Order, both operative and speculative: the terminology of the building site combined with Biblical imagery. It stands to reason therefore, that by shifting the baseline of the ritual in the direction of the Temple, the writers cleverly squeezed out competing stories, a move placing greater emphasis on the fragile connection between the new "speculative" fraternity and its "operational" ancestor.

Practicality played a part too. The story of the raising of King Solomon's Temple was — and is — rich in potential symbolism, which could provide the evolving Fraternity with an inexhaustible supply of "construction" material, metaphor and imagery, an immense compendium of detail that could be exploited by those penning "new" ritual to maximum effect. Whilst aiming for tighter imagery and practicality are both distinct possibilities behind change, a definitive answer may never be known, for, like the question of the "missing" construction detail, the reason behind the ritualists desire to shift Masonic ceremonial in the direction of King Solomon's Temple was something that neither the ritual explains, nor for that matter historical research has ever revealed.

Aside from the obvious connections to be drawn from the story of constructing the "ideal" building, there is also the symbolic importance of the Temple story's principal character, King Solomon. Alongside his father, David, Solomon has, over the last three millennia, been the best known of the rulers of ancient Israel, a celebrity primarily centered on one characteristic in particular: Wisdom. Over the centuries the king has been credited with almost super human powers of reason, and his renown has survived until the present day, especially in the Jewish and Christian world, although at certain times and places within this common culture an even deeper fascination with the King has also developed.

England at the time when the Grand Lodge of England was founded was one such place, although why a western European country at the height of the enlightenment should develop a fascination with a Middle Eastern Monarch from Biblical times is a mystery. One would have thought people like Sir Isaac Newton, his assistant Desaguliers or the map-maker Senex had enough to do pulling Britain out of its ignorance, although on the other side of the coin there is the symbolic importance Solomon could hold for such men, and others, in the vanguard of contemporary English intellectual thought. The cultural and scientific works of Augustan England were littered with references to the King's name — or a derivation of it — and, by extension, the religious building with which he is associated. Indeed, the frequency with which Solomon and the Temple appear in factual and fictional books and pamphlets between 1660 and 1760 was complimented only by the prominence of those who invoked his spirit, and it is a fact that many of the great thinkers of the Enlightenment — or at least its English variant — were impressed enough by the King's abilities to cite him as a symbol representing Wisdom or Knowledge in their works.

Enlightenment name dropping extended to the Temple, which, like Solomon, also made frequent appearances in the written works of the age. For instance, in 1688, John Bunyan, author of *A Pilgrims Progress*, published *Solomon's Temple Spiritualised* which, incidentally, was also an early example of the kind of allegory and symbolism later characterizing much of the "new" Masonic ritual. Forty years after *Solomon's Temple Spiritualised*, Newton's *The Chronology of Ancient Kingdoms Amended*, published posthumously in 1728, devoted one-fifth of its contents to a visionary description of the building, whilst sandwiched between Bunyan and Sir Isaac's works was the reconstruction of Saint Paul's Cathedral, the layout of which has led some to speculate that Sir Christopher Wren incorporated Temple influences into the building's design[28]. The aforementioned are, of course, a very small sample, and whilst it would be foolish to infer from them that many of the country's finest minds were obsessed with the Old Testament Building, they do however illustrate the level of awareness present amongst the likes of Bunyan, Newton and Wren, and how seriously such men valued the Temple as a symbol, to bear it in mind in their respective fields.

It wasn't only England's great and good nursing a curiosity about King Solomon's Temple, for poetry, paintings, engravings plus newspaper reports and advertisements from the late seventeenth and early eighteenth centuries again illustrate how deeply ordinary people shared the fascination as well. Amongst scores of examples, one instance of this phenomenon was in the wooden models of the Temple exhibited in London when the rituals of the Freemasons were undergoing their most fundamental change. At least two Georgian entrepreneurs had seen the way the wind was blowing, and constructed scale imitations of the Temple, the returns coming from public display, augmented by an additional charge for an accompanying booklet. The latter model went on show during 1759 and 1760; whilst the former, the work of a man named Schott, appeared before Londoners in 1723 and 1730 respectively.

The curiosity surrounding the Temple was, naturally, instrumental in determining whether Schott's brainwave would be successful or not; although a measure of his self confidence can, of course, be inferred from the advertising the businessman was prepared to splash out on. For on the Model's second outing — coincidentally the same year that *Masonry Dissected* first saw the light of day — Schott was obviously sure enough of a sizable financial return to place the following advert in the *London Daily Courant*:

> To be seen at the Royal-Exchange every Day, The model of the TEMPLE of SOLOMON, with all its Porches, Walls, Gates, Chambers and holy Vessels, the great Altar of the Burnt Offering, the Moulton Sea, the Lavers, the Sanctum Sanctorum; with the Ark of the Covenant, the Mercy Seat and Golden Cherubims, the Altar of Incense, the Candlestick, Tables of Shew-Bread, with the two famous pillars, called Joachim and Boas. Within the model are 2000 Chambers and Windows, and Pillars 7000; the Model is 13 foot high and 80 foot round. Likewise the Model of the Tabernacle of

---

28 Gilbert, *The New Jerusalem*

MOSES, with the Ark of the Covenant, wherein is the law of *Moses*, the Pot of Manna and the Rod of *Aaron*, the Urim and Tumin, with all the other Vessels. The printed Description of it, with 12 fine Cuts, is to be had at the same place at 5s. a Book.

N.B. The Publick is desired to take Notice, that the Sanctum Sanctorum, with all the holy Vessels is new gilt, and appears much finer and richer than before.[29]

If Schott's advertisement illustrates the man's confidence in his venture, the intricate detail he felt compelled to include in the model is a clear statement of "publick" awareness about the Temple. The model maker was obviously reacting to a level of popular knowledge in tune with the spirit of the times, in that the first exhibition fell during the forty years that separate *Solomon's Temple Spiritualized* and *The Chronology of Ancient Kingdoms Amended* whilst the second took place a mere two years later. Simultaneously, but on a far larger scale, this era also witnessed the completion of Saint Paul's Cathedral in 1710 and, seven years later, the foundation of the Grand Lodge.

It is therefore inevitable that Masonic researchers[30] have suggested there was almost certainly a connection between the popular fascination with the building, the change in emphasis within the ritual, and the adoption of the Temple as a symbolic representation of a Freemason's Lodge. This is highly likely, given the cultural and social crossovers between the Order and English society in general were very tight indeed at the time. Apart from the fact that scores of Masons (and would-be Masons) undoubtedly walked past — or even visited — Schott's model, and many of the contemporaries of Newton, Bunyan and Wren were joining the Fraternity, familiarity was reinforced by the "new" Order's birth at the very center of the "scene" in London, and nothing summed up the geographical and social nexus of Official Freemasonry more than the fact the Grand Lodge itself had been formed from Lodges based at the four London ale-houses mentioned previously. This in turn brings us to a *further* influence on the "Symbolic Temple" and its importance to the Masons: the physical restraints on Masonic assemblies during the years when the changes to the ritual were at their height.

---

29 Cited in Jones, *The Freemasons' Guide*
30 See W. J. Chetwode-Crawley.

IV

Even whilst the ritual was starting to undergo the transformation from its *Masonry Dissected* incarnation towards the modern version, ordinary Masons were, due to financial constraints, still confined to using chambers hired for the evening to conduct ceremonial, the room in question being decked out with Masonic features to imitate the Temple. One of the shortcomings inherent in this approach was a private room at an inn or coffee house was subject to use by others, and therefore the "Symbolic Building" assembled at Masonic meetings had to be temporary in character. Evidence — from contemporary *exposures* — indicate this often took a form of lines drawn on the floor, the materials used being Chalk, Charcoal and Clay, although an *expose* of 1766 points to a far more exotic mix of substances employed:

> The drawing is frequently made with chalk, stone-blue and charcoal intermixed...At the time of making (a mason), the room is very grandly illuminated; and, in some lodges, pwder'd rosin, mixed with shining sand, is strewed on the floor, which (together with the extraordinary illumination of the room) has a pretty effect... which in some lodges resembles the grand Building, termed a Mosaic Palace, and is described with the utmost exactness...[31].

The advantage of a drawing "made with chalk" was the simplicity of its removal. At the end of each assembly, all that was needed was for members present to wipe or wash away the design[32]. However, assuming cleaning up operations were carried out with varying degrees of success, one can imagine frequent altercations between publicans and Masons over the state of the wooden or stone floor, smeared with the chalk, charcoal or clay remnants of the Mosaic Palace. To circumvent this, some Lodges replaced the chalk and charcoal lines with tapes nailed to the floor, although hammering nails into floorboards cannot have been much more conducive

---

31 *The Freemasons' Guide*

32 Like everything else in Masonry at the time, the method of drawing the 'Grand Building' on the floor of whatever room was being used entered an experimental stage, even to the point where the eradication of the 'Mosaic Palace' at the end of the meeting became significant. Exposures indicate that this was a duty retained for the newest member to carry out, starting on the night of his initiation: 'as soon as the ceremony of making is over, the New-made Mason (though ever so great a Gentleman) must take a Mop from a Pail of Water, and wash it out'. Cited in Jones, *The Freemasons' Guide*

to good landlord-Masonic relations than messy clay and charcoal. A solution acceptable to all was required, which was found in the employment of carpets or floor cloths that bore the illustration of the symbolic building, which became more commonplace as the 1730s wore on.

But space limitations and privacy apart, there may be a third reason why the "Mosaic Palace" was, until purpose built Masonic halls were built, depicted on the floor of the Lodge in a one dimensional manner: the origin of the word "Temple" itself. W J Williams' research clearly infers that Freemasonry circa 1730 was already heavily colonized by some of the most intellectual minds in the country. It is inconceivable that these men were unaware that "Temple" is drawn from the Latin *Templum*, the literal translation of which is "open, or consecrated place"[33]. The word *Templum* appears in the ritual of the Royal Arch degree[34]; and bearing in mind the presence of individuals like Stukeley and Desaguliers, plus the existence of Schott's model at the Royal Exchange, it is feasible that the one dimensional "Palace" was deliberately laid out in this manner.

These travails, and experiments with clay, nails, tapes and carpets, highlights the fact early Freemasons were forced to conduct their ceremonies in premises reliant on the goodwill of others. To an outsider — and indeed many of the "Brethren" — all that really existed was a small English fraternal society, with a membership of, at most, a few thousand, and whose main claim to fame was they conducted ceremonies on a pattern of chalk lines meant to represent some kind of "Symbolic Temple." But was a fundamentally shallow analysis? For, in a deeper sense, a far more formidable movement was already taking shape. Whilst hundreds of other fraternities rose and fell, the Masonic Order, with its broad conditions of membership, was spreading through English society like a virus, although some sections were clearly more prone than others.

Whilst the laborers of England were poorly represented in Masonic ranks, at the other extremity of society, the Order was expanding in leaps and bounds. Members of Parliament, lords, dukes and even members of the royal family were queuing up to join, an accumulation of power and

---

33 *Concise Oxford Dictionary*
34 *Perfect Ceremonies of the Supreme Order of the Holy Royal Arch*, 1907, page 63

influence that over time merely emphasized the central contradiction at the heart of the Order. For, if Schott could build his model single-handedly, and Christopher Wren design Saint Paul's, then why couldn't a fraternity boasting some of the most intelligent and influential people in the most advanced nation in the world reconstitute the Temple itself?

In a physical sense reconstruction, of course, never happened. There is no structure anywhere on Earth that approximates to, or even resembles, a rebuilt Temple, regardless of whether its dimensions and features originate in the Bible, the rituals of the Freemasons, or for that matter, both. Even so, the non-existence of a physical building misses the point about the Masonic Order: it expresses itself through allegory and symbolism, rather than bricks and mortar. It therefore stands to reason any construction would be symbolic in character rather than stone, and if such a building were raised — or even considered — at least some conclusions as to its nature can be identified from the Masonic experience to date.

Firstly, the location of the site would, logically, be somewhere relatively manageable, where building could proceed with a minimum of interference regardless of whether it took the Biblical seven, seventy or seven hundred years to complete. This, theoretically could be anywhere, but ideally, would mean Britain, or somewhere compatible with, or influenced by, British culture, especially its Masonic strand.

Secondly, the method of laying out the dimensions and characteristics of the "Symbolic Temple" during the early years — lines on the floors of London Taverns — could be reprised for *the* Temple, i.e. geometric lines and shapes laid out on a flat — or relatively flat — surface. This approach would also have the added advantage of confirming the "building" as a literal translation of *Templum*, "an open or consecrated space".

Thirdly, the Temple's fixtures and features would be a synthesis of the influences that had gone into its makeup: features drawn from the Bible, the operative stoneworkers Lodges, crossed with the characteristics of the topographical background to be "worked". Fourthly, to harmonize with these changes and indeed to emphasis the important features, the ritual would be rewritten, thus allowing for the buildings quirks, methodology of construction, and limitations due to physical reasons. The "rewrite" would also confirm a rough date for commencement of construction: after the foundation of the Grand Lodge in 1717, in particular following the ritual rewrites that began in the 1730s;

Finally, five: to be as close a representation of its Old Testament predecessor as possible, the Temple would not only have to be built without the use of "tools of iron", as laid down in *Kings*, 6:7 "and the house, when it was in building, was built of stone made ready before it was brought thither: so that there was neither hammer nor axe nor any tool of iron heard in the house, while it was in building", but even more testing, the completed structure would have to be of dimensions enormous enough to accommodate people of "all nations", as prophesized in two books of the Old Testament:

> And it shall come to pass in the last days, that the mountain of the LORD's house shall be established in the top of the mountains, and shall be exalted above the hills; and all nations shall flow unto it. (Isaiah, 2:2)

> But in the last days it shall come to pass, that the mountain of the house of the LORD shall be established in the top of the mountains, and it shall be exalted above the hills, and people shall flow into it. 2 And many nations shall come, and say, Come, and let us go up to the mountain of the LORD, and to the house of the GOD of Jacob... (Micah, 4:1)

Inigo Jones

Elias Ashmole

William Stukeley

Anthony Sayer

Chapter 3. "Geometry in the Original Sense, is the Art of Measuring Land..."

> Simon: Why were you made a Mason? Philip: For sake of the Letter G
>
> Philip: What does it signifye?
>
> Simon: Geomitry
>
> Philip: Why Geomitry?
>
> Simon: Because it is the Root and foundation of all Arts and Sciences
>
> Part of *A Dialogue Between Simon, A Town Mason, & Philip, A Travelling Mason* (1740)[35]

I

Serendipity had played a significant role with regard to the birth of modern masonry. For the fraternity obsessed with construction site symbolism and the raising of the "ideal building" emerged in an era and country where the science of architecture and its related fields were experiencing unprecedented change. This process had already been gathering pace for some time, but during the Seventeenth century it accelerated, as Britain realized several innovations in the technology of construction

---

35 An Expose of circa 1740, published in Knoop, Jones and Hamer's The Early Masonic Catechisms, 1963, p.177

that by 1717, were already leading to a complete upheaval in design of the nations' architecture, landscape and streets.

Like all revolutions, it is impossible to define a date when the underlying causes behind radical change began to manifest themselves, although, undoubtedly, one key year was 1610, when Inigo Jones pioneered the use of architect's drawings to fine tune designs prior to construction. The fundamental importance of blueprints were that, rather than the traditional reliance on builders' intuition in the raising of buildings, they lead to a more scientific approach within architecture, incorporating greater use of physics and geometry. Blueprints also meant that in addition to more intricate designs being attempted, standardized plans could be copied on a far greater scale, spreading new ideas faster and further than before.

Professional drawings called for skilled draughtsman ship, and it was no coincidence that England in the seventeenth century also witnessed the genesis of the first generation of native born professional architects. There are several individuals who could lay claim to have been the most notable proponent of the profession during this time, although posterity remembers four names in particular, Jones, Christopher Wren, Nicholas Hawksmoor and John Vanbrugh. All of the former were destined to take the science of building — in Britain at least — to unprecedented heights, and would make full use of pre-construction plans in their designs, not only for buildings such as St Paul's Cathedral or Blenheim Palace, but also for reconstruction of Cities like London, Oxford and Bath.

The example of London following the fire of 1666 threw a further innovation into the mix: legislation aimed at greater regulation of Britain's urban development. Whilst the idea of designed street layouts was already millennia old by the seventeenth century, the city of London — especially the materials it was constructed of — had developed haphazardly, a central reason behind conditions causing the conflagration in the first place. To ensure such a situation didn't occur again, the capital's resurrection was defined by the Rebuilding Act of 1667, which laid down far tighter regulations that had hitherto existed before. This law demanded the "New" London be built from stone and slate, at the expense of the more fire-friendly timber and thatch, a trend that was, over time, gradually copied by other towns and cities across the Country.

Inevitably, these innovations were instrumental in triggering stylistic change as well, for coinciding with the reconstruction was a movement in English architecture towards the utilization of more classical influences, especially from ancient Rome and Greece. Undoubtedly, one cause behind this was that exiled Royalists, on the run across Europe from Oliver Cromwell's Republic, were exposed to far greater array of architectural styles than they had hitherto been used to, and brought new ideas back to Britain after 1660. Particularly influential in this respect was the Italian architect, Andrea Palladio, who's *The Four Books of Architecture*,[36] extolling the adoption of classical ideas for domestic architecture, was translated into English in 1676.

Over the next fifty years, the *Four Books* were joined by further works in a similar vein. These ranged from well known publications such as Campbell's *Vitruvius Britannicus* (1715), Kent's *Designs of Inigo Jones* (1727) through to more obscure texts such as Robert Castell's 1728 *The Villas of the Ancients Revisited*. These books, plus the scores of others on similar subjects, obviously meant stiff competition, in terms of influence, for Palladio. It was therefore an indication of the long dead Italian's impact that it was his name, rather than that of Campbell or Kent, which became synonymous with the design of many great houses and buildings erected during the century and a half following the publication of the *Four Books*: the Palladian style.

But it wasn't only the buildings of Britain which benefited from these new trends. Other facets of the man made environment subject to design, from town streets to gardens and furniture, were also affected by new science, innovative legislation and imported styles. For instance, a side effect of the 1667 Rebuilding Act had been to give the concept of town planning a huge push forward. For the first time since the Roman Empire, an opportunity existed for the street pattern of London to be laid out to a pre-drawn plan, a situation the authorities were initially keen to exploit. A competition to find the best design for the New London was held,

---

36 Originally called *I Quatttro Libri dell 'archittura*. Andrea Palladio was born in 1508 and died in 1580.

which attracted submissions from amongst others, Christopher Wren. Wren's idea was for a City of large, straight thoroughfares, set at geometric angles from one another, a design not dissimilar to the one devised by Baron Hausemann for Paris a century and a half in the future. Regardless of how revolutionary or sensible this was, on this occasion, Wren, along with other contestants, was to be disappointed. Far from seizing the opportunity, conservative elements amongst the powers that be decided that London was to be rebuilt using the streets existing prior to the fire.

Even so, notwithstanding this setback, the idea that towns, cities and other large areas could, via sophisticated geometry, be planned in advance now existed in the English consciousness. From the late seventeenth century onwards, the increasing use of this science meant the chaotic Tudor townscapes of England began to be replaced with a degree of order, symmetry and standardization not seen before. Whilst all of these changes may have only been witnessed in a fragmentary sense by the man in the street between 1660 and 1760, their collective impact was far more fundamental. For Great Britain, the quasi-instinctive desire to pre-plan work, cross fertilized with new influences, not only raised the aesthetic standard, but also the science of design too. Combined with acts of parliament and increasingly sophisticated measuring instrumentation, by the time of the foundation of the Grand Lodge of England in 1717, the country was already beginning to exhibit to the World a far more orderly and elegant face than had been the case a century earlier.

II

The experience of Britain was decisive in proving geometry could be drawn upon to promote order and elegance. It also posed a further question: could the science galvanizing Britain's designers to ever greater achievement be employed defining and delineating far larger projects, specifically the boundaries between states, provinces and spheres of influence? Such an idea was, and would continue to be, fanciful across mainland Europe, where national and provincial borders were forged through processes far removed from scientific application. Even on the British mainland, the answer would also be no, in that the boundaries between England, Scotland, Wales and their constituent counties and boroughs were already long in place by the time geometry could be applied to their design.

Nevertheless, Great Britain did differ from Europe in one crucial way with regard to cartography and geometry, and this was because early eighteenth century England was a time and place of marked improvement in the science of measuring far greater distances and areas, and the reason for this lies in Britain's status as island nation. From the sixteenth century onwards, the country was on its way to becoming the world's most powerful ocean-going power, a dominance relying heavily on the ability of its shipping to define location away from *terra firma*. Without such technology in place, Britain's Imperial interests in the Americas and elsewhere would be severely compromised, for not only the Royal Navy, but the merchant fleet too, would struggle to keep the bounds of Empire together. Following the triumph over the Spanish Armada in 1588, it was to be expected the search for better definition at sea could be put on the back burner for a while; but a bruising naval war against the Dutch between 1665 and 1667 again pushed it to the front of the minds governing England, even that of King Charles II, who created the Royal Astronomical Society during 1674, with the aim — apart from pure scientific research — of tightening up the technology of identifying position on the high seas.

The fundamental difficulty facing scientists and seafarers was the capability of existing instrumentation only stretched to measuring latitude, which only provided a clear definition of location with respect to North and South, the great unknown being a tried and tested method for ascertaining longitude, the key to position in terms of east and west. Such knowledge was naturally crucial to Britain's naval fortunes, though even the support of King Charles II wasn't enough to crack the mystery, and well into the eighteenth century ships' officers could only guess their position using latitude, a situation that on occasion had catastrophic consequences.

One such calamity was the destruction of *The Association* and other ships of the British Fleet off the Scilly Isles in 1707. So shocking did the country find this disaster, the Admiralty was forced to really get a grip on the problem, leading to the passage, seven years later, of the Longitude Act, which offered a prize of twenty thousand pounds to whoever devised a method of calculating longitude. Such an enormous sum in 1714 would see a man through life very comfortably indeed; so it is again a measure of the problem faced that no one claimed the prize for many years to come[37]. For the next forty-five years, those concerned with defining position on the high seas were still confined to technology and maps only showing them the ship's position in relation to the parallel lines of latitude circling the world from east to west.

For Britain, the importance of surveying wasn't confined to the sea. On dry land, especially those portions ruled from London, the art of defining territorial areas accurately was again crucial, as the country metamorphosed from a feudal society into the hub of a capitalist empire. From the fifteenth century onwards, land maps became increasingly important as "who owned what" — in both a political[38] and economic sense — became vital to the country's fortunes, something of such importance that it even attracted the attention of the monarch, Elizabeth I, who ordered the cartographer Christopher Saxton to produce the first accurate map of Britain, *Anglia*, during the 1570s.

Apart from its Royal endorsement, *Anglia* was also a breakthrough in English cartography in a secondary sense. Prior to Saxton, British map making was characterized by the production of merely symbolic representations, and even though such maps tended to be highly decorative — take for example the *Mappa Mundi* — they were usually worse than useless for the purposes of property and political definitions. In this respect, the English lagged behind the Dutch and Flemish who were drawing modern descriptive maps as early as the 1470s. Led by people such as Gerard Mercator and Abraham Ortelius, the low-countries maintained this lead well into the seventeenth century, although the creation of *Anglia* and application of the science behind it, planted the seeds of a new industry that gradually closed the gap on England's map making competitors.

---

37 Not until John Harrison developed his navigational clocks in 1759, in fact. See Dava Sobel's *Longitude*.

38 As early as the Sixteenth Century, military surveyors also needed increasingly accurate cartography, for the defence of the Kingdom.

As the sixteenth century gave way to the seventeenth, this new industry started to notch up some important successes, starting with the publication, in 1607, of William Camden's *Britannia*, which in turn was followed four years later by John Speed's *The Theatre of the Empire of Great Britaine*. Naturally, the spur to much of this activity were contemporary advances in the science of surveying, and notwithstanding the Low countries map making lead, England had got off to an early start in this field with Leonard Digges's invention of the Theodolite in the 1560s. The basic tool of the surveying trade, the Theodolite was — and is — basically a tripod-based instrument, with a rotating telescope on top. It is usually made from Brass, because instrumentation wrought from other metals like iron were vulnerable to changes in temperature, affecting accuracy. Such an invention, which could accurately define horizontal and vertical angles, naturally heralded a quantum leap forward in the science of map making and the definition of areas, and from *Anglia* onwards, British cartography started to undergo a continuous improvement, a process that continues to the present day.

Although the invention of the theodolite plus the new descriptive maps meant English cartography would gradually erode Mercator and Ortelius's lead, Christopher Saxton and his colleagues faced one intractable problem when it came to mapping Britain and its political subdivisions. And this was that by the time the science of surveying was up and running, the bulk of the country's estate, town and county boundaries were already in place, which meant the country's surveyors and cartographers were left with the task of simply reacting to what already existed.

Even though this may have suited cartographers happy simply to record or modify, one can imagine how stifling it could be for those who saw in surveying the chance to do something creative. For what has been overlooked by history is the science of identifying and marking boundaries could indeed be an *art*, so long as the right conditions existed for the surveyor, in that his technology could be applied to landscapes without the nuisance of political or physical interference. Of course, Britain — or anywhere in Europe for that matter — couldn't meet such criteria, for the reasons already stated; so there was only one place Anglo-Saxon surveyors of the seventeenth and eighteenth centuries could make full creative use of the science: the colonies in America, and it was here, across Britain's possessions in the New World, that the science of surveying, aided by astronomy, was to make its greatest impact.

The late American historian Daniel Boorstin described the effect of surveying technology on the developing economic map of America when he said:

> that to survey small town-lots and farm boundaries in long settled Europe, arithmetic with a smattering of trigonometry sufficed, but America offered a whole continent to be measured. The property lines of extensive tracts in the wilderness could not be drawn from a large rock or the stump of a familiar tree; they had to be defined by the astronomical dimensions of latitude and longitude.[39]

Boorstin was, however, only looking at part of the picture — economic development — for the application of the new science in the colonies differed from Europe in another way that would eventually be crucial to the political cartography of the United States, and this was the application of geometry to the boundaries of counties and provinces, in addition the more traditional farms and towns. Apart from the fact that carving up America geometrically represented a logical shift to a superior technology, a secondary reason behind surveying for political purposes was expediency: the need to map huge areas quickly for strategic and diplomatic purposes, on a continent subject to the attentions of Europe's three most aggressive imperial powers.

More fundamentally however, it was also the inevitable outcome of a situation where the world's most advanced surveying and cartographic science came into contact with a landscape where no one (from a European perspective) claimed formal ownership. Opinions of indigenous and slave populations were irrelevant, whilst the homogenizing effect that living in America had on British, Irish, Dutch, Swedish and German settlers meant sensitivities due to ethnicity could be ignored with impunity. This proved a sharp contrast to the Old World experience, where a settled but ethnically diverse population plus fierce competition for territory were instrumental in the siting of political borders and predated them, factors that were to play a much smaller role in the drawing of America.

---

39 Boorstin, *The Americans: The Colonial Experience.*

The creation of boundaries based on geometry was also necessary because of the scant knowledge Europeans had of the interior, especially its natural features. Although maps of the Continent had been plotted since the arrival of Christopher Columbus two hundred years earlier, cartographical analysis was handicapped by an inability to describe in detail much of the country inland from the coast. To be fair, every mapmaker was handicapped this problem, though one example that stands out was in the works of John Sellar, who produced the first collection of maps covering the eastern seaboard, *The English Pilot, Fourth Book*, during 1689[40].

Whilst Sellar accurately plotted the East Coast, he stumbled badly attempting to define the interior, a persistent problem throughout American history, for though inland features — such as the mountain ranges — were known about in a general sense by 1750, detailed mapping of huge chunks of country, especially the West, remained an impossibility as late as the second half of the nineteenth century.

Even so, and regardless of the difficulties such a situation posed for the powers that be, conditions were ideal for those who wished to survey, map and apply geometry to the design of America. Ignorance of the interior, the neutrality of public opinion, plus no meaningful military threat meant that as early as 1700 many of the colonial borders on the Eastern seaboard were already illustrating the hand of the surveyor and his new-fangled technology.

---

40 The dominance of the Dutch and Flemish mapmakers during the first half of the Seventeenth Century began to be seriously challenged by Britain following the restoration of Charles II in 1660. Conflict between Britain and Holland forced the British to act over the Cartography issue, which resulted in the first of Sellars' works, The English Pilot, being published in London during 1670. *The English Pilot* relied heavily on the Older Dutch maps, and was therefore flawed in that it produced some, if not all, of their mistakes. Nevertheless, Sellar had made a breakthrough. The English Pilot — which came out in several volumes over time — meant that anyone in Britain who wished to study the most up-to-date maps of the World was now able to do so.

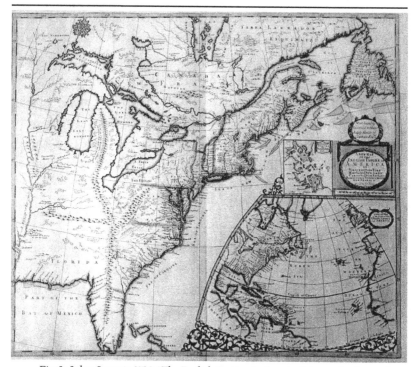

Fig 3: John Senex's 1719 *"The English Empire in America"* not only shows how important parallels and meridians were, but also the use of mathematical lines for the boundaries of the individual colonies.

Straight lines abounded everywhere, already reaching hundreds of miles in length in some cases, and not deviating — on paper at least — by as much as an inch. Two and a half centuries on, the culmination of this process — the political map of the Union of fifty sovereign States — was to be a highly geometric design that contrasted sharply with the twists and turns that are a permanent feature of the political cartography of Europe.

As if to emphasize the central role geometry played in the evolving imperial map were the claims Britain made to North America as a whole. As a society that already valued the rule of law, each colony organized its affairs under a charter, which, apart from defining various aspects of government, also outlined territorial limits of the said colony. These definitions were usually stated in a north–south and east–west manner: north–south in that the colony existed between two fixed points on the Eastern seaboard, whilst "east–west" was far more grand and abstract, in that the Crown awarded the colony the land rights from the two points on the Atlantic coast right across North America to the "South Seas", as the Pacific Ocean was then commonly referred to[41].

Such grandiose awards even existed during the earliest days. For example, the 1609 Charter for Virginia, granted the Colony all lands in North America between the thirty-forth and forty-fifth parallels north. This legal precedent was repeated and built upon[42] throughout the seventeenth and into the eighteenth century, as new provinces were born, all the way to the last, Georgia, which, according to its charter of 1732:

> ...lies from the northern stream of a river, there commonly called the Savannah, all along the seacoast to the southward unto the most southern stream of a certain other great water or river called the Altamaha, and westward from the heads of the said rivers, respectively, in direct lines to the South seas, and all that space, circuit, and precinct of land lying within the said boundaries.[43]

Such generosity on the part of the Crown was, however, marred by the fact these territorial claims were unilateral and represented a form of wishful thinking on the part of the Government in London. In reality, everyone knew that things were quite different in practice, and regardless of British aspirations, the formal owners of much of the territory to the West — especially west of the Mississippi River — was, by international agreement, the empires of France and Spain.

Nevertheless, by the early eighteenth century there existed, conceptually, an image of a potential Anglo-Saxon Empire in North America that stretched from coast to coast. Although this theoretical entity only lurked in the imaginations of a few individuals in England's ruling class-

---

41 Some colonies — Delaware, New Jersey, Rhode Island and Connecticut — had no open space to the west, because other colonies boxed them in, and were therefore defined differently.

42 Some Charters — notably that of Massachusetts in 1629 — claimed territory as far north as the 48th degree north. Generally however, the 45th degree was the accepted norm, in that it not only was the position claimed by the original Virginia grant of 1607, but also by the Dutch in their New Amsterdam claim — in effect from 1624 to 1664 — and formally accepted by Britain in the wake of the seven years war (1756–63), and lasting until the end of the colonial period. It was also used by the early USA to mark the northern boundaries of New York and Vermont.

43 Anthony Stokes: *A View of the Constitutions of the British Colonies in North-America and the West Indies*, London, 1783.

es, it was not only remarkable for the sheer size of its ambition, but also the way it was defined, for in the North, the forty-fifth parallel, marking the Northern border of the Massachusetts colony and French Canada, crossed the continent to the Northern boundary of what is today the state of Oregon, the Columbia River, whilst in the South, the thirty-fourth parallel bisected the continent from Charleston, South Carolina to meet the Pacific Ocean South of modern day Los Angeles.

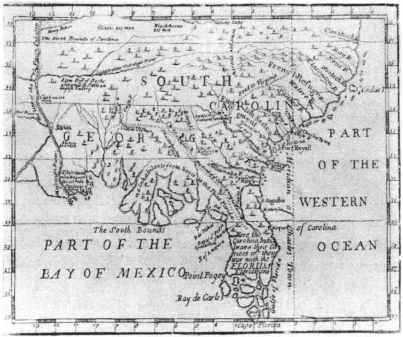

Fig. 4: A Senex map from 1732 showing the "parallel lines" arrangement for the north and south boundaries of Georgia, South Carolina and Virginia. Note how they extend west of the Mississippi — into French Louisiana.

For the first time in history, geometry rather than expediency defined a large part of the Earth's surface, and it was this idea — and aspiration — that fell within the jurisdiction of the new Secretary of State for the Southern Department, Thomas Pelham-Holles, First Duke of Newcastle[44], when the Prime Minister, Sir Robert Walpole, chose him to replace the existing Secretary, Lord Carteret, in 1724.

---

44 One of the curious facts about the British Government during the Eighteenth Century was that the Office of Secretary of State, second in power only to the Prime Minister, existed until 1782 as two separate departments, each respon-

III

"Permis" was the insulting nickname coined by Lord Hervey for Pelham-Holles. The observation arose because of the Duke of Newcastle's obsequiousness at the court of King George I, in that he always preceded anything he said to the Royal family with the rather pompous, "Est-il, Permis?"[45]. The scorn of the court might have been a price Newcastle thought paying if his sycophancy had worked on its principal target, the royal family; but unfortunately for the Duke, the courtiers' contempt extended as far as the monarchy as well. George I himself saw fit to deride Newcastle on occasion, notably at the christening of his son, the Prince of Wales, in November, 1717. a royal habit that was in turn inherited by George II, who, on his accession to the throne in 1727, sarcastically pronounced Pelham-Holles "unfit" to hold the office of Lord Chamberlain. In an era when Royal patronage could make or break a political career, it might appear that Pelham-Holles had the cards stacked against him, if it wasn't for one important fact: and that was, regardless of whether he was widely disliked, or simply a figure of fun, what no one disputed was the Duke of Newcastle's establishment credentials.

Born in London on the 21st July 1693, Pelham-Holles was the eighth child of Thomas Pelham and Lady Grace Holles. He was educated at Westminster School and Clare Hall College, Cambridge, from where he left without graduating in 1710. The failure to collect a Degree was however, sharply outweighed by the power of the hereditary principal in deciding his future. A seat in the House of Lords fell to him upon the death of his father in 1714, and a year later, aged twenty-two, he succeeded to the Dukedom of Newcastle upon the death of his uncle, John Holles. The country estates that came with both of these titles would see Pelham

---

sible for a specific geographical area. On the one hand there was the Northern Department, which had responsibility for Northern England, Scotland, and relations with the Protestant Countries of Europe. On the other was the Southern Department, the brief of which covered Southern England, Wales, Ireland, the Colonies, plus relations with the Catholic and Muslim countries of Europe. These two departments were Home and Foreign Office combined, and although nominally equal, the Southern, with its responsibility for relations with Britain's major opponents in Europe, France and Spain, plus the Empire, was considered the senior Office of the two.

45 French for 'If it is permitted?'

Holles through life regardless of his future career, but perhaps the indifference and contempt of the Royal family and their courtiers hit home. For, in what looks like defiance, throughout his life Pelham-Holles continually added to his titles and offices, as if to reinforce his position at the top of Britain's establishment. Two years after his Dukedom, he married Lady Harriet Godolphin, the granddaughter of John Churchill, Duke of Marlborough, and was made a member of the Privy Council. This pace of events was maintained: in the following year, 1718, he was made a Knight of the Garter, and so on and so on for the next thirty five years, until he succeeded his brother into the highest office of State, that of Prime Minister, at the age of sixty one.

For twenty-three years following Newcastle's initiation into the Order in 1731, the theoretical empire in America was, therefore, the political responsibility of a member of the Masonic fraternity[46]. Apart from providing a further example of the influence being accumulated by the movement, this fact alone may not appear particularly significant: the British establishment was already tightly entwined with Freemasonry by 1731, and the odds were stacked in favor of at least one future Secretary of State responsible for America being a "brother". Even so, Newcastle's appointment and Masonic membership did illustrate something interesting, and that was how geometrically identical the territory administered by the Southern Department was to a section of the *Explanation*, the soon-to-be-written "new" ritual describing the Layout of a Masonic Lodge[47], and by extension, the Symbolic Temple of Solomon:

> In all regular, well-formed, constituted Lodges, there is a point within a circle round which the brethren cannot err; this circle is bounded between North and South by two grand parallel lines"[48].

Naturally, it would be logical to view the similarity between this section of "new" ritual and the planned Empire in America as mere coincidence. For such an argument to be sustained however, it would be essential to discard two vitally important and contemporary occurrences.

---

46   The details of Pelham-Holles Masonic background are from Denslow's *10,000 Famous Freemasons*

47   For the best analysis of the role the Explanation plays in Freemasonry see Robert Lomas' *Turning the Hiram Key*

48   *The Perfect Ceremonies*

Firstly, the "new" ritual was written by men who could have quite easily been familiar with the abstract concept the Government had regarding North America, and at one extreme there is nothing to say it wasn't added by the Secretary of State and Freemason Thomas Pelham-Holles himself, and secondly, there is the sequence of events, for, according to all available research, not only the "parallel line" fragment but all of the *Explanation* was written after *Masonry Dissected*, dating its provenance to sometime after 1730. This meant that chronologically, the theoretical British North America, bounded between North and South by two parallel lines of latitude, either predates or evolved contemporaneously with the concept of a Masonic building "bounded between North and South by two grand parallel lines".

The mystery deepens with recognition that research into the beginnings of Masonic ritual has continually failed to provide a proper answer for the origins of the "Parallel Lines" fragment. Indeed, the reason for the inclusion of the "parallel lines" has been so elusive that one Masonic historian, Henry Coil, has put on record that "Of all the symbols of Craft Masonry, this one offers the greatest problem for the symbologist", a position generally accepted by other researchers in the same field.[49] Even so, it would still be remiss not to present a summary of the plethora of theories put forward to explain the "parallel lines", and taking it from the top, one idea is "the lines" are a symbolic acknowledgement to the two Saint John's[50], the dual claimants to be the patron saint of Freemasonry. Each have their own Saints days — June 24 and December 27 — which are sometimes referred to as "The Two Great Parallels" that occur in a calendar year.

This obscure possibility is, however, in competition with an alternative: that the "Parallel Lines" emanate from the operative building tradition. The initial laying out of a building — either on paper or in the open air — would, in the majority of cases, include the use of parallel lines, regardless of whether they were of string or the product of Sir Christopher Wren's pencil. By adding the "Two Grand Parallel Lines" to the ritual when they did — after 1730 — the writers could therefore claim to

49 *Coil's Masonic Encyclopedia*, p.479
50 Bernard Jones, *The Freemasons' Guide*, p.338-339

have included an architectural technique not only drawn from operative practice, but of speculative symbolism too, for the "parallel lines" also emphasized the "New" Fraternity's fascination with the greatest — in their view — of the liberal sciences, geometry.

But whilst there are several (possible) precedents for the inclusion of "parallel lines" in the ritual, when they are combined with the other geometrical feature from the fragment, the Circle, the picture becomes far more confusing. Naturally, explanations have been attempted, although what is curious is that, traditionally, research into the "Parallel Lines/Circle" fragment has seen the symbol as a one-dimensional figure. The essential point about this interpretation is that the (flat) circle only connects with the parallel lines at two points on its circumference — in this case the North and South:

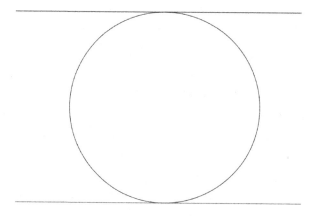

Fig. 5: The traditionally accepted interpretation of "...a circle bounded between North and South by Two Grand Parallel Lines..."

This analysis could, of course, be correct, and if so, then the Circle should again have symbolic meaning. Certainly, researchers have thought so, and it is not surprising that like the "parallel lines", the Circle, and the point within it, have also been the subject of several theories, as pointed out by Bernard Jones:

> The circle, having neither beginning nor end, is a symbol of the Deity and of eternity, and it follows that the compasses have been valued as being a means by which that perfect figure may be drawn. Everywhere, and in every age, the circle has been credited with magical properties, and

in particular has been thought to protect from external evil everything enclosed within it. Folklore contains thousands of examples of people, houses, places, threshed corn etc; being protected by the simple means of describing a circle around them. The innocent child could be placed within a circle, in which it was thought to be safe from any outside malevolent influence. The virtues of the circle were also attributed to the ring, the bracelet, the anklet, and the necklace, which have been worn since earliest times, not only as ornaments, but as a means of protecting the wearer from evil influences.

The completed emblem — the point within a circle — has been borrowed, consciously or otherwise, from some of the earliest pagan rites, in which it represented the male and female principles, and came in time to be the symbol of the sun and the universe. Phallic worship was common throughout the ancient world, simple people being naturally inclined to adopt as the foundation of their religion so great a mystery as the generative principle. The symbol came to be regarded as the sign of the divine creative energy. Freemasonry adopted the symbol, and easily gave it a geometrical explanation:[51]

But even the conjunction of a feature that *may* have originated in medieval building practices combined with "a symbol of the Deity" has failed to satisfy researchers. Henry Coil even went as far as to write off all of the above explanations (for both the "parallel lines" and the "circle"), describing them as "trite", and one can almost feel Coil's annoyance in his inability to find a logical explanation when he says: "it [the parallel lines/circle fragment] came into the ritual quite late without explanation, and no one has ever developed a satisfactory one [theory] for it"[52]. What is left in Masonic research is therefore a void. The only conclusive facts about the "Circle bound North and South by Two Grand Parallel Lines" is that it appeared sometime after 1730, and that nobody — even today — has come up with an answer to explain it.

Across the Atlantic meanwhile, there existed a theoretical (or symbolic) Empire that could, at the time, be described in an identical manner to part — the parallel lines — of the same fragment of ritual. Was there a connection? Of course, there was nothing to stop the Duke of Newcastle — or another Freemason — familiar with the claims made by the British in North America recognizing the geometrical significance of what they were looking at in the map collections of the British Government, and

---

51 *ibid*, p.406–407
52 *Coil's Masonic Encyclopedia*, p.479

harnessing its potential for the "new" ritual being rewritten at the same time. Even so, whilst this idea offers an alternative origin for the "parallel lines", where does it leave "The Circle"?

Perhaps the answer can be found by taking a fresh look at the entire fragment. As already mentioned, previous researchers have always viewed the "parallel lines/circle" ritual as a one dimensional figure. Whilst this approach is understandable, it is also feasible that this idea simply represents a misunderstanding of things written two hundred and seventy years ago, for W.J Williams' research into Freemasons of the time (1723–1739) eminent enough for the *Dictionary of National Biography* refers to six Architects. These men, schooled in design and active professionally at the time the ritual was rewritten, would have been familiar with the pre-construction diagrams pioneered by Inigo Jones, illustrating aspects of buildings in a *three* dimensional manner, and would have recognized the "parallel lines/circle" fragment as such. This means that if the ritual is looked at through the methodology of a blueprint, a completely different interpretation from what has traditionally been mooted comes to light, and here, the whole circle is "bounded to the North and South" by the parallel lines, which is, of course, a more accurate description of what was written:

North

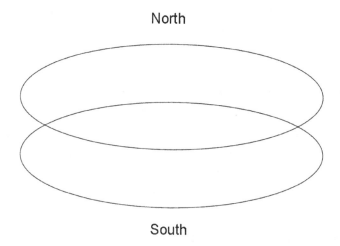

South

Fig. 6: A three dimensional analysis of the same section of ritual.

The "3-D" version of the fragment looks something like a wedding ring or cylinder. This doesn't mean it is cylindrical, of course, because another "gap" in the ritual is that nowhere does it state the two lines are the same length. This can, naturally, be interpreted in several ways: non-inclusion for the purpose of word use economy, or because blueprint definitions don't necessarily demand equilaterals, except, perhaps, for the purposes of neatness. What it doesn't exclude however is the idea the "parallel lines" could be a reference to something else entirely, specifically geographical parallels. None of these are the same length, due to the curvature of the earth, although the fact they circle the world suggests at least some individuals in the eighteenth century — such as Desaguliers' acquaintance John Senex — could have viewed them as "grand" in their own right.

As a globe maker, Senex would have recognized the only "circles" defined North and South by parallel lines were sections of the Earth's surface. It isn't inconceivable therefore that the ritual writers — amongst which Senex could possibly be included — saw the "circle" as a metaphorical description of the world. Certainly, evidence from two other sources indicates this could be so. The first port of call is the ritual itself, specifically the preceding line, which refers to "a point within in a circle from which the brethren cannot err". Definitely one "circle" the brethren — or anybody else for that matter — couldn't "err" from in the 1730s was the Earth's surface, whilst the second potential inspiration comes from somewhere that has — inexplicably, considering how much reliance other Masonic research has placed on it — been ignored by previous studies: Biblical precedent.

Contrary to popular opinion, the spherical nature of the Earth has been recognized by more enlightened individuals and societies for thousands of years. Greek civilization certainly saw it as such, with men such as Plato, Archimedes and especially the mathematician and philosopher Eratosthenes working out a fairly accurate stab at its dimensions[53]. It isn't surprising therefore the Bible itself occasionally refers to the World in the same way. For instance, *Isaiah 40:22* states, "It is he [God] that sitteth upon the circle of the Earth, and the inhabitants thereof are as

---

53 Eratosthenes was the first man to use the word 'geography', and went on to develop a system for measuring longitude and latitude.

grasshoppers", a concept reinforced in *Proverbs 8:27*: "When he prepared the heavens, I was there: when he set a compass on the face of the depth."

Both quotations come from the King James Bible, the version familiar to the men rewriting the ritual. Other Bibles have interpreted the "Circle" in *Isaiah* and *Proverbs* as a sphere, globe, or, in some contemporary editions, even dropping it from the text altogether. But it is interesting that at least one Victorian Bible historian, John Eadie, not only saw the "circle" as a metaphor for planet Earth, but also as a product of a design process, a point that could previously have been recognized by the Masonic ritual writers:

> CIRCLE: (Isa.XL.22) The word means, in this passage, the line within which the earth is supposed to revolve, or figuratively describes a position on its boundary from which every part of its surface can be seen. In Prov. VIII. 27 the same word is rendered compass, and denotes the boundary or mound within which the waters are restrained. The Creator is represented as marking out the habitation of the vast expanse of waters, with the same ease with which a designer or draftsman delineates the plan of a building or an estate.[54]

Contemporary cartographical practice and Biblical precedent apart, there is yet another reason to believe this section of ritual describes something geographical: and that is what is excluded from it. For an institution that put such store by geometrical terms, it is certainly odd that the ritual writers never got around to including *vertical* lines in their Temple specification. Nowhere in *The Explanation*, or the rest of the craft ritual for that matter, are the geometric dimensions of the Eastern and Western aspects of a Masonic Lodge ever referred to, even though a "Royal Arch" is supposed to dominate the east. This could be a simple oversight, or even an attempt to invest the North and South sides of the Lodge/Temple with an aura of mystique drawn from other sources. Even so, it is also possible that for the writers, the eastern and western sides of the building had to be excluded for the straightforward reason they were subject to some form of irregularity of such size and immovability that the emphasis on geometry within the *Explanation* would be compromised by their inclusion.

---

54 Eadie, *Bible Encyclopedia*

IV

If the "parallel lines" in Masonic ceremonial allude to the thirty-third and forty fifth parallels, especially where they straddle North America, then this suggests not one, but two explanations as to why the East and West sides of the building were ignored by the ritual writers. The first was the limits of eighteenth century technology. In the 1730s, the British were, of course, still struggling to find an accurate method of identifying longitude. Even if they could measure it, a vertical straight line drawn north to South would exclude nearly all of the settled area along the eastern seaboard, because the coast curves in an easterly direction north of Savannah. This in turn leads to the second reason: that the Eastern and Western sides, shaped by the forces of nature, were simply too irregular to be defined in a geometric manner, and were thus excluded.

Naturally, one counter argument to the above is *all* countries exist between two parallel lines; after all, every nation in the world has a North and South. Even though this is true, it must also be remembered that no other nation or colony was — or has ever been — defined in the way British America was prior to 1776, and nowhere else was destined to develop so neatly along these, or any other two parallels in the two hundred and thirty years since.

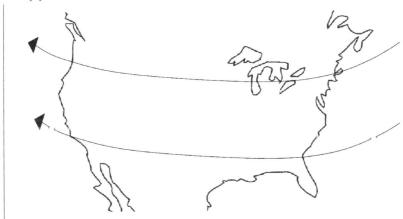

Fig. 7. The Virginia Charter of 1609 stated the colony's northern frontier ran along the forty-fifth parallel "from sea to sea". The charter for the most southerly and last province, Georgia, continued this tradition in 1732, in that the colony's southern limits were defined as the thirty-third parallel, "to the south seas". This arrangement came into existence prior to the "two grand parallel lines" fragment being added to the *Explanation*

The question remains, could it be possible that Pelham-Holles was inspired to include the Two Grand Parallel Lines in the ritual from what he knew about America? Or was the ritual *actually* referring to America? Certainly, another peculiarity of Masonic ceremonial in comparison with its Biblical inspiration was the absence of numerical divisions in its interpretation of the Temple. Whilst *Kings* and *Chronicles* refer to cubits, the Masonic ritual is silent on the matter, although Williams' six architects — and others — would have recognized the absurdity of attempting to define a building without tightly defined dimensions, unless their idea of a "cubit"[55] was something far removed from what was accepted in the Bible, and that *size*, probably the most crucial element in construction methodology, had to be left out deliberately.

So, could the ritual written in the 1730s and 1740s be describing a sizable portion of the Earth's surface for the site of the Freemasons symbolic Temple? Without doubt, the technology was in place: the science of drawing accurate maps and defining ownership and dimensions of huge, empty spaces was, by 1730, already an integral part of British policy making. Equally significant was the fact that this science had created a situation not seen before in human history, and that was from now on, men *could* define the boundaries and internal political divisions of a territory or nation without actually having to inhabit the said area. Add to this science the idea of pre-construction diagrams or blueprints, and the tendency towards design and order in the Anglo-Saxon mind. Armed with this arsenal of advantages, a unique scenario faced the men of the enlightenment: the chance to plot a *designed nation*, one constructed to a plan.

But where on Earth could such an enormous design be executed? Certainly not England or Europe, where a large, insitu population had been settled since ancient times, culminating in boundaries that had emerged gradually over hundreds of years. To put it bluntly, Wars, plagues, economics and population movements were long established as the deciding factors behind the Old World's political borders, rather than science. In some respects, Asia and Africa repeated this experience, for they too were already populated by people with cultures of their own, and were

---

55 A Biblical Cubit was considered to be a forearms length, or just over a foot.

therefore hardly likely to welcome the attentions of the West, however benign they may appear to be.

What was required was an empty — or virtually empty — space; but even in the 1730s these were starting to become thin on the ground. Siberia was far too cold and inhospitable and anyway, was on the verge of falling under Russian influence; whilst Australia and New Zealand still hadn't been formally claimed by anyone, and would remain so until the explorations of James Cook, forty years in the future. Even in the New World, territory was becoming scarce, for the Spanish and Portuguese already dominated the landmass to the south of the thirty-third parallel, whilst north of the forty-fifth, the French were making inroads into Quebec.

This left America, and, luckily enough, the territory claimed by Britain in 1732 had the ingredients needed. For not only were the colonies overwhelmingly Anglo-Saxon in their ethnicity, society and economy — and therefore tuned to English enlightenment thought — but the settled area only covered a small fraction of the total landmass with the British confined to the eastern fringe of the Continent. Crucially, everything to the west was more or less empty, or (apart from a few Spanish missionaries and French trappers) inhabited by scattered Native American tribes, who numbered, at the most, around three quarters of a million people[56].

The physical setting was ideal too: because, unlike Europe, with its myriad seas, inlets, islands and mountain ranges, the part of the North American continent free from French and Spanish incursion offered a rough rectangle, bounded by the Atlantic and Pacific Oceans to the east and west and the thirty-third and forty-fifth parallels to the south and north, three thousand miles by one thousand miles, to be worked on. The topography within this rectangle couldn't be bettered, either: large plains dominated, whilst other features, such as the Great Lakes and the Appalachian and Rocky Mountain ranges, presented minimal disruption, and even, with forethought, could be incorporated into the design.

So, if in the early eighteenth century a group of like-minded people were to design an Empire or Nation using geometry and architectural science, America was the place to do it. The physical backdrop, especially the unsettled west, formed the site thanks to the spirit of individuals such as Francis Drake, Walter Raleigh and William Penn; the likes

---

56 Niall Ferguson, *Empire*, p.66. Phillip Jenkins states that around 1500AD a population of two million was likely for the whole of North America north of Mexico *A History of the United States*, p.3

of More, Campanella and Bacon had, via their written works, contributed the theoretical basis; whilst the technology to make it happen came courtesy of the efforts of Leonard Digges, Christopher Saxton and the Royal Astronomical Society.

To execute such an extensive enterprise, all that was missing was the design itself and the architects to carry out the work. But what design should be followed? It was all very well to have the motive and means, but they wouldn't be much use without some sort of plan to work to, so what was needed was a blueprint capturing the essence of the enlightenment, a template Francis Bacon, Christopher Wren and Isaac Newton could appreciate; a diagram as valid upon completion of the project as it was at the beginning. To compromise, and follow something straightforward and functional, would lack the majesty, romance and elegance characteristic of the era. Essentially, it had to be symbolic of the *ideal*.

And who was going to execute the design? What was needed was a group, small in number to keep the project secret but durable enough to work over the generations it would take to complete. Certainly, the one fraternity recognizing that the science of geometry was applicable to geography was the Freemasons. Amongst the many thousands of documents held by the Library of the Grand Lodge of England is one named *Short Sketches in Craft Masonry*, by a certain John Knight. Dating from 1815, *Short Sketches* is an irregular, hand written description of the (now largely defunct) ritual that was practiced in Redruth, Cornwall around the time of the Napoleonic Wars. Like all Masonic ceremonial descriptions, *Short Sketches* covers a wide array of subjects, but interestingly enough it has the following to say about the relationship of geometry and geography:

> Geometry in the Original Sense, is the Art of Measuring Land, it is a Science which had its rise Among the Egyptians, who were by Necessity Compelled to invent Something of the Kind, to prevent the Disputes and Confusions Caused by the innundations of the River NILE, in the rapidity of which usually carried away all boundaries and effaced all limits of their possessions. Euclid was the first who made any Considerable Improvement in the Science of Geometry but since his days the refinements it has undergone, and the additions it has received, renders its importance in this age in a tenfold proportion. It now extends itself almost to every act and science. By the help of it Geographers determine the figure and Magnitude of the whole earth. Delineate the extent and bearings of Kingdoms, Provinces, Contenants, Lakes and harbours.[57]

---

57 Lecture to FC's: Library of the United Grand Lodge of England, BE 210 KNI, Section 152.

Part II. *Entrance*

Chapter 4. The North East Corner of the Building...

Therefore thus saith the Lord God, Behold I lay in Zion
for a foundation stone, a tried stone, a precious cornerstone,
a sure foundation.

— *Isaiah 28:16/17*

I

Seventeen thirty-three isn't notable in either the story of the British or American people. For England, the year lies in the relatively directionless period between the political upheavals of the previous century and the industrial revolution that characterized the latter half of the eighteenth. Across the Atlantic, 1733 again fell between two stools, equidistant from the hit and miss experimentalism of the later East Coast settlements of the sixteen hundreds and the full blooded revolutionary fervor that was to rip America from British rule fifty years in the future. Superficially, this appeared not to be a time of fantastic change in the Anglo-Saxon world, for there were no wars, battles or revolutions — scientific, social or political — to invest the thirty-third year of the eighteenth century with anything approaching the pivotal feel of, for example, ten sixty-six, seventeen seventy-six or nineteen forty-five.

Even so, the absence of a world-changing event does not mean that a specific year is a void, with nothing occurring during its twelve months to mark its place in history. Something of note *always* happens in each cycle of three hundred and sixty five days, and Seventeen Thirty-three was no different from any other. For Britain, some notable events of the year were, in chronological order, the invention of the "Planetarium" by a certain Doctor Desaguliers, publication of one of the World's first science fiction novels, Samuel Madden's *Memoirs of the Twentieth Century*, and the patenting of the Flying Shuttle Loom. Each of these carries some historical value in their own right, although it would be naive to imagine that the inventions or Madden's novel as having a revolutionary impact on the country's history or fortune.

This left Britain's colonies, and it was there that the importance of 1733 lay, specifically with the actions of two Masons who left London in late 1732 and early 1733 each bound for the extremities of the Empire in North America. One was James Edward Oglethorpe, Member of Parliament and humanitarian, who journeyed west in late 1732 to found the new Colony of Georgia, to the south of the already existing twelve provinces. The other man was Henry Price, a tailor in the northern City of Boston, who was travelling home after a business trip to the British capital. Superficially, Price didn't have a great deal in common with the MP, except that he, like Oglethorpe, was also heading to the New World to found something new during 1733, for, within a few months of his return to Boston, the tailor presided over a small ceremony that has, in the centuries since, become recognized as the establishment of a movement that today can boast the membership of, amongst others, at least seventeen former Presidents of the United States[58].

Official American Freemasonry was born at a Lodge meeting held at the *Bunch of Grapes* Inn on King Street, Boston during the evening of July 30th 1733. The assembly began with Henry Price, the representative of the Grand Lodge of England, reading out a deputation stating that the Grand Lodge had granted him authority over all Masonic activities in New England. Having established the authority under which business was to be conducted, Price then moved onto the rest of the agenda, the initial item being the initiation of new candidates into the Order. Today, it would only be possible to deal with the applications of one or maybe

---

58   The sixteen are: Washington, Monroe, Jackson, Polk, Buchanan, Andrew Johnson, Garfield, McKinley, Theodore Roosevelt, Taft, Harding, Franklin D Roosevelt, Truman, Lyndon Johnson and Ford.

two candidates a night, due to the length of the ceremonial. It is again an indication of how different the ritual was in 1733 (see chapter two) that Price was not only able to initiate an astonishing *eight* new Freemasons, but also leave enough time during the evening for two more vitally important changes.

The first of these was the establishment of a basic framework for what would become the Grand Lodge of Massachusetts. Over time, this organization would evolve into the "management" of Masonic activity in the colony, although due to the evening wearing on and the primitive nature of the Order in Boston and its environs, only a handful of appointments were deemed necessary to fill at *The Bunch of Grapes*. Price, backed up by his authority from London, appointed himself Grand Master for Massachusetts, with Andrew Belcher his Deputy, whilst two other men, Thomas Kennel and John Quan, were proposed, seconded and then nominated to more junior posts in the organization.

One reason why Henry Price only went as far as he did with regards to "management" that evening was because the primary unit of Masonic activity wasn't (and isn't) the Grand Lodge, but rather the ordinary Lodge. Without these fraternities, there would hardly any need for governance, and it was the establishment of one such entity at the *Bunch of Grapes* that was Henry Price's last and most important item of business. In his role as London's representative and newly installed Grand Master of Massachusetts, Price, alongside Belcher, Kennel and Quan, received a petition from eighteen local Masons who sought recognition as a regular Lodge under the authority of the Grand Lodge of England. Price granted the petition, and in accordance with Anderson's *Book of Constitutions*, the first official Masonic fraternity in America — St John's — was constituted, soon to be entered as number one hundred and twenty six on the register of the Grand Lodge in London.

For all its portentousness and businesslike quality, the establishment of St John's Lodge did however only mark the arrival of the official Order in America. The decades leading up to the assembly at the *Bunch of Grapes* had already witnessed increasing Masonic activity in the Colonies, albeit of the unofficial variety that had characterized English Freemasonry up to 1717. Like its British counterpart, this was again a shambolic affair, so the answer to the question of *when* "unregulated" Masonry actually arrived in America is unknown, although this hasn't prevented several theories being put forward to clear up the issue. At one extreme, some have speculated that the Order landed on the Eastern Seaboard as early as the Jamestown colony in 1607[59], although concrete evidence, in the shape of surviving documentation, points to the fraternity arriving much later, probably sometime around the year 1700.

References to the Order started to appear with increasing frequency following this date, starting with Jonathan Belcher[60] — father of Henry Price's deputy Andrew Belcher — who was initiated into a London Lodge whilst on a trip to England during 1704. It is highly unlikely that Jonathan Belcher was alone either, for sixteen years later, further confirmation of irregular Masonic activity comes via a record of a Lodge meeting that took place in Boston during 1720, and within twelve months, the presence in Boston harbour of *Freemason*, a sloop registered in the port[61].

Events now began to escalate. As the 1720s progressed, colonial newspapers like the *Boston Newsletter* and the *Pennsylvania Gazette* occasionally mentioned the "secret society" and its meetings across America, which was all the more remarkable considering that this branch of the Order still hadn't been recognized by the Grand Lodge. Greater clarity was also evident in the type of men who were joining too, for the *Pennsylvania Gazette* was actually edited by a Mason: Benjamin Franklin, who, like Jonathan Belcher, had signed up to the Order whilst living in London.

Franklin's initiation had taken place sometime in 1731, a point in history when the American "unofficial" fraternity was already approaching the "official" status enjoyed by its English counterpart. Undoubtedly, increasing fraternal activity in the colonies was central to encouraging the Grand Lodge to move on the issue of American Freemasonry, even to the point where London could even be accused of acting in haste. Like any organization, on occasion the Masons' supreme body was going to appoint someone who wasn't up to the job, and that is exactly what happened with their first attempt at exporting "official" masonry to America.

---

59 See Knight and Lomas.

60 Jonathan Belcher was the Governor of the Massachusetts Colony during the 1730s

61 From the official record of the port of Boston for 18th September, 1721

The problem began when the Grand Master for the year 1730, the Duke of Norfolk, deputized one Daniel Coxe to act as "Provincial Grand Master of the Province of New York, New Jersey and Pennsylvania". Whilst Coxe's elevation again illustrated the Grand Lodge's willingness to set up shop in the Colonies, on this occasion expansion ended in failure. The Duke had miscalculated, for not only did his man Daniel Coxe fail to lay a foundation for American Masonry, he didn't even bother to turn up in the Colonies at all, electing to remain in England to pursue a ridiculous claim to half of North America on the grounds it had been granted to his father, physician to both Charles I and Charles II[62]. Such a cavalier attitude by Daniel Coxe meant that by the time of Benjamin Franklin's initiation, it was clear a new Grand Master was needed, and the stage was now set for the Boston tailor Henry Price to get Official American Freemasonry off the Ground.

II

Henry Price was born in the London area around 1697. As a youth, he was apprenticed to a tailor, a trade he mastered well enough to secure admission to the City's Company of Merchant Tailors in July, 1719. Being good at something doesn't necessarily mean that success will follow, and for this particular twenty-something Englishman, the fierce competition that faced any business operating in the largest city in the world must have proved daunting. Luckily for Price though, he had served his time mastering a trade that could be practiced anywhere, provided there was sufficient demand, and it is highly likely that it was the pursuit of stronger commercial opportunities that persuaded Price to emigrate, when, in 1723, he sailed away from London, bound for the port of Boston, Massachusetts.

Once safely arrived in the new world, Price set up shop at *The Brazen Head*, on Cornhill, midway between Water and State Streets. Unlike some emigrants, the whole risky game of crossing the Atlantic actually paid off for the Londoner; for Henry Price's tailoring business — in partnership with one Francis Betheilhe after 1736 — was a enterprise evidently conducted with considerable success over the next twenty or so

---

62 *The Builder Magazine*, May, 1915, 'The establishment and early days of Masonry in America' — Melvin M Johnson

years. Price became well established in the town, and notwithstanding a disastrous fire in 1740, his businesses were certainly profitable enough to ensure that the one-time tailor's apprentice found space in his schedule for other passions, most notably his three marriages, fathering two children when well into his seventies, and involvement with the embryonic Masonic Fraternity, having joined the Order back in London years earlier.[63].

Price naturally juggled his business commitments and family with time spent on Masonics. For a man in his position there was no alternative; although on at least one occasion he succeeded in combining Masonic activities with the demands of his livelihood. This took place during the trip back to London mentioned earlier, when Price seized the opportunity to lobby the new Grand Master, Viscount Montague, for the deputation over Freemasonry in New England. Montague, possibly mindful of the urgent need to have someone in place to succeed the disastrous Daniel Coxe, accepted Henry Price's application, and on 2nd April, 1733, the Grand Lodge of England recorded:

> We have nominated, Ordained Constituted and appointed and do by those Presents Nominate, Ordain, Constitute and appoint our said Worshipful and Well Beloved Brother Mr. Henry Price, Provincial Grand Master of New England aforesaid and Dominions and Territories thereunto belonging....to Constitute the Brethren (Free and Accepted Mason's) now Residing or who shall hereafter reside in those parts, Into One, or more Regular Lodge or Lodges, as he shall think fit, and as often as Occasion shall require[64].

The establishment of the first Official Lodge in the America's within walking distance of Henry Price's residence therefore made sense. Communications across the colonies in 1733 were, like everywhere else, based on the staying power of the horse, and would remain so for at least a century to come. Had Price established the fraternity scores, or even hundreds of miles away from Boston, the foundation would mean a major expedition on his part, with all of its attendant costs in terms of time

---

63 Membership records held by the Grand Lodge of England record that Price was a member of Lodge number 75, which met at the Rainbow, a London Coffee House. Today this is Lodge 33, 'The Britannic'. All biographical information on Price is culled from the 1961 edition of *Coil's Masonic Encyclopedia* (pp.484–485) and his entry in Denslow's *10,000 Famous Freemasons*

64 Melvin M Johnson, The Early Days...*The Builder Magazine*, May, 1915

and money. Supposing the tailor been at the top of his profession, counting amongst his clients the fops and "men of fashion" of contemporary London, such a journey may have been within the realms of the possible; but for someone engaged in "trade", especially in a small provincial backwater like Boston, such a trip would have represented extraordinary expenditure, coming as it would just after an expensive visit to the Capital.

Realistically, money wasn't the only thing such an expedition would cost — there was time as well. In 1733, Price was still three years away from his successful partnership with Beheille, meaning a suspension of business had he announced another odyssey, so soon after returning from Europe. Price's time and money, never mind any other domestic considerations, may appear mundane, but they undoubtedly played a decisive role in deciding the location of the birth of American Freemasonry. It would, however, be naïve to believe that for an organization so well versed in the use of multi-layered symbolism, they were to be the only ones.

For marshalling all available evidence, circumstances surrounding the founding of Saint John's Lodge where and when it was strongly suggest there were other reasons involved besides practicality and convenience. The first Masonic outpost in the Colonies was obviously symbolic in so much as it not only marked the arrival of the Order in the New World, but also amongst the largest concentration of people of Anglo-Saxon extraction outside the British Isles. The significance of this cannot have been missed by the Grand Lodge — or at least parts of it — an organization not only placing symbolism at its core, but in some respects making it the working medium.

Logically, therefore, London would have wished to mark such a momentous occasion with something highly symbolic, and deputized their local representative, Henry Price, to carry this out. This argument does rely of course on the assumption that the tailor had a good grasp of contemporary Masonic symbolism, and although the level of Price's awareness is mere conjecture, it stands to reason this particular Mason had at least some knowledge, simply from the confidence that Montague had shown in him. Not one to repeat the Duke of Norfolk's mistake, "Ned" Montague would have been well aware developments in New England were far too important to entrust to a complete novice, especially after the Daniel Coxe debacle, so the authority could only be vested in someone familiar with the intricacies of the Order, and Price's ability in this area can therefore be inferred from his appointment.

In conclusion, and with Henry Price calling the shots, conditions were now perfect to guarantee that Montague and the Grand Lodge of England got the beginning it wanted in America. The tailor, armed with a mastery of the rituals and protocols of the Masonic fraternity, was, either at his own instigation, or more likely that of the Grand Master, under orders to invest the foundation with as much symbolism as possible; and, in hindsight, he was successful, for the question is not how little Masonic imagery appears around the birth of Saint John's Lodge, but how much.

III

Long before Saint John's Lodge, Boston, or even America had been thought of, the opening stages in the raising of a building in Britain normally followed the pattern outlined in chapter one. Firstly, the site of the proposed structure was cleared of encumbrances like trees and rocks, and leveled. This task completed, a wooden peg would be hammered into the ground to mark out one of the corners, and then a length of cord strung from this peg to others to define the outline and principal points of the edifice. A third duty, possibly carried out at the same time as the first two, was the construction of the Masons' temporary home and workshop, the Lodge.

Whilst these three jobs could be carried out as a sequence, there was, of course, nothing to stop them being undertaken simultaneously, so long as enough men were on hand. The Lodge could be built away from the main site, whilst vegetation and boulders could be uprooted even as the dimensions of the structure were defined. Time and experience hasn't really changed these procedures, and they apply just as much today as they did in the era of William of Sens and Thomas Crump.

From a Masonic perspective, the continuity inherent in building site procedures undoubtedly played a part in ensuring the above functions were included amongst the "new" rituals written during and after the seventeen thirties, although it is also possible at the time they were added to bolster "speculative" masonry's claim to operative origins. Even so, and regardless of their historical provenance, what are noticeable about the "opening procedures" are only those that could be reused to make a symbolic point made the transition to the "new" ritual. Those that couldn't, for instance the clearing of the site — which demanded no skills whatsoever — failed to survive, in so far as this work isn't mentioned in any of the rituals or ceremonies written after 1717.

The other two duties — the establishment of the Lodge and the identification of a corner to start from — did make it into "new" ritual. The Mason's retreat, of course, got detailed coverage, being the subject of the lecture allied to the First Degree, *The Explanation of the First Degree Tracing Board*, and it is significant that in the body of this same Degree that it furnished a precise geographical location where a Masonic Temple should always be commenced, when it states that:

> It is customary at the erection of all stately and superb edifices to lay the first or foundation stone at the North East corner of the building.[65]

In keeping with the multiple symbolism characteristic of the Order, events at *the Bunch of Grapes* therefore harmonized neatly with operative practice and the ceremonial directive for the beginning of a Masonic building. The Masons' Lodge was the first structure to go up, as it would have done at the site of England's cathedrals. Simultaneously, this Lodge — Saint John's — was quite clearly at the "north east corner" of the theoretical British Empire in America, the enormous rectangular territory "bound north and south" by the "two grand parallel lines", the forty-fifth and thirty-third lines of latitude.

From this, it could, of course, be assumed Henry Price, had ten years earlier, consciously relocated to Boston with the aim of one day conducting the foundation in accordance with standard Masonic practice. Such a theory however, not only depends on the farfetched assumption that Price altered the course of his entire life to meet the needs of the Fraternity, something Daniel Coxe wasn't even prepared to consider, but in addition the ritual directives mentioned above existed for him to work to. It is therefore intriguing that when Price left England for America — 1723 — neither the "north east corner of the building" or the "two grand paral-

---

lel lines" cropped up in the rituals of the Masons. Even when the "north east corner" did make an appearance for the first time — in *Masonry Dissected*, seven years later — it wasn't in relation to the laying of the first, or any other cornerstone.

In the absence of a contemporary directive for guidance, the alternative scenario is that Price drew inspiration from either, or both, of the primary sources behind much of the Masonic ritual, the Bible and the traditions of the medieval stone cutters. Like Pritchard's *Expose*, however, neither the Old Testament nor operative methodology answers the question either. Taking the two sources chronologically, whilst laying cornerstones are indeed mentioned in several books of the Bible — *Ezra, Hebrews, Isaiah, Joshua* and *Kings* — nowhere is there an indication, or even a hint, of any particular geographical preference to the positioning of the first stone[66].

Biblical ambiguity was a precedent — or lack of one — in turn repeated within the practice of operative stonemasons. Drawing on records of stone laying ceremonies relating to notable medieval buildings across Britain[67], several Masonic researchers have, over time, attempted to discover whether the "north east corner" held special significance with regard to the place where the first stone was laid. Inevitably, with so many large buildings erected during this era cases do exist. One is Croyland (Crowland) Abbey, Lincolnshire, where, in 1114, "The venerable Abbat Joffird himself laid the first corner-stone on the eastern side, facing the north."[68] Whilst nearly two hundred years later, around 1304, a further example can be found within the walls of the famous Rosslyn chapel in Scotland.

The potential significance of these two occurrences are, however, swamped by an equivalent number of occasions where the first cornerstone was laid at the South East, South West and North West corners

---

66 *The Freemason's Guide*

67 The laying of a cornerstone at any one of the four corners of a building has been a characteristic of British construction throughout the last thousand years. Possibly the best example from the immediate pre-1717 era was the new Saint Paul's Cathedral in 1675. The cornerstone was laid in the south east corner. (source: Hutchinson, *Sir Christopher Wren*, p.84)

68 From the *History of Croyland* by the medieval writer Peter of Blois, Quoted in *The Freemasons Guide*.

of buildings built across Great Britain. Lacking clear Biblical or "operative" precedent therefore, researchers have, from time to time, aired other theories to explain why the "north east corner" suddenly took on a new significance to the "speculative" Masonic Order. One such idea has it that the "north east corner" originated within an archaic Catholic ritual for the consecration of a Church, a ceremonial beginning with the Bishop standing at the north east corner of the building, whilst a further possible operative precedent was also re-examined in the idea that the starting point of a Masonic building originates with the Sun rising in the North East on St John's Day, 24th June. This theory rests on the idea that an operative Mason, starting work at daybreak, would commence construction at that point; but in Bernard Jones' own words, he, like other Masonic authorities, finds this possibility "far from convincing"[69].

So if the "north east corner" didn't originate in either the Bible or medieval practice, where could it have come from? Certainly one common denominator in previous research into the "north east corner" is that they have all assumed an origin lying in the past (i.e., before the foundation of the Grand Lodge). The central problem with this approach is that it ignores the social and economic developments of Freemasonry's *present* at the time of its greatest changes. As already mentioned, the ritual was starting to absorb a far wider array of subjects within itself by the time the eighteenth century reached its fourth decade. Within this context, failure to shine in *Masonry Dissected* suggests that, like the "parallel lines" the "north east corner" was again added — or beefed up — sometime after 1730. Officially, the last time this could occur was 1816, the year the Grand Lodge of England completed "Modern" ritual. Unofficially, however, external material — *exposes* — point to the addition of the "north east corner" to Masons' ritual taking place at least fifty years earlier, during the middle third of the eighteenth century.

The evidence lies within *Three Distinct Knocks* and *Jachin and Boaz*, two *exposés* published in London during 1760 and 1762 respectively. Unlike *Masonry Dissected*, both mention the "north east corner" in the modern sense, with respect to a new initiate. "The Master Call'd me up to the North-East Corner of the Lodge, or at his Right-hand," is how *Three Dis-*

---

69 Jones, *The Freemasons Guide*

tinct Knocks illustrates the point, a virtually identical sequence of words to *Jachin and Boaz*. Far from origins centuries or millennia old therefore, the logical conclusion is that whatever inspired the elevation of the "north east corner" within Masonic ceremonial occurred around the time the ritual was rewritten. This point to the years after the publication of *Masonry Dissected* and before *Three Distinct Knocks*: somewhere between the years 1730 and 1760.

There are three possibilities. Firstly, is that the rewrite represents nothing more than an act of pure inventiveness by one of the (anonymous) men who rewrote the ritual, whilst the second is that the "north east corner" owes its origins in the conventions and habits of operative stonemasons during the first third of the eighteenth century. But the problem with both of these explanations is that if either is true, the ritual is essentially meaningless. At worst, the ceremonial would carry no symbolic value at all, whilst at best all it would commemorate was a mundane detail of contemporary building technique, for which, of course, no evidence exists.

For the ritual to have proper gravitas, the symbolic importance of the "north east corner" had to be either an illusion to an event or occurrence out of the past still significant enough between 1730 and 1760 to warrant inclusion, or to the most significant contemporary Masonic foundation of the day. For something so historically important to Freemasonry to be lost in the intervening two hundred and fifty years is, of course, highly unlikely, especially when one bears in mind the time and effort already spent scouring for an answer. This leaves a contemporary foundation, of which evidence, from all of the countries the Order had spread to by the publication of *Three Distinct Knocks*, brings us full circle to the Boston tailor Henry Price, because between 1730 and 1760, the sole Masonic establishment beginning at the "north east corner" of "something" "bound north and south by two grand parallel lines" was Freemasonry in Britain's American Colonies.

The location of American Masonry's birth is intriguing in the way it corresponds with the modernized ritual. However, *place* is not the only aspect of the foundation recognizably symbolic: for the *timing* was highly significant too. The Lodge held in 1720 and the presence of the *Freemason* in Boston harbor strongly infer "unofficial" Freemasonry in the colonies that pre-dated the Grand Lodge, whilst contemporary articles from the *Boston Newsletter* and *Pennsylvania Gazette* illustrate how geographically widespread the phenomenon was across America. It stands to reason therefore that across the Atlantic, English Masonic authorities must have been aware of the potential inherent in the "unofficial" movement in America, and the opportunity it offered to export "official" Masonry to the New World.

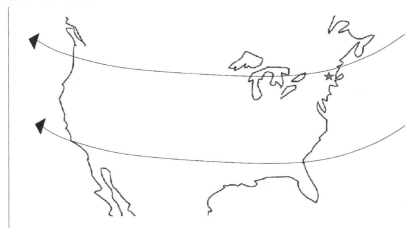

Fig.8: "The North East Corner of the Building" Outline map of British Claims in North America, circa 1733. This illustrates the respective positions of the 45th and 33rd Parallels, the Colony of Massachusetts and the city of Boston, home of the first official Masonic Lodge in America.

Even if London had ignored this "unofficial" activity — which was highly unlikely as it had provided the basic building blocks for the Order in England — American colonists still constituted the largest Anglo-Saxon population outside of the British Isles, a fact that cannot have been overlooked by an organization reliant on fresh recruitment. So it is all the more puzzling why America was ignored during the 1720s, whilst other, less promising countries got "official" Masonic outposts. To put it bluntly, for some undeclared reason, American Masons were kept on ice for sixteen years following the assembly at the *Goose and Gridiron*, before the Grand Lodge, in the shape of Henry Price, made its move: during the thirty-third year of the eighteenth century.

Throughout Masonic history, "thirty-three" or "thirty-third" has always enjoyed a special, if undefined, importance. One obvious manifestation of this is the number of degrees in the Scottish rite branch of the Order. Back in 1730, Pritchard's *Masonry Dissected* had, of course, defined the full body of Masonic ritual as three degrees in total, Entered Apprentice, Fellow Craft, and Master Mason. Before long, however, further degrees were added culminating in the modern total of thirty-three.

It is also important to define what we mean by "degree", although typically for the Masonic movement, the term again has a multiple meaning. At one level, "Degree" represents a level of knowledge or understanding, in the same sense as an academic qualification. Alternatively, and in keeping with Masonry's close connection with geometry, the Order also views "degree" as a geometric entity, a "unit of angular or circular-arc measurement"[70]. Using the "thirty-third degree" as the example, then as a unit of measurement it must relate to everything greater than thirty-two (degrees) as far as thirty-three degrees exactly. Thirty two point five degrees would be part of the thirty-third; but thirty-three point one degrees wouldn't, as it belongs to the thirty forth. For the purposes of simplicity, the minutest fraction above thirty-two degrees exact symbolizes the beginning of "thirty-third", whilst thirty-three degrees represents its end. Geometrically, therefore, "thirty-third" is more important than the number thirty-three, which indicates the culmination of the geometrical degree.

Like so many things Masonic, there is again no identifiable origin for the use of "thirty-three" or "thirty-third" as a symbol. This doesn't mean that there weren't precedents that couldn't have been recognized and utilized in the eighteenth century. The Enlightenment was an era when the "speculative" minded were sucking in ideas from abroad, and the adoption of "thirty-three" or "thirty-third" possibly represents another attempt by "speculative" Masons to link the new fraternity with another operative tradition, in this case that of Ancient Egypt.

The Pyramid builders made extensive use of thirty-three degree angles, and it is conceivable that one of the men of the enlightenment brought the idea back after a "Grand Tour" of the Middle East. Even if this is true, far from being an invention of the Grand Lodge, available evidence suggests "thirty-third" actually precedes 1717. As previously stated,

---

70 *Concise Oxford Dictionary*

there are two days a year devoted to Saint John, the patron Saint of the Order; so it cannot be any coincidence that the foundation of the Grand Lodge of England took place on the thirty-third Saint John's Day of the eighteenth century[71].

Going back even further, it is also possible "thirty-three" and "thirty-third" held some symbolic significance for the operative masons. Out of this tradition comes the *Regius* Poem, widely recognized as the first written reference to a medieval fraternity of stone cutters, for *Regius*, at thirty-three pages long, laid down the rules by which such a "union" would be organized. Coming back to the eighteenth century, there were further potential reasons for the adoption of the number and its sequential, this time drawn from the immediate surroundings stonemasons found them in. The first was that at the time, English Stonemasons were paid roughly the rate of 32d a day. The thirty-third penny could therefore easily come to symbolize proper remuneration, or even the end work being carried out, whilst another reason was something else important to the "physical" builders of the 1720s: the fact that the sun disappears over the horizon at a thirty-three degree angle — marking the end of the working day.

More importantly, these potential "operative" sources were complimented by further possibilities being culled from the main source of the Masons' ritual, the Bible, especially the frequency "thirty-third" crops up around the Temple story:

- Thirty-three represents truth, or the triumph of good over evil;
- The thirty-third parallel line of latitude north runs across Israel, the theoretical site of the Temple;
- *Chronicles* state Temple construction started on the "second day of the second month" — the thirty-third day of the year in modern calendars;
- The Temple overseers numbered three thousand three hundred;
- The Human vertebrae has thirty-two parts, with the thirty-third, the skull, a repository of wisdom;
- *Micah*, one of the books prophesying the rebuilding of the Temple, is the thirty-third book of the Old Testament;

---

71 Taking the start of the century from 1st January 1701. All dates are the ones used at the time i.e., Julian calendar up to 1752, Gregorian after.

- And crucially, the geometrical depiction of "thirty-three" is the double triangle, or hexagram, one variant of which is the Seal of Solomon:

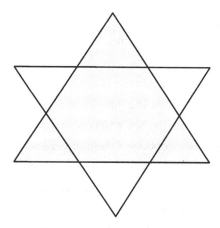

All of the above undoubtedly played a part, to a greater or lesser degree, to why "thirty-third" and "thirty-three" were incorporated by the Masonic Order into its imagery. It is also possible, however, that usage of thirty-three or thirty-third by modern Freemasonry originated outside the Order, because in many mystical and religious systems, the number is, along with eleven and twenty two, a master number, one of the few that numerically possesses special powers:

> [Thirty-three] This number is probably too powerful to work with in simple magic. It signifies the adept or spiritual leader, someone who has accepted the responsibility for making major changes in the world in which we live. It is unlikely that it can be worked with unless such responsibility has been accepted, since it will usually revert to the number six, its simplest form. It normally requires acts of great sacrifice (making life sacred)[72].

The Judeo-Christian tradition is no exception to this rule, master numbers — whether they be eleven, twenty two or thirty-three — playing an important part in both the old and new Testaments. Probably the most important example was the death of a "spiritual leader", Jesus Christ, at the age of thirty-three, although the number, or multiples of it, also shows up in other books of the Bible and has symbolic significance

72 Pamela Ball, *Spells, Charms, Talismans and Amulets* p.329

in other religions, such as Hinduism, where the population of the World at its beginning was three hundred and thirty million, and Islam, where the dwellers of Heaven exist forever aged thirty-three.

The significance and potential origins of "thirty-third" could therefore go on and on. Nevertheless, regardless of whether it was the number of Saint John's days the Grand Lodge was founded on, the double triangle of geometry, or even operative stonemason earnings around 1717, whatever inspired the inclusion of "thirty-third" into Masonry isn't particularly important. What is however crucial, is that each, in their own way, illustrate one thing in common: and that is symbolically they all represent *Truth, Excellence* or *Achievement*.

IV

Naturally, the Freemasonic Order's arrival in new territory was an *achievement* meriting the use of "thirty-third" in as many ways as it could be applied. This had been the case back in London, when the formation of the Grand Lodge had taken place on the thirty-third St John's day of the century; so it was reasonable to expect the same numerical symbol to turn up around events in Boston too. Even so, what was curious about Freemasonry's beginnings on American soil was just how often "thirty-third" manifested itself in the temporal vicinity of the meeting at the *Bunch of Grapes*. The first — and most obvious — appearance was that the meeting of 30th June took place in the thirty-third year of the eighteenth century; whilst a second, more subtle and undeniably Masonic related use was in the number of Saint John's days that had passed since the formation of the Grand Lodge of England.

There was nothing particularly innovative about this: mention has already been made of the world's first Masonic Authority being created on the thirty-third Saint John's Day of the seventeen hundreds, back in June 1717. So the same idea was applied to America, the thirty-third "period" of Saint John following the birth of the Grand Lodge took place between 24th June and 27th December 1733, the six months during which Henry Price and Saint John's Lodge first came together to conduct their business at *The Bunch of Grapes*.

This double entanglement of thirty-third around the birth of Saint John's Lodge, Boston does, of course, have a common denominator: time.

It could therefore be inferred that the emergence of the Masonic Order in America was deliberately put off during the 1720s and early 1730s by influential members of the Grand Lodge of England. Realizing their most important foundation was yet to come, such men could have easily stalled until the summer of 1733, when the laying of a symbolic stone at the "north east corner" could take place on a date that had maximum symbolic significance.

The double occurrence of "thirty-third", alongside the simultaneous appearance of the "north east corner" and "parallel lines" references in the ritual, and their corresponding imposition on the map of colonial America, suggested the beginnings of Freemasonry in the New World held a greater importance to the Order — or sections of it — than anywhere else on the planet. Without doubt, no other Masonic beginning, in any other country, was to have as much symbolism invested in it as America, hinting that Britain's territorial claims had a special, if unspoken meaning, to Henry Price and some — if not all — of the Grand Lodge of England.

But what was it? It was all very well to pile symbolic feature upon symbolic feature, enshrine them in the ritual of an Anglo-Saxon fraternal society, and then duplicate the lot at specific locations across England's American Colonies. Whatever was going on, the whole process was meaningless unless some specific objective was the aim, and to be fair, Price, Montague, and the symbol-manufacturing Desaguliers weren't stupid men, accustomed to spending their time on foolishness; for by the very nature of the way they had already conducted their lives, they knew how to recognize an ambition, and formulate a plan to realize it.

It was crystal clear that Montague and Price had, so far, acted with a quiet but deliberate determination to engineer the beginning they wanted, so it would be logical to assume the same mind-set would again be brought to bear for their next move, the foundation of the second Official Masonic Lodge in America. Without question, practicality and common sense suggested that once the fraternity was up and running in Boston, the next Lodge to be fully warranted would again be relatively local, for there were, in a material sense, certainly enough "unofficial" Lodges already in existence across New England, New York and Pennsylvania ready and willing to be absorbed by the Grand Lodge of England.

To contradict this pattern, and for Price to look further afield, was to ask for the kind of trouble the creation of Saint John's Lodge had avoided, for, alongside the difficulties of physical communication alluded to earlier, for it stands to reason the greater the distance from Boston to the next Lodge, the greater the problems of administration would be. Even so, considerations such as practicality all rested on the conventional and mundane idea that the reasons underpinning events in Boston would repeat themselves during the expansion of Freemasonry in America. It was all the more intriguing therefore that Henry Price was to pay no attention to practicality and common sense whatsoever, electing, instead of a logical progression through New England, a pattern of expansion striking in how closely it harmonized with something far more architectural: the construction imagery and symbolism central to the Masonic Order.

It was these rituals — especially those written at the time of Henry Price's activities — that clearly stated where the first cornerstone should be laid, a foundation the Boston tailor had dutifully carried out. This left a question: could Price — and the Grand Lodge of England — be looking at the distribution of the first two Masonic Lodges in America as symbolic cornerstones — or more likely, William of Sens style corner pegs? If so, then the Freemasons symbolic string — to the second fully warranted Lodge — could only be uncoiled in the direction of only three possible locations: the Southeast, Southwest and Northwest corners formed by the parallel lines of latitude defining the huge rectangular territory claimed by the British.

Price's options were limited however, for planting the second "peg" at one of the western corners — on the Pacific Coast in modern day Southern California and central Oregon — was out of the question, for not only were these places three thousand miles from areas of English influence, but they weren't even properly "settled" in the European sense at all. This left Price with only one choice, the Southeast corner, and significantly, it was to this region of the theoretical Empire he next turned his attention.

In December 1735, *ye Lodge of Savannah*, in the infant colony of Georgia, became the second Masonic Lodge in the Americas fully warranted by the Grand Lodge of England. Crucially, its founder was none other than James Oglethorpe, the other English Freemason who left London in 1732. Significantly, Oglethorpe had established the thirteenth province two years earlier in the thirty-third year of the eighteenth century; his colony straddled the thirty-third parallel line of latitude, and to reinforce the symbolism behind Georgia, named it in honor of the reigning King, George II, the thirty-third Monarch to rule England since the first of the great castle builders, William the Conqueror[73].

---

73 The thirty-three were: William I, William II, Henry I, Stephen, Henry II, Richard I, John, Henry III, Edward I, Edward II, Edward III, Richard II, Henry IV, Henry V, Henry VI, Edward IV, Edward V, Richard III, Henry VII, Henry VIII, Edward VI, Lady Jane Grey, Mary I, Elizabeth I, James I, Charles I, Charles II, James II, William III, Mary II, Anne, George I and George II. A possible source for this chronology was the author of the *Constitutions*, Doctor Anderson, who wrote *Royal Genealogies or the Genealogical Tables of Emperors, Kings and Princes, from Adam to These Times*, published in London during 1732.

Chapter 5. The South East Part...

> And it came to pass in the four hundred and eightieth
> year after the children of Israel were come out of the land of
> Egypt, in the fourth year of Solomon's reign over Israel, in the
> month Zif, which is the second month, that he began to build
> the house of the Lord.
>
> — Kings, 6:1

I

Henry Price had obviously done the right thing in the eyes of the
Grand Lodge, for a year after his appointment over all Masonic activity
across New England promotion was again in the air, on this occasion to
the new, but far more powerful, office of Grand Master of His Majesty's
Dominions in North America. Such exalted status meant the Boston tailor was now positioned to maintain the momentum of the fraternity's
spread along the Eastern Seaboard, a development he clearly anticipat-
ed when, early in 1734, he appointed the Philadelphia printer Benjamin
Franklin to be the Order's Grand Master for Pennsylvania.

Franklin's elevation was one of Price's most astute moves, for within
a year, the printer had published the first Masonic book in America, a
reprint of Doctor Anderson's *Constitutions*, and was almost certainly involved with the construction of the first Masonic Temple in Philadelphia.
Having had the foresight to recognize Franklin's indefatigability, and the
mature state of Pennsylvanian Masonry, on the surface it looked logical

for Price to conclude that the next official Lodge should be warranted there, or at least one of the other well-established provinces. Indeed, Benjamin Franklin was certainly thinking along these lines, for he wrote no less than two letters on the subject to Price — one official and one personal — arguing for recognition by the Grand Lodge of England, one of which, the informal, is reproduced below:

> Dear Brother Price, I am glad to hear of your recovery. I hoped to have seen you here this fall, agreeable to the expectation you were so good as to give me; but since sickness has prevented your coming while the weather was moderate. I have no room to flatter myself with a visit from you before the Spring, when a deputation of the Brethren here will have an opportunity of showing how much they esteem you. I beg leave to recommend their request to you, and to inform you, that some false and rebel Brethren, who are foreigners being about to set up a distinct Lodge in opposition to the old and true Brethren here, pretending to make Masons for a bowl of punch, and the Craft is like to come into disesteem among us unless the true Brethren are countenanced and distinguished by some special authority as herein desired. I entreat therefore, that whatever you think proper to do therein may be sent to me by the next post, if possible, or the next following.

> I am, your Affectionate Brother and humble servant,

> B. Franklin, GM Pennsylvania Philadelphia, Nov. 28, 1734[74]

Unfortunately for Benjamin Franklin, his plea fell on deaf ears, for although the Order was indeed destined to spread to Pennsylvania and the other eleven long settled colonies during the late seventeen thirties and forties, Henry Price and the Grand Lodge had already decreed the second Official Lodge in America was to be founded on the southern frontier: in Georgia, Great Britain's thirteenth, and newest, province.

London's Fleet Prison may seem an unlikely location for the genesis of an imperial adventure, but it was within its walls that the story of Georgia began. A jail had stood off Farringdon Street from 1197, and despite destruction twice, the second time in the Great Fire of 1666, by the early eighteenth century "The Fleet" specialized in the incarceration of London's debtors and bankrupts. To put it in context, it is a measure of how property-centered English law was during that time that offences merely resulting in a restriction on credit today were deemed serious enough

---

74 Johnson, *Ibid*

to merit a custodial sentence three hundred years ago. Indeed, to make matters worse, the authorities viewed "innocent" debtors as culpable as the "guilty" for their predicament, and what was more, treated them the same as other felons residing within the system. The upshot was the same miserable conditions were the lot of those in debt as they were for the prostitutes, pickpockets and footpads who, at the time, constituted the bulk of England's prison *clientele*.

For the debtors, the horror of sharing cells with the truly criminal was compounded by the virtual non-existence of anything promoting their welfare. All prisons suffer from unsanitary conditions, for the obvious reason human beings are forced together, although conditions in England's jails three hundred years ago must have ranked amongst the worst. Disease and poor food competed with rampant corruption amongst officials to rack up the misery, and in so pernicious an environment, basic necessities came at a premium that was often beyond the means of those in debt. Squalor on such a scale resulted in a high mortality rate from both natural and unnatural causes, and it is a measure of how little interest Parliament took of the matter that prison conditions within the Fleet were not only tolerated, but considered acceptable.

This was, however, an age in British history before ordinary people had either a vote or a voice in the affairs of the nation, one consequence of which was the state of the prisons, along with other social ills, was a low priority to those in power. Indeed, in the absence of any kind of public discourse, this state of affairs could, in theory, have continued indefinitely, so long as it didn't impinge on the lives of the rich and influential; and so it remained until the death in the Fleet of a bankrupt writer, one Robert Castell, during 1728. The author of *The Villas of the Ancients Revisited*, a work on classical architecture, Castell had originally been imprisoned for debts totaling less than £400; so when the warder, Thomas Bambridge, demanded £5,200 for preferential treatment, the author found himself sharing a cell with another inmate suffering from "jail fever" — smallpox — which in turn led Castell to succumb too, a fatality that in normal circumstances would have gone virtually unnoticed.

In contrast to many of his fellow inmates, however, Castell had enjoyed good connections prior to conviction. A respected figure in London "society", the writer counted amongst his friends James Oglethorpe, the Tory Member of Parliament for Haslemere. Outraged at his friend's death, Oglethorpe demanded "an inquiry should be instituted into the state of the jails in the metropolis"[75], a call carrying some weight, bearing in mind not only the MP's membership of the Parliamentary Prison Discipline Committee, but his experience too; for, unlike many of his fellow MPs, the Member for Haslemere had intimate knowledge of England's prisons, arising from his own incarceration six years earlier in 1722, when, according to the London *Daily Journal*[76]:

> Yesterday Morning about 6 of the Clock James Oglethorpe, Esq., lately chosen at Haslemere in Surrey a Representative for the new Parliament, had the misfortune to go into a Night-House of evil Reput, without Temple-Bar (being overcome with Wine), where mixing with a promiscuous Company of Hackney-Coachmen, Shoe-Blackers, and Linkmen, Mr. Oglethorpe missed a piece of Gold, and charging a Link Fellow with having taking it from him, high Words arose, and the Linkman struck Mr. Oglethorpe several blows with his Link, who resenting such usage drew his Sword and gave the Fellow a mortal Wound in the Breast, for which he was seiz'd and carried before Mr. Justice Street, who committed him to the Gate-House.

The perversity of a legal system that put property before people was again demonstrated by the sentence the Honorable Member for Haslemere received, for Oglethorpe served a grand total of five months in prison. What was more, there were to be no long term repercussions for Haslemere's representative by running through the link man, in either his Parliamentary career or life in general. Such were the standards of England in the early eighteenth century that an act of violence culminating in a man's death was considered less of a crime than Robert Castell's inability to pay his debts.

It would, however, be a mistake to view James Edward Oglethorpe as a prototype roughneck. Although notorious for his volatile temper, this particular Englishman had already enjoyed all the advantages in life that could be amassed by a member the ruling class. The seventh of nine children, he was born into a wealthy family, that of Sir Theophilius Oglethor-

---

75 Cited in *Biographical Memorials of James Oglethorpe*, Thaddeus Mason Harris, 1828

76 Edition dated 25th April, 1722. Cited in 'This Day in Georgia History', the Carl Vinson Institute of Government, The University of Georgia

rpe, on 1ˢᵗ June, 1689. The family seat was the rather grand Westbrook Place, in Godalming, Surrey, an estate one day to be inherited by him due to the deaths during his childhood of his father and eldest brother in the wars of the Spanish succession. Family mortality didn't however deter him from also following a military career following his matriculation from Corpus Christi College, Oxford, in 1714. Oglethorpe initially started his career within in the British Army, although latterly he acted as a volunteer on behalf of various rulers in Eastern Europe, being involved in the Turkish campaign and the siege and capture of Belgrade in 1717.

Family tradition apart, Army life didn't mean that James Oglethorpe was evolving into a one-dimensional military type. He was also well known as a philanthropist, helping poor children and also making public his opposition to slavery at a time when enforced servitude was widely accepted, a charitable nature soon acknowledged by one of the foremost poets of the age, Alexander Pope, in his *Imitations of Horace*:

> One driven by strong benevolence of soul shall fly like Oglethorpe from Pole to Pole[77].

This "strong benevolence of soul", reinforced by Robert Castell's death and his own incarceration, was undoubtedly a secondary reason behind a developing personal interest in the reform of Britain's jails, although this was one enthusiasm of Oglethorpe's that was to have a specifically American ending, for his zest not only led to involvement in the committee set up to administer the proposed new colony of Georgia, using inmates of England's debtors' prisons to settle the region, but also the MP's physical presence, and authority, throughout the entire process of colonization.

It was the committee's opinion that because debtors weren't "criminals" in the conventional sense, they could be offered the chance of early release, on condition they were prepared to start afresh in the new colony, a position reiterated in the members petition at the time, which stated:

> that the cities of London, Westminster, and parts adjacent, do abound with great numbers of indigent persons, who are reduced to such necessity as to become burthensome to the public, and who could be willing to seek a livelihood in any part of his majesty's plantations in America, if they were provided with passage, and means of settling there.

---

77 *Imitations of Horace*, Epistle II, 1733–37

To be fair, the creation of what was, in effect a penal colony wasn't a new concept, for the idea Georgia could become home for England's destitute wasn't originally Oglethorpe's nor for that matter, the Committee's. Over a decade earlier Sir Robert Montgomery had written a pamphlet extolling the climatic and natural virtues of the region south of the Carolinas, and how, via colonization, these wonders could be harnessed for the benefit of the settlers, and in the long term, the Empire. In a nutshell, Montgomery's long term plan was that the colony would eventually emerge as a substantial economic asset for the British, but when his ideas were first mooted back in 1717, the concept of a thirteenth colony failed to attract widespread support.

Fifteen years later, the scheme was re-examined by the Government, who realized settlement represented a "win–win" situation: the colonists would profit from the process of rehabilitation, whilst the nation would not only save public money on the cost of incarceration, but also bathe in the satisfaction of watching the boundaries of the Empire in America expand west and south. Buoyed up by enthusiasm, most of the necessary ingredients ensuring a successful colonial experiment were in place by 1732; and the Committee, armed with James Oglethorpe's drive, the blessing of King George II, and a grant of ten thousand pounds from Parliament, was ready to make Sir Robert Montgomery's idea a reality.

II

To round off the administration, the Duke of Newcastle's Southern Department granted a Royal charter for Georgia on 9th June 1732, and appointed a board of trustees to manage the enterprise. One immediate and pressing concern facing the Committee at this time was, of course, the annexation of enough territory on which to establish the colony. A solution to this difficulty was found via a treaty with the Chief of the local Creek Indians, Tomochichi, who was, conveniently enough, sympathetic to the idea of British settlement. To this end, the Creek leader went as far as to grant the Committee a large strip of country between the rivers Altamaha and Savannah on the East Coast between South Carolina and the Spanish colony of Florida.

The generosity of the Creek people was not, however, reciprocated by the British. The Charter defining Georgia — which carried legal weight in London — unilaterally laid claim to all lands directly west of Tomochichi's grant as far as the South Seas, the Pacific Ocean. Territorial Georgia was therefore destined, from the point of view of the Crown, to be no different from any of the other British colonies with an open border to the west, in that it was defined by English law as a trans-continental entity, even though such a claim was purely unilateral, and ignored the internationally accepted rights of those with formal title to the west, which at the time were France and Spain.

Short of going to war over the issue, Britain's claims were therefore doomed to remain a theoretical construct, of interest only to a few hundred people. Even so, they are an indication of the awesome ambitions England had in North America at the time, for the size and boundaries of the region claimed by London in 1732 were indeed truly staggering. Although largely unsettled, the theoretical Empire now stretched from the East to West Coasts in a rectangle that, with the addition of Georgia south to the thirty-third parallel, roughly three thousand miles long and one thousand miles wide.

Grandiose though Britain's aspirations were in 1732, their fulfillment would remain an Imperial daydream without the most vital ingredient: people. Bolstered by Oglethorpe's recent publications *A New and Accurate Account of the Province of South Carolina and Georgia* and *An Essay on Plantations*, plus the chance to cross the Atlantic for nothing, assembling enough willing volunteers was largely successful by the end of the autumn, and when the 200 ton frigate *Ann* sailed out of Gravesend on November 16, 1732, there were, according to the *Gentleman's Magazine*, one hundred and fourteen passengers on board, "thirty-five families, consisting of carpenters, brick-layers, farmers etc.,"[78] ready to start a new life in Oglethorpe's colony.

---

78 *Gentleman's Magazine* for 1732, p.1029 'Account of their setting forth'. There were two additional passengers: the chaplain, Rev. Henry Herbert, D.D., and a Mr. Paul Amatis, a Piedmontese silk specialist.

Disregarding the fact that none of the passengers on board were actually released debtors[79], the transatlantic crossing was considered successful for the time. The journey took just under three months, and was
marked by the deaths of two "infirm children" and a single birth by the
time the *Ann* docked at Charles Town, South Carolina, from where a relieved Oglethorpe wrote to the trustees:

On board the Ship Ann 8 of the

Clock Jany. 13 1732/3

This Lte from James Oglethorpe Esqr. to the Honbl. Trustees

Gentlemen:

We just now discover the Cost of America and it proves to be the Land
which lyes off Charles town We are now within nine Miles distant and
can from the Deck with the naked Eye discover the Trees just above the
Horrizon No disagreeable sight to those who for seven weeks have seen
nothing but Sea and Sky We have had a very favourable Passage considering that we passed the Tropick of Cancer and Stood to the South ward
till we came into 20 Degrees and then Stood back again to 32 where we
now are By this meons t.e lengthened our Navagation from England above
a third which was done to avoid the fury of the North west Winds that
generaly rage in the Winter season on the Coast of America We have lost
none of our People except the Youngest Son of Richard Cannon aged
Eight Months and the Youngest Sone of Robert Clsrke Aged one Year and
an half both of whome were very weakly when I came on Board and had
indeed been half Starved thro' want before they left London as many others were who are recovered with Food and Care but these were so far gone
that all our Efforts to Save them were in vain Doctor Herbert and all on
Board are in perfect health except Mr. Scott who was bruised with a Fall
in the Last Storm At present we ere all in a hurry so must beg leave to refer
you for a fuller account to my next Letters Wee intend to take in a pilot

---

79 The opportunity to cross the Atlantic gratis — even to an unknown like
Georgia — must have been irresistible to many people who weren't in debt,
only poor. For instance, the plot of the novel *Kidnapped* — set less than twenty years after the creation of Georgia — begins with an attempt to 'export'
one of the main characters, David Balfour, to the Carolinas as an indentured
laborer. Such a term usually meant service as a slave for a period of seven
years, an identical period of time to that of the concept of 'apprenticeship'
served in England. Balfour was to be sold in America as a 'twenty pounder',
a term which illustrates how much a transatlantic crossing cost. To avoid
such a fate, it would take a stonemason paid 32d a day (see chapter IV) in
1717, nearly six months to accumulate such an amount and arrive in America
a free man.

at this place for to conduct us to Port Royal where we shall hire Imberka-
tions to carry us to Georgia I am

Gentlemen

Your most obedient humble Servant

James Oglethorpe

Less than a month later, following a temporary sojourn on Tench's
island, the small group of settlers, ably assisted by South Carolina rang-
ers, were headed up the Savannah River, which was destined to mark the
boundary between the new colony and South Carolina to the North. On
the evening of the 1st of February 1733, the party landed at Yamacra Bluff,
on the Georgia side of the river, and under orders from Oglethorpe, immediately began to raise tents in which to sleep the night.

Far from an oversight, the absence of released debtors on the *Ann* was
probably a blessing in disguise. As other ships gradually arrived bringing
amongst others those for whom Georgia had been dreamt up in the first
place, it painfully became clear Oglethorpe's idealistic experiment was
already doomed to failure. The problem was basically Oglethorpe's myo-
pia when it came to human frailty, for even though no one could deny the
Parliamentarian's aims were laudable and progressive, others recognized
his inability to see *why* authorities back in England had incarcerated so
many of his colonists in the first place. Oglethorpe may have claimed
that debtors were "undone by guardians, some by lawsuits, some by ac-
cidents in commerce, some by stocks and bubbles, and some by surety
ship...may reduce the rich, and industrious, to danger of a prison, to a
moral certainty of starving!"[80], but this was only part of the picture, for
he failed to acknowledge that others had succumbed due to self-inflicted
crises like incompetence, gambling or drink.

With the rationale behind the colony inextricably linked to such
people, it was inevitable their weaknesses were exported out to Georgia
alongside those of a more hardworking disposition. In an environment
where it was vital everybody pulled their weight, such a situation was
bound to lead to disaster, facts well known to Oglethorpe, for even then
the human challenges facing his venture were widely recognized, take

---

80 Oglethorpe, JE: *New and Accurate Account of the Provinces of South Carolina and
Georgia*, London, 1733, p.30-33

for example, the sharp-eyed Benjamin Franklin a few hundred miles to the North, who espied what was wrong with Georgia, and noted in his *Autobiography:*

> The settlement of that province [Georgia] had lately been begun, but, instead of being made with hardy, industrious husbandmen, accustomed to labour, the only people fit for such an enterprise, it was with families of broken shop-keepers and other insolvent debtors, many of indolent and idle habits, taken out of the jails, who, being set down in the woods, unqualified for clearing land, and unable to endure the hardships of a new settlement, perished in numbers, leaving many helpless children unprovided for. [81]

Such an impasse would have spelled disaster in well-established provinces like New York or Rhode Island, but for something as embryonic as Georgia, colonization by unsuitable people was utterly ruinous, although it wasn't a problem that could be blamed on the settlers alone. For to be fair to the "broken shop-keepers" and their associates, the realities of life in Georgia differed fundamentally from the version sold to them back in England. Although sincere in their opinions, both Montgomery and latterly Oglethorpe were guilty of emphasizing the positives over the negatives of the country to the south of the Carolinas in order to stimulate emigration, some aspects of which overlooked, or minimized, the struggles the settlers would face.

Take one specific example, the weather. The climate differences between England and the American South were given scant attention, dooming early Georgia to limp along as a colony of people used to the cold and damp of England having to toil in an atmosphere that, even at the best of times, could be described as hot and muggy. Compounding environmental shortcomings was the gulf between the social and economic background of many of the settlers and the type of work vital to successful establishment of the colony. The new settlement was naturally going to be agrarian in nature, even relying on subsistence farming to get it off the ground, especially during the early days. In such straitened circumstances, a simple division of labor targeted at survival would therefore have been the sensible course of action, the management of which wasn't beyond Oglethorpe's capabilities.

---

81 Franklin, *Autobiography*

Rather than follow such a program however, a situation where "every man for himself" was allowed to reign. Each family that arrived was immediately given a tenancy over five hundred acres of land, which they were expected to clear themselves and plant crops on. Such a start in the New World would have been onerous enough for people who'd spent their formative years on a farm in the English countryside, but Oglethorpe and the Committee's careful planning had again let them down, for many of the emigrants' lives had been played out against the backdrop of the hustle and bustle of London.

Decisions reached by the Committee and Board of Trustees exacerbated the difficulties of environment and human nature. For one thing, the nearest the Colony had to Government placed extremely restrictive conditions on the ownership and use of land. The five hundred acre tenancy issued to each family stated the land could not be owned outright, sold on to anyone, or inherited, unless by a male heir, a prohibition that was to sap the enterprise of many colonists over the next few years.

Another ill thought out scheme was the idea of dictating what the settlers should actually grow. Montgomery and others assumed that because of its warm climate, Georgia would be an ideal location to cultivate olives and grapes, foodstuffs England was forced to import from the Mediterranean. This was an idea picked up enthusiastically by Oglethorpe, who had taken advantage of the warm summer of 1730 to plant vineyards at his home at Westbrook. Even so, the unexpected failure of these crops in Georgia still didn't stop the interference. The trustees knew Britain during the 1700s was increasingly dependent on imports from Italy to meet domestic demand for Silk, and the Committee — possibly seduced by Montgomery's description of the fertility of the region — decided it would be another good idea if Georgia were to provide an alternative source of the material.

On paper, the plan looked sensible, in that home-grown Silk neatly fused national self-reliance and imperial expansion together in one move. But the scheme was doomed to be a further example of how a theory drawn up in London could founder in the face of American experience, for mulberry bushes, the basic source of food for silkworm cocoons, and cultivated by the sweltering settlers, paradoxically found the Georgian climate too cold to thrive. Like the earlier motion to grow grapes and olives to help England's balance of payments, the initiative behind silk was again, in time, quietly dropped.

All in all, the authoritarian attitude of the Committee only added more problems to those already crippling the fledgling province, and further pushed the colony towards economic stagnation. For hardworking settlers, never mind those of "indolent and idle habits", the situation, natural and man-made, was becoming impossible, and as early as 1740, dissident Georgians, resident in Charleston, were already commenting bitterly:

> By these and many other hardships, the poor inhabitants of Georgia are scattered over the face of the earth, — her plantations a wild, her towns a desert, her villages in rubbish, her improvements a byword, and her liberties a jest, an object of pity to friends, and of insult, contempt, and ridicule to enemies".[82]

III

Notwithstanding these setbacks, it is however plausible the establishment of Georgia marked the successful first stage of a far grander enterprise. The early years in the colony — 1733 and 1734 — were naturally a time of hardship and struggle, even had the additional handicaps peculiar to Oglethorpe's experiment been absent. Ground needed to be cleared, crops planted, and houses built, and, to put it bluntly, this wasn't a time for diversions, such as the founding of yet another Masonic Lodge in America, which could, in theory, wait until later, more settled times.

But this wasn't to be the case. Barely a year after the arrival of the *Ann*, the Freemasons of the new province were already organized enough to found a Lodge, albeit of the "unofficial" variety[83]. Undoubtedly, James Oglethorpe's forceful nature played a part in these rapid turn of events, and, in the long run, was certainly a factor in the successful petition to make the Lodge "official" in the eyes of the Grand Lodge of England. In

---

82 *A True and Historical Narrative of the Colony of Georgia*, Patrick Tailfer, Hugh Anderson, David Douglass and others, Charleston and London, 1740

83 21st February 1734 was the date cited in Denslow's *10,000 Famous Freemasons*, published in 1959. According to *Coil's Masonic Encyclopedia*, which came out in 1961, the date traditionally accepted by the Lodge, culled from a Lodge minute dated 21st December 1858, was 10th February, 1734.

this respect, the brethren of Savannah were only doing the expected by requesting "official" status; although, on the other hand, the same cannot be said for the Grand Lodge, who, ignoring the aspirations of well-established unofficial Lodges further north — as well as practical considerations — granted the petition of the Savannah Masons early in the year of 1735[84]. *The Lodge at Savannah in Ye Province of Georgia* was duly entered into the roll books of the Grand Lodge in London as number one hundred and thirty nine, and once notified of this a few months later, the Masonic brethren of Savannah met "officially" for the first time on the following 2nd December.

Part of the reason behind the extraordinary speed Savannah Lodge was accepted by the Grand Lodge was certainly linked to Oglethorpe's membership of the self same governing body. Nevertheless, what was also remarkable was how neatly the second lodge in America again harmonized with the "modern" ritual. St John's Lodge in Boston had duplicated the ceremonial — if it even existed at the time — and now, two years later, the progression was adhered to at Savannah, only twenty miles from the Atlantic Ocean, and a mere five miles north of British America's self-styled southern boundary, the thirty-third parallel:

> you were placed in the North East part of the Lodge, to show that you were newly admitted; you are now placed at the South East part, to mark the progress you have made in the science[85].

Events leading to the warranting of Savannah — after Boston but before anywhere else — clearly indicate the establishment of the first and second "Official" Lodges in America were following the sequence of laying the eastern corners of the symbolic Temple outlined in the "new" ritual. Even more intriguingly, in the same manner the "parallel lines" and "north east corner" appeared to post-date — or were contemporary with — events in America, the same applied to the "South East Part": Pritchard didn't mention a second corner — or cornerstone — in *Masonry Dissected* written in 1730, a mere five years earlier. Within a quarter of a century of the arrival of the *Ann*, however, the 1760 exposé *Three Distinct Knocks* not

84 *Coil's Masonic Encyclopedia*, p.275. The Grand Master at the time was Lord Weymouth. Grand Masters served a year — Montague 1732-33, and Weymouth 1734-35.

85 *The Perfect Ceremonies of Craft Masonry*, p.116.

only referred to a second cornerstone but also its "modern" position, the south east corner.

The mystery as to why the distribution and formation of Masonic Lodges in America pre-empted the emerging ritual was compounded by the outwardly inexplicable actions of the participants in events. Although part of the reason for the rapid birth of "Official" Freemasonry in Georgia was doubtlessly due to Oglethorpe's domineering personality, it still doesn't explain why Price and the Grand Lodge agreed to the petition from the Savannah Masons when there were many more deserving cases to the North. Of course, the Boston tailor had the excuse that St. John's No. 1 was on his doorstep, giving him a rock solid reason for starting there; but the same argument couldn't justify the creation of the Savannah Lodge, several hundred miles to the south.

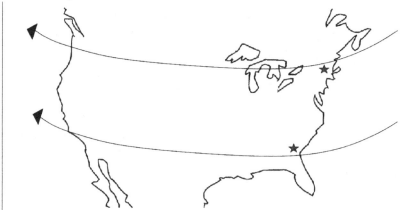

Fig. 9: St. Johns lodge was founded in Boston in 1733, and was followed by "Ye *Lodge at Savannah*" two years later. Note the identical pattern to the founding of the two cornerstones mentioned in the ritual, and in addition the proximity of the "*Two Grand Parallel Lines*".

Even if one assumes that Price and Oglethorpe were laying down the future parameters of American Freemasonry, by harnessing the boundaries of British influence as a guide, such a plan still flew in the face of practical considerations. The mail services across the colonies in 1735 were as bad as they were in England, condemning the two already existing Lodges to function an impossibly enormous distance apart. There was also the great unknown about the future of Britain's new province to contend with as well: for due to its instability, there was no guarantee Georgia — and the Savannah Lodge — would survive, especially during the years when the colony struggled.

Significantly, Price and Oglethorpe weren't the only Brethren making a special case out of Georgia, for the rest of England's Freemasons were pulling out all the stops to ensure the successful establishment of the colony too. This movement began at a Lodge in the northern city of Newcastle-upon-Tyne around Christmas, 1732, where, according to the *Newcastle Courant*[86], the brethren "ordered a considerable sum of money to be distributed among the poor families sent to Georgia". Of course, the Masons of Newcastle had already missed the boat, in the shape of the *Ann*, which had sailed six weeks earlier. This makes it all the more likely the northerners were thinking of the long term future of the colony, an idea picked up by the Grand Lodge in London twelve months later, as Georgia's problems began to bite.

London's Masons were certainly aware of the difficulties facing the thirteenth province by the end of 1733. Going on existing evidence, at least six of the twenty trustees — Lord Carpenter, Oglethorpe, James Vernon, commissioner of Excise, and Members of Parliament George Heathcote, Roger Holland, and John Laroche were proven Masons, alongside Thomas Pelham-Holles, His Majesty's Secretary of State with responsibility for the Colonies[87]. Undoubtedly all of these fretted about the difficulties engulfing Georgia at Masonic assemblies, even if only to assuage their anxiety over the issue; for the success or failure of the venture could be instrumental in deciding whether they all — Pelham — Holles especially — kept their jobs or not.

Even if the details of such fretting will never be known, their general thrust can, for the Grand Lodge itself decided to lend its weight to James

---

86 Edition dated 30th December 1732

87 The other fourteen were Viscount Percival, Edward Digby, Thomas Tower MP, Robert Moor MP, Robert Hucks MP, William Sloper MP, Sir Francis Eyles MP, William Beletha, John Burton D.D, Richard Bundy D.D, Arthur Blaford, Samuel Smith, Adam Anderson and Captain Thomas Coram. It isn't known whether any of these were Freemasons at the time. All references to the Masonic involvement with Georgia are drawn from *The Builder Magazine*, June 1928, Volume XIV, No. 6, the article titled 'General James Oglethorpe: Benefactor and Freemason' by Gilbert W Daynes.

Oglethorpe's experiment. At the quarterly meeting on the premises of the *Devil Tavern*, Temple Bar, London, held on Tuesday, 13th December, 1733, senior Masons considered Georgia's survival, and the result of their deliberations was a plan to augment the colony's population with an encouragement to emigration of their own, passed onto individual Lodges via the *Quarterly Communication*, the periodical Anderson mentioned being "revived" back in 1717:

> Then the Depy Grand Master opened to the Lodge the Affairs of Planting the New Colony of Georgia in America, and having sent an Account in Print of the Nature of such Plantation to all the Lodges, and informed the Grand Lodge that the Trustees had to Nathaniel Blackerby Esqr. And to himself Commissions under their Common-Seal to collect the charity of this Society towards enabling the Trustee's to send distressed Brethren to Georgia where they may be comfortably provided for...that it be strenuously recommended by Masters and Wardens of regular Lodges to make a generous collection amongst their all their members for that purpose. [88]

> Which being seconded by Bro. Rogers Holland Esqr. (One of the said Trustees) who opened the nature of the settlement, and by Sir William Keith, Bart., who was for many years Governour of Pennsylvania by Dr. Desaguliers, Lord Southwell Br. Blackerby and many others, very worthy Brethren it was recommended accordingly.

By pursuing this course of action, the Grand Lodge was not only saving Brother Pelham-Holles' political career but also fulfilling one of the stated principles of the Order, charity. Georgia was "an instance of generosity and public spirit...which few ages or nations can boast"[89] in 1733 and the interest and influence of a contemporary and local fraternity, one of whose aims was *relief* was therefore inevitable. Indeed, looking to the longer term, such an innovation could even have marked the Orders' initial excursion in using *relief* to spread Freemasonry around the World, using the Georgia experience as the model; for even though subsidized emigration was only likely to be offered to men (and their families) already members of the fraternity, such largess on the part of the Grand Lodge placed it alongside other organizations encouraging emigration to America, an idea that could, in theory, be replicated anywhere the British went.

---

88   Cited in Oglethorpe's entry in *10,000 Famous Freemasons*, as well as the above.
89   *Account of the first planting of the colony of Georgia; published from the records of the Trustees; by BENJAMIN MARTIN, their secretary*, London, 1741, p.11

Oddly, however, Georgia was to be a one off in Masonic history, because the offer of free travel to Britain's colonies was never made again. In the two hundred and seventy years following Oglethorpe's great experiment, much of North America, South Africa, Australia and New Zealand amongst others have been settled by people originating in Great Britain, yet no further offer to these countries, or any other, was ever forthcoming, either to Freemasons or anybody else.

So why was this? Undoubtedly, one reason is, with hindsight, the whole idea with Georgia was extremely ill thought out. Not only were costs prohibitive, but there was also the question of the *type* of people who were members of the Order, and their ability to adapt to a far more rough and ready lifestyle. It was highly unlikely the men of fashion, sculptors, poets *et cetera*, identified by W J Williams, would easily exchange life in London for the privations of a frontier colony no matter how poverty stricken they were. Common sense, even at the time, suggests the other twelve colonies — although still considered hopelessly provincial by metropolitan standards — would have provided far better refuge for "distressed brethren" than the primitive conditions prevalent on the Southern fringe of the Empire.

From a practical point of view, the policy of sending the wrong people to the wrong place therefore looks like breathtaking naivety on the part of the Grand Lodge, though doubtless part of this was because many of the members of the supreme assembly were ignorant of conditions in Georgia, Even so, there were others — George Shelvock, Thomas Pelham — Holles and Sir William Keith, the former Governor of Pennsylvania for example — who would've been fully aware of the potential pitfalls of experimenting with emigration to the thirteenth province, and who would have recognized the Grand Lodge's logic was flawed, leading to a bizarre discrepancy between a sensible course of action and what actually transpired.

Again, practicality was ignored, because for the Grand Lodge to allow the resolution without qualification, and to commit "distressed brethren" to populate a place where, as Benjamin Franklin noted, many settlers "perished in numbers" suggested there had to be a deeper reason for their interest and commitment. Certainly, one common denominator within all of the dispirit strands existed, and that was whilst Oglethorpe's efforts can be seen to establish his colony, Price's to further Freemasonry in America, and the Grand Lodge, an opportunity to exercise one of the principals it was founded on, a recurring theme tying them all together was the survival of Georgia as an *entity*, and the reason behind the determination to secure the future of the colony was not only because success was vital to a harmonization with the rituals being rewritten. For it was also apparent that by creating Georgia when they did, and where they did, Freemasons triggered the emergence of a numerical symbol not only affecting the thirteenth province, but the other twelve as well.

IV

From James Oglethorpe's membership of the Grand Lodge of England it can be safely assumed that, like Henry Price, at worst he had a basic knowledge of Masonic symbolism, and at best be fully conversant with it. Much of this imagery is, of course, a variation on practices of the operative stonemasons of the middle ages, and it is interesting to speculate whether Oglethorpe interpreted these practices to again mark the foundation of the new province. Undoubtedly, much of the symbolism surrounding Georgia's birth has an alternative Masonic explanation, in particular the multiple occurrence of "thirty-third", the Masonic mark for "Truth" or "achievement", which cropped up three times in the creation of the colony: established in the thirty-third year, bisected by the thirty-third parallel and named after the thirty-third monarch. If Oglethorpe saw the birth of Georgia as some sort of Masonic achievement, then by carefully weaving "thirty-third" into Georgia's symbolism he had succeeded in molding all of the characteristics of the colony's foundation: the name, place and time it came into existence.

Naturally, it would be naive to ignore the fact that these occurrences have non-Masonic explanations as well. Seventeen thirty-three was the most realistic time, the thirty-third parallel the logical place, whilst naming the colony after the thirty-third monarch was obviously an exercise in keeping the enterprise's most important supporter happy. And even if the multi-occurrence of "thirty-third" was deliberate, there is nothing to say it was not simply at the initiative of James Oglethorpe himself. The

Member of Parliament was well known for his enthusiastic nature, and it is plausible he again worked Masonic imagery into his own creation simply for his own satisfaction[90]. Certainly the idea of Oglethorpe acting alone would form a neat and acceptable ending to the story of Georgia's symbolism, if it weren't for one crucial point: and that was, by creating his colony where he did, and when he did, the MP triggered the emergence of a *second* numeric symbol which had ramifications not only for Georgia, but the rest of the Empire too: the number thirteen.

Generally speaking, thirteen has had a poor press. For centuries the number has been maligned as a symbol of bad luck, an association fostered by proximity to dark events ranging from the persecution of the Knights Templar to the near-disastrous Apollo mission to the Moon. However, this analysis is more a product of popular imagination rather than anything esoteric, for practitioners in the fields of religion and mysticism see thirteen as having a totally different connotation from negativity, in that it is often allied to ideas such as completion, union, intelligence, change, rebirth or consciousness.

The most obvious example of this deeper meaning lies in the measurement of time. Many societies around the world have employed thirteen for chronological measurement, its usage undoubtedly derived from the Moon and its thirteen lunar cycles in a year. Such cycles were a straightforward way to measure annual change in primitive societies, and it is clear the number and its use became so deeply entrenched that some civilizations continued to use thirteen as a measure even into the last millennium, like the Aztecs for example, to whom thirteen was a representation of time itself, their 'age' being four cycles of thirteen, and their week thirteen days in duration.

Like any numerical symbol, the strength of thirteen again lies in its adaptability, and it has been used in other ways to represent completion, union *etcetera*. Mediterranean and Middle Eastern societies of two or three thousand years ago certainly viewed thirteen in this way, from Greece, where thirteen was considered the most powerful numbers, to

---

90 If this was the case, the Oglethorpe was in illustrious company. His fellow Mason Wolfgang Amadeus Mozart incorporated cycles of thirty-three into his highly Masonic opera, *The Magic Flute.*

Rome and Old Testament Israel, where it often symbolized groups of people comprising twelve individuals plus one (special) other, such as Romulus and his twelve shepherds, Jacob and his twelve sons, and of course, Jesus and his twelve disciples.

Staying with the Biblical theme, the number also made further appearances, always suggesting completion, union or change, in both the Old and New Testaments, and even, when filtered through the science of geometry, one of the most famous Biblical shapes of all:

Crucially, Anglo-Saxon culture also co-opted this idea: the witches' coven, King Arthur and his knights, plus Robin Hood and his Merry Men are all examples of how this specific formula was again absorbed into the mythology of the British people. Of course, popular awareness of thirteen's esoteric value withered — or became more negative — as society matured, meaning that at the point when the eighteenth century was reaching a third of its span, few in England would have realized the num-

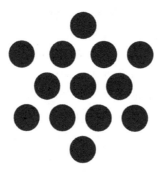

ber was again emerging as e symbol of completion, only his time it was across the Atlantic, and specifically around the birth of Britain's newest colony, Georgia.

And this was because once Oglethorpe started laying out Savannah, the colonies totaled thirteen, the highest figure they would reach; Including Georgia, Britain's provinces also stretched across thirteen parallel lines of latitude, from the forty-fifth on the border with Canada to the thirty-third in the South; an finally, these events took place between 1727 and 1737, in other words between one hundred and twenty and one hundred and thirty years after the Jamestown colony was founded in 1607, the thirteenth decade of Britain's Empire in America.

This multiple conjunction could, of course, be explained away as a mere accident of history, if it wasn't for one highly significant fact, and that was that each occurrence of thirteen also co-existed within a tightly defined relationship with the sequential "thirty-third", representing truth and achievement:

TIME	NAME	PLACE
All events took place during the 33rd year of the eighteenth century	Georgia: the Colony named after the 33rd Monarch	Savannah, on the 33rd Parallel
13 Decades	13 Colonies	13 Parallels
First British settlement at Jamestown, 1607	Northernmost Colony: Massachusetts	Most Northern Parallel: 45th Degree

Fig.10: The foundation of Georgia in 1733 illustrates the emergence of a numerical formula appearing in the makeup of the British Colonies.

The tight juxtaposition of "thirteen" and "thirty-third", and their multiple and simultaneous emergence in the relationships and spatial fabric of the colonies can, of course, be written off as coincidence, or possibly the work of one man. Nevertheless, Haslemere's MP was, like Price, Montague and Pelham-Holles, a member of a fraternity employing symbolism and imagery, numeric or otherwise, to make a point; and the point made on this occasion was "completion" and "achievement" had arrived with respect to the British Empire in America. For the remaining years of rule from London, no new colonies were born, and for good measure, the line of settlement didn't expand much North and South beyond the thirty-third and forty-fifth parallels.

In a deeper sense however, events concurrent in America and the changes to the ritual also suggested something far more important had taken place. The sum of the ceremonial fragments — apart from one — defining the exterior of a Masonic Temple, the "north east corner", the "south east part", the "parallel lines", all bound together by the sequential and numerical "thirty-third" and "thirteen" now existed on the map of colonial America, and their presence, far from the cartography of imperialism, hinted that something *architectural* was the result. The question was, if thirteen represented *completion,* and thirty-third *truth,* and together a symbolic stonemason mark stating *"this section of the work is true and complete",* then what aspect of "the building" had been erected?

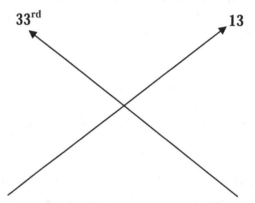

Fig.11: The numerical symbol appearing in America's makeup following the creation of Georgia

CHAPTER 6. "THE ROYALL ARCH WAS CARRIED BY TWO EXCELLENT MASONS..."

Mathematics resemble a well built arch; logic, a castle; and romances, castles in the air.

— Jonathan Swift, 1728

I

Less than two years after the foundation of Georgia, over the Christmas and New Year of 1734/35, the Duke of Montague hosted a house party at his home at Ditton, in the County of Surrey. The idea of such a gathering at a large country house — at least for the well to do — wasn't unusual for the era, and the guests, who started arriving on the day after Christmas, soon began to unwind in a boozy revelry that would continue until New Year. Indeed, so typical was Montague's hospitality that any record of the party ever happening would almost certainly have been lost to posterity, if it wasn't for two notable occurrences. The first was Montague possibly attempted to introduce a whiff of novelty to proceedings by the inclusion of several "brethren" from the Fraternity he had previously been Grand Master of, whilst secondly, and more specifically, the celebrations are remembered — at least in Masonic circles — for the actions of one partygoer in particular, an individual who went by the rather un-aristocratic name of Mick Broughton.

Mick was a well known mixer in society, a "noted lover of good living" who, far from his rather proletarian sounding name, was actually a clergyman, and possibly Jonathan Swift's successor as chaplain to the Lord-Lieutenant of Ireland, Lord Carteret. Although not a Mason himself, he must have been on good enough terms with the Duke's Masonic colleagues to have developed at least some familiarity with the Order they were members of, for during his stay at Ditton he sobered up sufficiently to pen a letter to the Duke of Richmond, in which he wrote:

DITTON, New Years Day, 1734–5

...I am sorry the weather has not been kinder for your Sport; bad as it is, it has not hindered ours, without doors or within: Rowing every day to old Windsor or Dachett, and within, Hollis and Desaguliers (who came hither on his Crutches on Saturday, and able to go without them in 24 hours) have been super-excellent in their different ways, and often at one anothers. We have been entertaining sometimes with scenes out of Don Sebastian, Tamerlane, Love for Love, &c.; the chief actors Desaguliers, St. John, Bodens and Webber. Mick, having a bad memory, excus'd himself from Acting, and Seated, Solus, upon a large Sopha, Represented a Full Audience. To give Caesar his Due, this Jest was Spoken by the Master of the House. On Sunday Night at a Lodge in the Library St John, Albermarle and Russell [were] made chapters: and Bob [Webber] Admitted Apprentice; the Dr. being very hardly persuaded by the Latter, by reason of Bob's tender years and want of Aprons. My being out of this Farce likewise, excludes me the honor of styling myself Brother, and must be contented to subscribe myself

My Dear Lord Duke

  Your Grace's Most Devoted
  And Humble Servant
  M. BROUGHTON.[91]

What was curious about Mick Broughton's use of terms such as "Chapters" and "Super-Excellent" is that over time they became synonymous with a new Masonic degree that suddenly appeared during the 1730s, the Royal Arch. Indeed, the house party at Ditton — and specifically the Lodge meeting held in the library — are the first recorded occurrence of a Royal Arch ceremony, or at least an embryonic version of it. For some obscure reason, and in contrast to the three degrees of Craft Freemasonry mentioned earlier, the Royal Arch burst out of nowhere in

---

91 Quoted in Jones, *The Royal Arch*, (p.41), and *The Builder Magazine*, May 1925, Volume XI, Number 5, 'Dr. J.T. Desaguliers and the Duke of Montague, 1734

Montague's Library in 1735, as if it had been conjured up for some specific, albeit mysterious purpose.

So why were these men creating a brand new Masonic Degree? Published material indicates the existing ceremonial — Entered Apprentice, Fellow Craft and Master Mason — were beginning to undergo the frantic rewrite transforming all three within a generation[92]. Surely sense dictated concentration on their completion, rather than charging off in a completely new direction, although this assumption again rests on practicality being the driving force behind change, something Henry Price's Lodge foundations in America and the Grand Lodge's subsidized emigration program showed was of secondary importance. For some unexplained reason, the timing of the Royal Arch's birth, along with its attendant imagery, was again symbolic, and the key to the meaning behind this symbolism lay with the men assembled in the Duke's library that frosty Sunday night in January, 1735.

Of course, of the eight men mentioned in Broughton's letter, five can be discounted immediately from being privy to the Royal Arch's formulation on the grounds they were either initiated that night — St John, Albemarle, Russell and Bob Webber — or in Broughton's case, not even being a Mason at all. This leaves three: the host, Montague, and the "super-excellent" Desaguliers and Hollis. The former was undoubtedly the Reverend Desaguliers, second Grand Master back in 1718 and mastermind behind much of the "new" symbolism being incorporated into Lodges and the ritual, whilst the latter, "Hollis" was, bearing in mind the optional spelling of the time[93], the age and class background of the participants, probably Thomas Pelham-Holles, the Duke of Newcastle.

---

92 See chapter one of Jones's *The Royal Arch*, Hammill's *The Craft* and Coil's *Masonic Encyclopedia*

93 Apart from Thomas Pelham-Holles, the *Dictionary of National Biography* lists no one else called either 'Hollis' or 'Holles' who could have been present at Ditton in 1735. Whilst the *DNB* does list one Thomas Hollis, (1720 –1774), he can be ruled out as an attendee. This was on the grounds that not only would he have been 14 or 15 at the time, and therefore too young to be a mason, but was also to emerge as a political radical during adulthood. It is therefore unlikely that Montague and Desaguliers would have welcomed the teenage republican into their midst.

Does the key to the rationale behind the Royal Arch Degree therefore lie with these three, the Duke, the chief symbolist of the Order, and His Majesty's Secretary of State for the Southern Department? If so, what had Desaguliers and Hollis done to make them "super-excellent" in the eyes of Mick Broughton? And did Broughton's praise infer that the Party — in particular the ceremony held in Montague's Library — was, far from a celebration of a new addition to the canon of Masonic ritual, actually a commemoration of something that had already taken place?

Whatever the answer, neither the history of the Royal Arch ceremony or the ritual itself provides much of a clue. Like other construction allusions in the degrees of the Masons, the Royal Arch again celebrates an aspect of the Temple, in this case the entrance. Stylistically reminiscent of the Old Testament, the story is of the reconstruction (or repair) of this feature of the building, the anomaly being due to alternative interpretations developing in Britain and Ireland over time[94]. Even taking these differences into account, what is striking about this ceremonial in comparison with the other three Degrees is its uniformity. Whilst the first, second and third degrees contain allusions from possible operative sources overlaid with fragments of eighteenth century intellectual thinking, the Royal Arch by contrast is far more consistent, in its style and substance is almost entirely Biblical in character.

It would therefore be natural to think this greater level of cohesion would be paralleled by a significant improvement in the use of Biblical imagery. But on this point — the most important aspect of the entire Degree — the Masonic interpretation of the entrance to the symbolic Temple makes an abrupt departure from Old Testament precedent, because even though the Royal Arch correctly points out the entrance to Solomon's Temple was on the eastern side[95], the Masonic version is sub-

---

94 The Royal Arch evolved around the concept of repair in Irish Freemasonry, whilst its English counterpart developed a story based on a complete reconstruction of the entrance.

95 The theory goes that God's people would turn their back on the rising sun — worshipped by the unbelievers — as they entered the building. Bernard Jones, on page 349 of the Freemason's Guide, summarizes some of the theories why Masonic Lodges' are laid out the way they are: 'why are Lodges placed East to West, with the Master's place in the East? It is a fair question because, whilst freemasonry corresponds to so many ancient Jewish prec-

ject to one massive inconsistency, a split with the Bible so fundamental there was absolutely no chance it was overlooked in 1735: and that is neither *Kings* or *Chronicles* mentions an Arch anywhere. Like so much of the Masonic ritual, the Royal Arch story is therefore left wide open to question; was it simply the result of some of the more fertile imaginations in the Grand Lodge — such as Doctor Desagliuers and his symbolism inventing colleagues? Or was its inspiration drawn from some other, non-biblical source?

Failure to dovetail with the Bible does indeed infer the Royal Arch has a rather more prosaic origin than generally supposed. Even so, its writers must have been inspired by *something*, for what they were doing was being taken extremely seriously, and whatever its genesis was, must have existed at, or prior to, Montague's party at Ditton. The first place to look is obviously at the ceremonial itself — official and unofficial — predating this particular year, although again this isn't much help. The most thorough examinations of Masonic terminology of the 1720s have, at most, only succeeded in finding the odd term destined for incorporation into the Arch ritual, and nothing could emphasis this more than the near-total absence from pre-*Masonry Dissected* Masonic vocabulary of the most important feature of the entire degree, the "arch" itself.

This is because during the 1720s, the use of the word "Arch" by the fraternity was minimal, which is all the more surprising considering the central role of Arches throughout the history of Architecture, and its importance within the dominant Palladian style of the time. More intriguingly, Bernard Jones' extensive researches have only produced one reference to "Arch" being used in a Masonic sense before the 1730s, and this wasn't even in the ritual, but a section of Doctor Anderson's *Constitutions*, which at the end of the day was simply the rulebook of the Order. Here,

---

edents, it apparently departs from them in orienting its lodges in a manner opposite to the example set by the Jewish tabernacle, which has its Holy place in the west and its porchway in the East. The Freemason's lodge follows the custom set for it through the centuries by the churches which, in the vast majority of cases, have their Holy of Holies in the east, the worshippers when they turn east in prayer thereby facing the altar. Many reasons have been given why Christians should face the east in this way. A thirteenth century writer explained that 'from the east Christ shall come to judge mankind; therefore we pray towards the east.'

there existed a solitary instance of the word, when Anderson, commenting on the concept of Brotherhood, stated a group of men, properly organized, "resembles a well-built Arch".

The fact the Royal Arch was a contemporary invention with no obvious origin was even recognized during the eighteenth century. During the 1770s, the Masonic authority Dr Oliver even went so far as to point the finger behind the fabrication at a certain Andrew Michael Ramsay, whom he claimed brought a number of additional Masonic degrees from Paris to London around 1740, and these included the Royal Arch. This continental explanation is supported by another Masonic historian, W. Redfern Kelly, although he doesn't go as far as to credit Ramsay with its authorship.

Even so, however obscure its beginnings, within eight years of the party at Ditton, the degree had spread throughout the British Isles and logically other places too. Bernard Jones mentions two occurrences in 1743, the first of the Stirling Rock Royal Arch Lodge in Scotland, and the second a report from *Faulkner's Dublin Journal* of a public procession carried out by a Lodge in Youghal, County Cork, where "The Royall Arch was carried by two Excellent Masons". So even though the "Royall Arch" was being paraded through the streets of Youghal during 1743, its beginnings, less than a decade earlier, are still shrouded in mystery. Why did Montague's houseguests create a degree around a non-existent feature of the Temple? Why did it emerge when it did? And could its inspiration, far from crossing the English Channel, come from a much greater distance?

II

One Mason who didn't make it to the Duke's party was James Oglethorpe, who, having returned from Georgia in May, 1734, was busy raising funds, and collecting new settlers, to keep the colony going. Like any other public-spirited enterprise, Georgia was totally reliant on enthusiasm, and Oglethorpe, keen to drum up support, was prepared to use every trick in the book to keep his idea in the public eye. To be fair, as a Parliamentarian, he had a strong base to start from, though he wasn't squeamish about using some of the darker political arts, such as boasting a little to secure interest, judging by the preamble of a letter he wrote to the trustees sometime in December, 1733:

> Gentlemen
>
> I cannot but congreulate You upon the great Success your Designs have met with being not only approved, of by all America but so strongly supported by His Majesty and the Parliament of Great Britain. Providence it self seems visible in all things to prosper your Designs calculated for the Protection of the persecuted, the relief of the poor and the Benefit of mankind.

Oglethorpe's ace in the hole with regards to publicity was, however, the presence of the ever obliging Tomochichi and his retinue in London. The chief, his wife and nephew, alongside a small number of warriors, had accompanied the MP back to Britain to see for themselves the kind of society they were getting involved with. The party visited Whitehall and Eton and various other places of interest, creating quite a stir as they did so, and an audience with none other than the King himself was also arranged. George II, as keen as everybody else to secure the success of the Imperial adventure named in his honor, received his new subjects on August 1st, a coup for Oglethorpe, especially as the Sovereign wrote to Tomochichi later in the year:

> I am glad of this Opportunity of assuring You of my regard for the People from whom You come, and am extreamly veil pleased with the assurances you have brought me from them, and accept very Gratefully this present as an Indication of their Good Disposition to me and my People. I shall always be reedy to Cultivate a good. Correspondence between them and my own Subjects and shall be glad of any occasion to shew You a Mark of My Particular Friendship and Esteem.

Amongst other presents from a grateful England, Tomochichi's wife Scanauki received that latest medical wonder, a glass eye; though the limitations of English medical science also became apparent when someone as eminent a physician as Sir Hans Sloane still couldn't stop Robert Castell's nemesis, smallpox, taking the life of one of Tomochichi's retinue. The Creeks, crushed by this turn of events, retired to Oglethorpe's estate at Westbrook, but still made occasional excursions, like the time they dined with Oglethorpe at the *White Hart Inn* in Godalming, an event that startled and bemused the local population.

Possibly too busy wining and dining Tomochichi to attend Montague's party, Oglethorpe still had plenty to celebrate himself by the new year of 1735. For his colony Georgia — notwithstanding its human and natural handicaps — was well on the way to becoming firmly, albeit erratically, established as the second anniversary of its foundation approached. Already, the original one hundred and fourteen settlers had been augmented by further immigration, not only of debtors, but also English Jews and people from further afield, such as the Salzburgers, a Protestant sect fleeing persecution in Southern Germany. Whilst the MP may therefore have mourned the fact the colony he envisioned in his original blueprint was already fading, he did at least have the satisfaction of knowing his creation, two years on, would endure.

Another Member of Parliament whose confidence had been vindicated and who could share in Oglethorpe's glory was Montague's fellow partygoer, Thomas Pelham-Holles. The Secretary of State for the Southern Department had doubtless monitored Georgia closely, and not only because the birth of the thirteenth colony represented the greatest single advance of British imperialism during his tenure to date. Like any other successful politician dependant on the patronage of the Crown, Pelham-Holles would have also been acutely aware that not only had Parliament invested the massive sum of ten thousand pounds in the venture, but failure would incur the displeasure of King George, who had been so supportive. The Duke couldn't afford to lose face at Court, and this was a near certainty had the colony named after the Head of State come to a miserable end.

By the time Pelham-Holles was enjoying Montague's hospitality however, this danger had passed. Relaxing in the convivial surroundings of Montague's home, it is highly likely that Newcastle, a noted chatterbox relieved at the partial success of the venture, brought up the subject of Georgia, and not only to crow about his role, and this was because there were several others present at Ditton who also had a direct connection with the new colony, even if it were only supporting the Grand Lodge's motion to supplement Georgia's population with "distressed brethren". These men, well versed in the politics of British imperialism and the symbolism of the Masonic Order, could easily have alluded to Georgia — and the colonies as a whole — in conversation that weekend, although for reasons completely different from those already mentioned; and that was how, symbolically, the Empire in America not only now resembled a common feature of the popular Palladian architecture of the time, but also the newest addition to a rapidly changing Masonic ritual, an Arch.

"The Keystone in the Democratic Arch" was how *Aurora*, an early American newspaper, once described the State of Pennsylvania. The reason for the nickname was, and is, straightforward enough. The emergence of Georgia during 1733 meant the number of British provinces on the eastern seaboard now came to a grand total of thirteen: six northeast of the "Keystone" and six to the south. Considering the extraordinary changes that have happened since, what is remarkable about Pennsylvania's "Keystone" relationship with the other states facing the Atlantic is that it is still as true today as it was during the reign of George II. Even with the addition of two new states to the original thirteen — Maine to the north and Florida to the south — the basic configuration has remained the same.

Perhaps the most interesting aspect of this symbolic architectural feature was how it came about in the first place, and the collective affiliation of the men who created it, for what would one day become America's "Democratic Arch" was indeed born out of the actions of members of a fraternity specializing in the use of architectural terminology for symbolic purposes. Whilst nobody could dispute that the main participants in the story of Georgia — James Oglethorpe, Thomas Pelham-Holles and Lord Montague — all had their own, very public reasons for the survival of the province, this still leaves the question of what their private — and collective — motivations were. Of course, without direct evidence, their involvement will always remain conjecture; but it was a fact the configuration of the thirteen colonies now imitated a contemporary architectural feature, complete with stonemason's mark that stated this aspect of the building — the entrance — was *complete* and *true*; and it was a fact that the same men, only months later, created a new Masonic ritual around the same "Arch" feature.

Their involvement may remain forever as purely circumstantial, though one thing is certain, and would have been recognized by them at the time, and that was an alignment of twelve — or any even number — wedge shaped stones, plus a central "Keystone" was the kind of arch eighteenth century operative stone masons were not only most familiar with, but also adept at raising. Part of the reason for this was the pivotal role that such arches played within the Palladian style; although it must also be remembered the "Keystone" arch had been in the ascendancy before Inigo Jones and Sir Christopher Wren popularized it. By 1735, conventional wisdom in building and architectural circles had long accepted this kind of arch held several advantages in comparison with other styles, most notably the Gothic[96], which, according to the dominant consensus of the eighteenth century lacked strength compared to the "keystone", in that the latter was far more capable of carrying and distributing a substantial load:

> As regards the other stones, some strength is borrowed from the presence of cement or mortar in the joints; but the real strength — the capacity of the arch to sustain a great weight bearing down on it — is due to the arch-stone or center-stone or keystone, as it is variously called, which functions independently of any mortar or cement, and transmits a load evenly through the other stones to the vertical supports, or abutments. An arch correctly designed and built should function without the cement or mortar joints, but, of course, is better for their presence[97].

Whilst the above is correct about the central importance of the keystone, it fails to mention the other stones in a keystone arch also have a crucial role to play. Remove a stone — or build the arch with inferior materials — and it was guaranteed the whole edifice would come crashing down at some point in the future. Nobody needed reminding that the same concept now applied to the symbolic arch on the eastern seaboard following the arrival of the *Ann*, for the British had already tasted bitter failure on occasion in their attempts to settle the east coast[98]. With these unfortunate precedents in mind, and as Georgia struggled to survive, there lurked in the background a strong possibility the "symbolic arch" could crumble backwards to twelve provinces in total, something

---

96 The latter had, of course, been a staple of English architecture throughout the Middle Ages, and was characterized by two, long tapering pieces of stone, which in theory, met at the top to close the Arch.

97 Bernard Jones, *The Freemason's Guide*

98 e.g., Raleigh's 1585 Roanoke colony and the abortive attempt to settle Newfoundland in 1610.

involved Masons must have been well aware of, though by late 1734, however, this eventuality had receded, and the Duke of Newcastle would have known -possibly via a face to face meeting with Oglethorpe — that Georgia was becoming well established after two successful harvests and a constant stream of immigrants. For "Hollis", Montague, and the symbolism creating Desaguliers, success was now firmly in the bag, and the way was now clear to start drawing up the rituals that would become the Royal Arch, ready for the Duke's party at Ditton.

III

Whatever the nature of the ceremony Desaguliers and the others conducted in the library, its embryonic nature can be inferred from the name they gave it at the time. Today, the formal title of the Royal Arch is the Holy Royal Arch of Jerusalem, but back when Montague, Newcastle and Desaguliers met in the library, they were calling their new ceremony something subtly different: the English Royal Arch. So why did they adopt this particular name? Certainly, accepted theories as to its origins are straightforward enough: "English" has usually been assumed to refer to the part of the world where the degree was developed — a view even taken by Doctor Oliver two hundred and fifty years ago — whilst "Royal" has been presumed to be an allusion to King Solomon (or possibly the House of David in general). This connection is potentially reinforced by the traditional and widespread use of such arches in Middle Eastern architecture, a fact well known to the academics and architects who were members of the Order at the time: for the eighteenth was also the century of the "Grand Tour", where men of wealth and education travelled extensively in search of new ideas and experiences.

Nevertheless, it was still an *English Royal* Arch, hinting at some form of Anglo-Saxon connection, and if this influence was colonial America, then the way to see the thirteen colonies as such is to take a closer look at *their* potential symbolic value.

Henry Price

James Oglethorpe

Anthony Browne
Lord Viscount Montague

Thomas Pelham-Holles
Duke of Newcastle

Taking "English" first, then one straightforward answer is that the colonies in 1733 were not only English in that their allegiance was to Great Britain, but ethnically too. Successive waves of immigrants from mainland Europe, plus slaves imported from Africa had still failed to dent the lead Britain had in providing the blood stock of the American colonies in 1733, a gap so great, that the country remained overwhelmingly Anglo-Saxon well into the nineteenth century.

With regard to the word "Royal", one obvious idea is it is an allusion to the thirteen colonies being the only part of America ever subject to the British Monarchy. This is unlikely however, for the rituals of the "Royal Arch" were published over forty years before the Declaration of Independence, a period in American history when the whole idea of political separation followed by republican government was only the desire of a small minority, something confirmed by Franklin's *Autobiography*, which suggested that loyalty to the Crown was the dominant political theme during the 1730s.

This allusion is further undermined by the fact that the rest of the territory of what was to become America was also under "Royal" authority in 1733: the King of France, Louis XV and Spain's King Phillip V. Britain's provinces were therefore no different to the rest of the Americas, north and south, in their relationship with Monarchical rule when the "Arch" ritual first emerged, although there is, however, one further potential "Royal" connection, impacting directly on the thirteen colonies: their individual names.

James Oglethorpe had already illustrated the potential symbolism inherent in a title when he named his colony after King George II. But was there a secondary reason for the MP's decision, one that like "thirteen" and "thirty-third" affected the other twelve provinces as well? Collectively, the names of the "thirteen originals" were a declaration of the wide array of people and motivations going into their evolution and establishment. Massachusetts and Connecticut were named for Native American tribes; New Hampshire and New Jersey for counties and islands of the British Isles, whilst the origins of Rhode Island lie with the Dutch for Red Island.

Of the remaining eight, the names of seven originate from English Royalty and Aristocracy. Starting from the South, there was Georgia, followed by the two Carolinas, north and south, named after Charles II, via the Latin for Charles, *Carolus*. Next is Virginia, named after Elizabeth I, "The Virgin Queen", whilst Maryland, named for Henrietta Maria, the wife of King Charles I. The last — and most northerly of these Royal colonies was New York, named after the Duke of York, the younger brother of King Charles II, who had, back in 1685, succeeded Charles as King James II. The strong emphasis on monarchy was tempered by Delaware, named after a mere aristocrat, Lord De la Warre. These royal names are concentrated south of New England, but if dispersed equally with non-royal titles either side of the Keystone, this is the pattern:

New York (Duke of York, later James II)
Massachusetts

Maryland *(Henrietta Maria, wife of Charles I)*
Delaware
Virginia (Elizabeth I)
Connecticut
PENNSYLVANIA (Keystone)
New Hampshire
North Carolina (Charles II)
Rhode Island
South Carolina (Charles II)
New Jersey
Georgia (George II)

Fig. 12. The thirteen colonies with "royal" and "non-royal" names equally interspersed.

All of the ingredients — timing, names, ethnicity, allegiance, position and number — clearly add up to an "English Royal Arch"[99] regardless of whether it was deliberate or not, although further confirmation this could indeed be a Masonic construction lies in the symbolism of the Keystone itself, for, apart from the cutting of a Keystone to get the right fit, operative stonemasons were often called upon to perform a second job on such stones: carving into their exterior face something illustrating the building's nature . This could range from the stonemason's own initials to the owners name, the year of construction, or something defining the building's use, a word or symbol for example.

In a Symbolic sense therefore, and accounting for the "new" Masonic Order's desire to maintain or invent connections with its operative forebear, it was logical that when "speculative" Freemasons built an arch, they would again cut the "keystone" to make a statement. And here they were lucky, for the capital city of this particular keystone, Philadelphia,

---

99 The Romans pioneered the construction of 'true' arches. During the first century, some spanned a width of eighty three feet and rose to a height of a height of a hundred and twenty one feet. Interestingly enough for the 'Royal Arch' model above, (Fig. 1) one of the characteristics of the 'Roman' arch — especially in the Middle East — was the use of alternate kinds of stone to get a light/dark/light/dark effect.

shared its name not only with a principal of Freemasonry[100], but also the most important one, the City of Brotherly Love. Named by William Penn to illustrate the type of human relationships he strove for in his colony, Philadelphia, fifty years into its existence, suddenly took on a new role, and that was because, if the "Arch" of thirteen colonies really were deliberate, and Pennsylvania a Keystone, then *Brotherly Love* was the obvious term to cut[101].

IV

To summarize, it had taken a handful of individuals — backed by affiliates throughout England, Europe and America — under three years to reconfigure the Empire into something symbolically architectural, and even more astonishing, this achievement was based on the philosophy and imagery of an English fraternal society that, formally, hadn't even reached the twentieth year of its existence. Without a doubt, 1733 to 1735 had certainly been a period of *completion* and *achievement* for Freemasons like Henry Price, Viscount Montague, James Oglethorpe and Thomas Pelham-Holles.

Even so, there was *still* something missing in the symbolism of Pennsylvania: the "thirteen crossed with thirty-third" imagery that pointed to *Completion* and *Achievement*. The Keystone was going to be of paramount importance if America was to be laid out to architectural principals, but back in 1733, the failure of the two numbers to appear anywhere in Pennsylvanian symbolism meant there was no evidence that what was to become the "Keystone State" was just that, a Keystone. However, the non-appearance of "thirteen" and "thirty-third" around the Keystone cir-

---

100 Brotherly Love, Relief and Truth.

101 It stands to reason that if the 'Keystone' has 'Brotherly Love' carved upon it, then the other two principles of the order should be found at the cornerstones of the 'Arch' — Georgia and Massachusetts. In the modern era however, there are no city, town or county names that reflect this. In terms of 'Truth', this is understandable in that it is not supposed to have a home: it should always be looked for. The situation is far more curious with regards to Georgia, which was created by Freemasons specifically for the purposes of 'relief'. Even more intriguing was the actions of the Salzburgers, the German Protestant sect that arrived in Oglethorpe's colony during 1734–35. The original name of their settlement was Ebenezer, the Hebrew word for 'Stone of Relief.'

ca 1733 again makes sense if one looks at the thirteen colonies — and by extension the rest of America — through the prism of architectural science. As the author of the *Freemason's Encyclopaedia*, Bernard Jones, has already said, "...the real strength — the capacity of the Arch to sustain a great weight bearing down on it — is due to the Arch-stone or Centre-stone or Keystone..." and the inference from this is obvious. If America was to be laid out architecturally, then Pennsylvania's proper keystone status, illustrated by "thirteen crossed with thirty-third" would only become recognizable upon *completion* of the entire building[102].

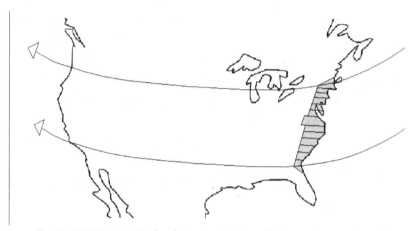

Fig. 13: *ROYAL ARCH.* The thirteen colonies and the northern and southern boundaries, the "parallel lines", the forty-fifth and thirty-third lines of latitude

But was this something brand new, or a symbolic representation of some older structure? Maybe the answer to this particular question could be found on the first few days of the Georgia settlement. According to one of the settlers, 34-year-old upholsterer Peter Gordon, "we sailed from Jones's Island, with a fair wind and arrived the same day at Yamacra Bluff in Georgia, the place which Mr. Oglethorp had pitched upon for

---

102 It would, however, be a mistake to believe that the symbolic importance of an Arch is peculiar to Freemasonry: many other mystical systems also put great emphasis on the Arch. The common denominator in all of these systems is that the Arch illustrates two important characteristics. The first of these is strength, in so much as part of the Arch's role in a building is to hold up the construction work above it. The second meaning is that the Arch acts as a symbolic gate or doorway, to a new life (or to be mystical) a higher stage of consciousness.

our intended settlement"[103]. Gordon's diary entry was for the 1st February, 1733; a date confirmed by Oglethorpe himself in a letter to the trustees dated 10th February, in which he stated that "The whole people arrived here on the first of February. At night their tents were got up" [104]. Even so, this wasn't the full picture, for Peter Gordon's diary had also stated:

> next morning, being the first of February...as Soon as we landed, we Sett immediately about getting our Tents fixed, and our goods brought ashore... Not being able to compleat the pitching of our Tents this night; ...Friday the 2nd we finished our Tents, and gott some of our Stows on Shore.[105]

Part of the failure to raise the tents may have been due to the entertainments the Creek chief Tomochichi laid on for Oglethorpe and his followers, or more pertinently, the liquor provided by a local trader named Musgrove, which, according to Gordon, overcame at least one settler, the colonists' apothecary Doctor Syms, who "got a little in drink." Conversely though, it is also possible that Oglethorpe timed everything to ensure that the colonists arrived during the hours of darkness, especially the darkness of this particular night. And that was because, as a stonemason in symbolism, Oglethorpe would have been well aware of the significance of commencing work at daybreak, especially the dawn of the next day, February 2nd, 1733. This wasn't simply because the establishment of the first British settlement in Georgia — and by extension the creation of the "Royal Arch" of thirteen provinces — could be said to begin on the morning of the thirty-third day of the thirty-third year[106]. As Doctor Syms nursed his hangover, James Oglethorpe also knew that the birth of

---

103 *Our First Visit in America: Early Reports from the Colony of Georgia, 1732–1740* (Savannah, Beehive Press, 1974) pp. 12–13

104 *Account of the first planting of the Colony of Georgia*

105 Peter Gordon 'An Account of the first settling of the Colony of Georgia with a journal of the first embarkation, under the direction of Mr. Oglethorpe' Box 09, Folder 47, Document 01, Keith Reid Collection, Hargrett Rare Book and Manuscript Library, The University of Georgia Libraries, Presented in the Digital Library of Georgia

106 The decision begin work in February is also another possible example of Oglethorpe's military precision being brought to bear. Prior to the arrival of the *Ann*, the time of year when the other twelve colonies were founded rarely followed a pattern, or sensibility. The Pilgrim Fathers had landed on Plymouth Rock in December; the Jamestown settlers had come ashore in May, whilst Sir Francis Drake's ill-fated Roanoke colony had been founded in June. Of these three, the last was a total failure whilst the other two endured extreme privations before emerging as long term successes.

his settlement, and by extension the completion of the entrance to the symbolic building, had taken place not only during the modern equivalent of "the month Zif, which is the second month,"[107] but also the contemporary version of the actual *day* Solomon started raising his Temple:

> And he began to build in the second *day* of the second month...

— 2nd Book of Chronicles, 3:2

A symbolic view of the British Colonies in North America after the 2nd February, 1733. This was during the 13th decade (1727–37) of Britain's involvement in the New World. The 33rd year of the eighteenth century witnessed the foundation of Official Freemasonry in America, plus the creation of Georgia, the 13th Colony, named after England's 33rd Monarch. Note the profusion of 33rds and 13s denoting "achievement" and "completion" and the position of the *Two Grand Parallel Lines*, the 33rd and 45th parallels.

It was therefore inevitable that by the 1730s the British had learned from these mistakes, and decided to establish their newest province at the optimum moment to ensure the colony's survival. So by founding Georgia in a February, Pelham-Holles and Oglethorpe were, from a practical point of view, taking advantage of the best time of year to start a new settlement in the Northern Hemisphere. The winter of 1732/33 was ending, presenting the settlers with time to plant crops and build habitations, and setting the colony maximum opportunity to get off to a flying start.

107   This argument relies on the Freemasons of the time employing the modern equivalents of Biblical months. In the ancient Hebrew Calendar, 'Zif' would have occurred in April or May. No allowance has been made for the change from the Julian to Gregorian calendars in 1752 on the grounds that numerically, February 2nd remained the thirty-third day of the year/ 'second day of the second month'.

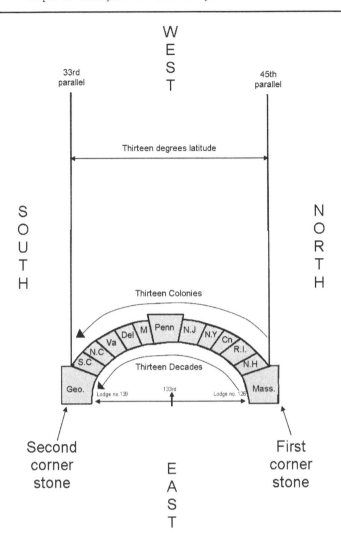

Fig. 14: The Entrance to the Temple

Part III. *Floor*

Chapter 7. "They determined to consult Vitruvius, Palladio, and all other writers of reputation in the art"

> Freemasonry has exercised a greater influence upon the establishment and development of this (the American) Government than any other single institution. Neither general historians nor the members of the Fraternity since the days of the first Constitutional Conventions have realized how much the United States of America owes to Freemasonry, and how great a part it played in the birth of the nation and the establishment of the landmarks of that civilization..
>
> — Heaton, *Masonic Membership of the Founding Fathers*

I

"The scene which that country presents to the eye of the spectator," exulted Tom Paine in *The Rights of Man*, "has something in it which generates and encourages great ideas". Whether this particular Englishman, author of *Common Sense* and other works that influenced America's insurrection against his homeland ever mused on the nature of the mysterious "something" will forever remain within the realm of speculation; although one thing was self-evident by the time *The Rights of Man* was published in 1792[108], and that was that "great idea" upon "great idea" found themselves on fertile ground in the former British colonies.

---

108   Thomas Paine, Introduction to *The Rights of Man*, 1792, part 2

Already, sixteen years had passed since the United States had broken with Britain and nine since a formal peace had been agreed between the two powers. Indeed, "to assume among the powers of the earth, the separate and equal station to which the laws of nature and of nature's God entitle them", as Jefferson elegantly put it, was doubtless one of the "great ideas" alluded to by Paine. Like everybody else, the Englishman was well aware that no colony had ever stood up to its European mother country before; and no other colony had ever had the nerve to go it alone.

Paine, the visionary, could see which way the wind was blowing, something eluding many of his fellow Englishmen. Across the British Isles, scorn was poured on the idea that mere *colonials* could be capable of running their own affairs, and still smarting from defeat, many Britons — and other Europeans — opined that by denying the social and political solidity provided by monarchism, the hot-headed revolutionaries were doomed to racial conflict, mob rule, or slink back to the orbit of one or more of the imperial powers with an interest in the continent.

Contrary to the doom-mongers' prognostications, by 1790 the thirteen states were, despite the inevitable disruptions thrown up by independence, enjoying not only an enviable domestic harmony but also proving adroit at keeping the surrounding predatory powers at bay. Part of the cause behind the latter was, undoubtedly, the fact that Europe's major nations were otherwise distracted. France, temporarily expelled from North America following defeat in the Seven Years War[109], was in the throes of its own revolution. The British meanwhile, recognizing the inevitable with regard to America, contented themselves by consolidating their grip on Canada.

The position of the third power — Spain — looked formidable enough, for the 1763 treaty had ceded France's Louisiana to Madrid, extending Spanish rule over everything west of the Mississippi, plus Florida. Hegemony on such a grand scale was however hollow, for whilst Spain's windfall may have meant something two hundred years earlier, by 1790 their empire was itself coming apart at the seams, and was facing nemesis within a generation.

---

109   This War — between Britain, France and Spain — lasted from 1756 to 1763

Fig. 15: Jean Lattre's Map of America, 1784

Equilibrium was reinforced by the revolution's hands-off approach to society and economy. Unlike the changes wrought by the revolutions of France and latterly Russia, all of the old colonial relationships in America — between capital and labor, master and slave, town and country, native and immigrant — carried on more or less as if nothing had happened in 1776. English remained the language of the Republic; English law its legal basis. Indeed, for many Americans probably the most noteworthy change apart from home rule was the replacement of monarchical symbolism with imagery drawn from a far wider array of sources throughout the states: The names of many towns, counties and public institutions were all divested of their connections with English kings and queens, although by contrast, and uniquely for a post-revolutionary society, the "royal" names of the thirteen states making up the symbolic Arch remained.[110].

---

110 Many countries and former colonies have changed their names, and those of their cities and regions, quite quickly after independence or revolution. Whilst this has been standard in Africa, the most obvious examples in Europe are Russia and Ireland. In Ireland, following the 1921 treaty with Britain, King's County and Queen's County became Leix and Offaly respectively, whilst ports like Kingstown and Queenstown were renamed Cobh and Dun Loaghaire. Russian cities like St. Petersburg and Ekaterinburg underwent an identical process after 1917, becoming Leningrad and Sverdlovsk, although these reverted to their original names after 1991. By contrast, and

Business as usual characterized the United States' international intercourse as well. Immigration, mainly from America's recent adversary, carried on uninterrupted; it was often British ships that brought slaves and manufactured goods into American ports; and cotton continued to be exported to Lancashire mills. The European merchant, newly arrived in Boston, New York or Charleston in 1790, haggled over the price of New England fish, backcountry furs or Carolina tobacco in much the same way he would have done twenty years earlier. All in all, the durability and maturity of American society in the 1780s dictated minimal interference with the mechanics of everyday life: Paine's "scene" was indeed ready for more "great ideas" but they were to be restricted to the spheres of politics, administration, and crucially, the physical growth and layout of America.

One of the first and foremost innovations was already underway: the creation of the Constitution. Whilst the Revolution had come about primarily because of the machinations of England's parliament, Americans were — and are — more inclined to blame the perceived tyranny of King George III. It was therefore understandable for representatives of twelve of the thirteen states[lll] meeting at the Constitutional Convention held in Philadelphia between 1787 and 1790 to devise structures making such a state of affairs unthinkable ever again. To this end, the governmental system agreed upon was divided into three parts — executive, legislature and judiciary — held in place, not only from each other, but from domination over the public, by a cunning series of checks and balances.

What the creation of the Constitution also illustrated was that the American republic had come to life in precisely the right time and circumstances for the application of as many rational and scientific ideas as possible. There were certainly enough lying around, for the Western intellectual tradition had long been in the business of accumulating "good ideas", which now, refined and honed from classical times to the renaissance and enlightenment, could be tested fully in America, as one future President, John Adams, recognized in 1787:

uniquely, American States retained their 'Royal' titles after 1776: only the names of towns (with the exception of Charleston), counties and public institutions were changed.

lll   Rhode Island declined to take part.

Called without exception, and compelled without previous inclination, though undoubtedly at the best period of time, both for England and America, suddenly to erect new systems of laws for their future government, they adopted the method of a wise architect, in erecting a new palace for the residence of his sovereign. They determined to consult Vitruvius, Palladio, and all other writers of reputation in the art; to examine the most celebrated buildings, whether they remain entire or in ruins; to compare these with the principles of writers; and to inquire how far both the theories and models were founded in nature, or created by fancy; and when this was done, so far as their circumstances would allow, to adopt the advantages and reject the inconveniences of all.

...Thirteen governments thus founded on the natural authority of the people alone, without a pretence of miracle or mystery, and which are destined to spread over the northern part of the whole quarter of the globe, are a great point gained in favour of the rights of mankind. The experiment is made, and has completely succeeded; it can no longer be called in question, whether authority in magistrates and obedience of citizens can be grounded on reason, morality, and the Christian religion, without the monkery of priests, or the knavery of politicians[112].

Adams, for all his architectural allusions, wasn't a Mason. Nonetheless, his argument, that organized human beings could, inspired by architectural and scientific precedent, influence the course of the new nation was a public declaration of something which, unbeknown to him, had already existed in America for over fifty years, because the tiny fraternal society of Price and Oglethorpe's day now had its adherents across all thirteen states and within every section of American society. George Washington himself was a Mason, and a former surveyor, too, and would have recognized the desire, and the science to achieve it, was now in place for the raising of a symbolic building across the North American continent. Her would have also realized that apart from possible intransigence from foreign powers or Native Americans, there was now nothing to stop these men and others, having consulted Vitruvius, Palladio, "and all other writers of reputation in the art" laying out the Republic to maximize "the advantages and reject the inconveniences of all".

---

112   From the preface of Adams's 1787 *Defence of the Constitutions of the United States*

II

One "great idea" that almost certainly attracted the attention of such men went — and goes — by the rather inaccessible title of "Lambert's Conformal Conic". To put it simply, the "Conic" is a map projection: which in itself is a mathematical formula that, when applied to a portion of the Earth's surface, is intended to maximize the accuracy of a map of that same area. This doesn't mean the Conformal Conic is the only projection in existence: projections come in many forms, depending on the shape, size and position of the territory to be mapped, and it is significant that when the Alsatian mathematician Johann Heinrich Lambert first turned his attention to the problems of mapmaking in 1772, that he was to devise at least five other projections in addition to the conformal conic.

Neither does it suggest that any projection delivers optimum results from the measurement of an area, for, as Wellman Chamberlin, a former Cartographer of the National Geographic Society, explains:

> There is no overall "best projection" for all maps. Each map presents a particular problem. The projection that is ideal for mapping Chile, which extends more than 2,600 miles north and south and an average of less than 150 miles east and west, is not the ideal projection for mapping an area like the former Soviet Union, which extended 5,000 miles east and west near the top of the globe[113].

It is also significant that particular types of projections are favored by different groups. Scientists, geographers, and others to whom a standard area scale is more important than correct shape prefer "equal-area" projections. Conversely, navigators, engineers, and military strategists are more likely to work with conformal maps of which, Lambert's Conic was, and is, an obvious example.

With regard to the origins of Lambert's theorem, its pedigree can be traced to an era long before his particular scientist was born, and in fact it was the Egyptian mathematician and astronomer Ptolemy, who, back in the second century AD, first devised a version of the conic, for mapping the Roman Empire. In simple terms, Ptolemy's projection was that of a ball (representing the Earth) within a cone, where the circumferences of both only meet at one point (the line of tangency). Theoretically,

---

113 Quoted in the *Mapmakers*, p.

along this line the map dimensions are true, with inaccuracy increasing the further one moves away to the north or south:

Fig.16: Ptolemy's projection.

The importance of Ptolemy's projection was that it proved, and proves, useful when mapping a large scale area — a region — in the middle latitudes: those areas of the world which lie between twenty and sixty degrees north and south of the equator. Ideal for mapping the Roman World therefore, Ptolemy's work was however largely ignored during the thousand years following the Empire's fall; but sprang back into fashion during the sixteenth century and after as the Spanish, Portuguese and latterly other powers, began their carve up of the newly found Americas, and latterly, other places, such as Australia.

In 1772, when Lambert turned his attention to map accuracy, he revisited Ptolemy's concept, and modified it in one crucial way: his projection was to be based along two parallel lines rather than one. With Lambert, the "cone" theoretically slices through the earth's crust. The importance of this innovation was that accuracy is maintained along the two parallel lines, rather than one, in theory greatly increasing — to the north and south — the map area that is true.

Like John Adams, no record exists to link Johann Heinrich Lambert with the Mason's fraternity, and neither was he ever a citizen of Great Britain or the United States. It is therefore highly improbable he was familiar with — or inspired by — the "two grand parallel lines" fragment embedded in the Masonic ritual less than forty years before, or for that matter the unilateral claims made by the English to America as a whole. What is far more likely is that this particular mathematician developed his theorem independently, in ignorance of the above, although "ignorant" was the last word that could be applied to interested parties once his ideas were published.

This was because Lambert's Conformal Conic could, if used as a tool to define America to the Pacific, re-emphasize the symbolic importance of the forty fifth and thirty-third degrees latitude north. Armed with Lambert's theory therefore, a highly fluid situation with regards to who-owned-what west of the Mississippi, and a nation now looking west rather than east, the question facing American Freemasons was could they actually achieve this extraordinary endeavor, and increase American territory to the point where it corresponded correctly, in a mathematical sense, to this particular theorem?

Fig. 17. Lambert's Conformal Conic

It was indisputable that, by 1800, the conventional tools behind territorial expansion, force and diplomacy, were in place. Washington's

Army had already exhibited its credentials, when it secured independence from the world's most powerful nation. Likewise diplomacy, of which America as a practitioner matured quickly during the war, for the straightforward reason the Republic needed allies — namely France and Spain — if liberty was to be achieved.

This list wasn't exhaustive, for there were other tools at hand too. One was another English legacy: an undying desire to secure the west. This idea, in its earliest incarnation, had its genesis two hundred years earlier with the Oxford Don, Professor Richard Hakluyt, who in his 1585 *Discourse on Western Planting* and 1589 *Principal Navigations, Voyages and Discoveries of the English Nation*[114], encouraged English colonization. Thinking along these lines continued via England's claims to the continent, and reappeared in the thoughts of America's leaders at the time, most notably Benjamin Franklin and Thomas Jefferson, who commented that whilst he believed America would one day stretch to the Pacific, it would take a thousand years to achieve.

Even so, none of the above would be of much use, or clumsy at best, if America was to be laid out in accordance with a mathematical formula. It was therefore necessary to call up something new in the history of nations — another "great idea" so to speak — that was not only to be unique, but was also destined, as an instrument of unsurpassed precision, to define America mathematically: commercial acquisition.

In 1803, to the west of the Mississippi lay the French owned territory of Louisiana. A rough and ill defined triangle of over eight hundred thousand square miles, this region, or at least the Southern tip around the Mississippi Delta, had begun to be settled by the French as early as 1682. Attempts to emulate British successes with immigration were, however, only partially successful, and by the year 1762, with both powers at war with one another, the interior of Louisiana still remained virtually untouched. As far as the Great Lakes to the North, and the Prairies to the West, French authority only extended to isolated trading posts and a handful of forts on the Mississippi[115]. France still enjoyed legal owner-

---

114   Published in 1584 and 1589 respectively
115   Names like Louisville, Detroit and Saint Louis are testament to this policy.

ship of the entire region however, or at least until military defeat[116] forced Paris to cede ownership of Louisiana to Spain.

There was nothing odd about this, for the swapping of vast territories from one colonial power to another was a characteristic of deals struck in the aftermath of eighteenth century conflicts. The practice arose because England, France, Spain and Portugal were already beginning to solidify into the shapes on the European map that endure to the present day. This inevitably made the transfer of European lands from defeated to victorious nations all the more difficult; and it was therefore far more practical for a "losing" power to cede an imperial possession, and a winning" nation to gain one.

So it was that defeat in 1763 saw France loose her possessions on the North American continent — Louisiana to Spain and Canada to Britain. But notwithstanding defeat in that particular war, France — like Britain — was a country in the ascendancy during the late eighteenth century, in sharp contrast to Spain, whose power and influence had waned since the Imperial heyday of the fifteen hundreds. The upshot of such mixed fortunes was that by the late 1790s, France, restored to aggressive virility by its ambitious new Emperor Napoleon Bonaparte, was strong enough to bully Spain into handing the Louisiana territory back via the secret Treaty of Ildefonso.

Naturally, the very idea of the French on the Mississippi had serious implications for the infant United States. America's third President, Thomas Jefferson, was certainly alarmed enough, and not only because France could pose more of a threat than Spain, who had already made a nuisance of themselves when, during the 1780s and 1790s they tried to withhold shipping rights on the river from the Americans. Jefferson and his cabinet harbored a legitimate fear France could reprise this tactic, with far more devastating results than just having their river commerce choked off. Faced with possible French awkwardness across the Mississippi, as well as American ambitions being boxed in by the river permanently, Jefferson immediately countered by sending a special envoy, James Monroe[117], to work with America's minister to France, Robert Liv-

---

116   1756 to 1763
117   For Monroe's Masonic connections, see Chapter 7.

ingston[118]. Monroe's brief was straightforward: he and Livingston were to press Napoleon for navigation and trading guarantees for the region, and the possible purchase of the city of New Orleans.

Jefferson instructed Livingston and Monroe to offer $5 million for New Orleans and its environs, so it was a surprise when Bonaparte offered the *entire* territory to the Americans for $15 million, or 4 cents an Acre. The French Emperor harbored good reasons for this tactic: an inability to crush the slave uprising on the Island of Santo Domingo had already drove home to him the perils of meddling in the Americas; whilst $15 million would be handy for paying for his wars in Europe.

For their part, Livingston and Monroe were far sighted enough to recognize the bargain this was; and closed the deal with Bonaparte in Paris without President Jefferson knowing. By doing things this way, the deal was, in theory, unconstitutional, but the Senate, seeing what Livingston and Monroe saw, rubberstamped the arrangement. It was unlikely Thomas Jefferson was particularly upset at how things turned out either, for doubling the size of the Country was by far the most popular act of his first term, and played a large part in his re-election in 1804.

All in all, two major lessons were learnt by the purchase of Louisiana. The first was that territorial acquisition could proceed regardless of whether the constitution sanctioned it or not, thus giving the government — especially the Presidency — the power to transform the geography of the country at will; whilst the second was that from now on America could grow by simply buying land from other powers: a new and novel idea, and one that would reoccur three times during the next sixty

---

118 According to Denslow's *10,000 Famous Freemasons*, Livingston was a member of Union Lodge, New York City and from 1784 to 1801, the first Grand Master of the Grand Lodge of New York. Born on 27th November 1746, Livingston Graduated from King's College (Now Columbia University) in 1765. He was elected to represent Dutchess County in the Provisional Assembly for New York during 1775, and was delegated from that body to the Continental Congress. He was one of the five — the others being Jefferson, Franklin, Adams and Sherman — who drew up the Declaration of Independence. He served in the Congress again in 1777 and 1779–1781. For the next two years, he was Secretary of Foreign Affairs. On 30th April 1789 he administered the Oath of office to George Washington. He was offered the position of Minister to France in 1794, and turned it down. He took the job up in 1801 however. He was a friend of fellow Mason, Napoleon Bonaparte.

four years, on each occasion with the notable, and significant, involve-ment of Freemasons. When combined with the traditional methods of acquisition, diplomacy and war, purchase was, in their hands, a precision instrument that would not only speed the country's shift to the west, but was destined to cut and trim America into exactly the shape they wanted.

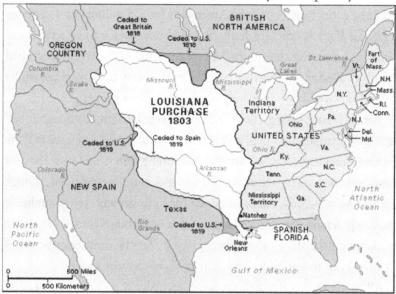

Fig. 18: America with the addition of the Louisiana Purchase, 1803.

III

Whilst in 1790 the application of Lambert's Conformal Conic to North America was the most realistic and scientific model that anyone could employ if they wished the United States to be laid out as a rect-angle, it was, in a construction sense, again highly symbolic. Tight defini-tions, worked out mathematically, were, and are, absolutely essential in ensuring the edifice to be raised conforms to what the builders, archi-tects and clients require: for, in any age, the cost of fouling up, in both financial and prestige terms was always too great to bear. Bearing this in mind, it was therefore vital that this specific pre-construction task was carried out with a great deal of accuracy.

For the medieval builder and architect William of Sens, a building's limits were measured by setting wooden pegs at the corners of a rectan-gular area and then stretching string between these points in order to correctly define and align the buildings limits. The central importance of this function is underscored by the fact that it is still used today, albeit backed up, during the last twenty years, by increasingly sophisticated electronic measuring equipment. Back in the Middle Ages however, even though the use of strings and pegs was also useful in measuring many of the buildings internal features — a row of columns, say — its usage became more limited during the cutting of individual stones.

The stonemason's eye would have to suffice here as the basic measuring instrument, backed up by tools such as the square and compasses, and the work's successful execution reliant on strength and a steady hand. No one was going to pay for shoddy work, so it was vital the medieval mason learnt how to get it right first time, and many — if not most — stonemasons working on England's cathedrals would only ever get as far as turning out square or rectangular blocks in their career. Only a minority of specialist workers, the most talented practitioners of the ancient science of masonry, would ever get the call from William of Sens to cut the fine detail vital to ecclesiastical architecture, for what this particular Frenchman, his builders, and anyone with eyes to see could not fail to recognize was that stonemasonry was, when done right, an art.

Far from the art of cutting stone, America circa 1800 did offer conditions that couldn't be bettered for those who partook in the employment, and potentially art, of surveying. George Washington himself had started his career this way, when, after only a few preparatory exercises, he was commissioned as surveyor for the frontier county of Culpepper in 1749. Naturally, with such a vast area to measure as America — even within its then boundaries — the trade of surveying was to be an attractive career option for many years to come. Washington himself had realized this when he complained that:

> The want of accurate Maps of the Country which has hitherto been the Scene of War, has been a great disadvantage to me. I have in vain endeavored to procure them and have been obliged to make shift, with such sketches as I could trace from my own Observations.[119]

---

119   John C. Fitzpatrick, ed., *Writings of George Washington from the Original Manuscript Sources, 1745–1799*, ed. (Washington, D.C.: Government Printing Office, 1931–44)

Washington's Republic would, over the next century and a half, require the services of thousands of individuals to map it, not only for the needs of commerce, transport or property reasons, but also for governmental and administrative purposes. This included, of course, the boundaries of counties, towns and cities, but also, most importantly, the political borders of the individual states, which would be laid with such accuracy, and mathematical precision, the likes of which the World had never seen before.

Five hundred years earlier, one thing William of Sens and many of his anonymous contemporaries would have spotted straight away in the Biblical descriptions of King Solomon's Temple was the lack of mortar or any other kind of bonding material between its component parts. The book of *Kings* stated that the individual stones were cut to the proper proportions at their quarry of origin, transported to the site of the Temple, and then laid with such accuracy, "that there was neither hammer nor axe, nor any tool of iron heard in the house while it was in building"[120] Taken at its most obvious level, this statement again neatly reinforced the idea of the Temple as an "ideal" structure, in that as a building of such perfection, bonding materials were completely unnecessary.

If Sens could have been introduced to the idea of American states serving as a symbolic reinvention of a Mason's work, then one aspect he would have recognized and admired straight away was that each "stone" again lay perfectly aligned with the stones lying next to it. Where the legal jurisdiction of Virginia ended to the south, North Carolina began; and where Massachusetts stopped in the west, the state of New York started and so on across the original thirteen states, and in time, the other thirty seven destined to join the union. Of course, as a modern interpretation of King Solomon's Temple this was entirely fitting: for this was a construction that, if everything went to plan, it would not — and should not — require mortar or any other bonding material to hold its stones together.

Whilst the Constitution had been understandably silent on the issue of expansion, to avoid upsetting the neighbors, so to speak, no such restriction was necessary with regard to America's internal sub-divisions. Indeed, the framers of the Constitution had even gone so far as to lay

---

120 I Kings vi, 7.

down a set of principals covering this contingency, set down in Article 4, section 3, clauses 1 & 2:

> Clause 1: New States may be admitted by the Congress into this Union; but no new State shall be formed or erected within the Jurisdiction of any other State; nor any State be formed by the Junction of two or more States, or Parts of States, without the Consent of the Legislatures of the States concerned as well as of the Congress. Clause 2: The Congress shall have Power to dispose of and make all needful Rules and Regulations respecting the Territory or other Property belonging to the United States; and nothing in this Constitution shall be so construed as to Prejudice any Claims of the United States, or of any particular State.

The above provisions for the creation of new political entities were very much in the spirit of times in that they were again minimalist in nature. The founding fathers were astute enough to recognize the future would be full of different circumstances demanding different approaches to the question of new states, even if America remained within the boundaries stipulated in the Treaty of Paris. It was therefore understandable that the Constitution was again silent regarding the future geometry, size, shape or date of accession to territorial, and then full statehood of new provinces. This was sensible in practice, in that nobody back in the 1780s knew when, where and how many settlers would head west to create a demand for new states; though it also meant if there was a collective intelligence acting in pursuit of an agreed plan, then these, in theory, enjoyed a free hand to design as they saw fit.

The idea isn't as far-fetched as it may first appear, for there were people in post-revolutionary America who already recognized the value of establishing political boundaries in specific shapes and patterns for their own purposes. As a republic bound by the rule of the people, the nation's electoral districts had to be constantly recalibrated to ensure as great a level of equality as possible. This process required activism at all levels, though during the 1780s to the early 1800s Elbridge Gerry, the Governor of Massachusetts, saw in it the chance to come up with something new, the idea of "Gerrymandering." Gerry soon became a master at drawing the boundaries of Massachusetts electoral districts to maximize his political chances, and *Gerrymandering* as a term of abuse was coined when his interference and manipulation led to one such district looking so snake-like it resembled a salamander.

Gerry's scam was however confined Massachusetts in the north east; so it was highly unlikely he had any influence on the eventual boundaries of Georgia, far away to the south. Even so, a similar way of thinking must have entered the minds of those charged with defining the limits of Oglethorpe's old stamping ground, albeit one with an architectural twist reminiscent of the style starting to dominate America's public buildings. By now, — 1818 — the United States was beginning to expand westwards politically, with new states joining the original thirteen. This meant the political boundaries of the originals had to be mapped and completed, as they no longer occupied frontier positions. Georgia was no exception, and as its western neighbor Alabama approached statehood, it became necessary to draw a boundary line between the two. When this border was drawn, Georgia, the colony created by Masons specifically to emphasize America's architectural underpinning, took on its final and highly symbolic shape: that of a Palladian Arch cornerstone.

Fig. 19: Map of Georgia, after 1819.

IV

The activities of Elbridge Gerry and the Georgia boundary markers apart, the idea of territory being "A" the ground on which the Temple would be raised, "B" the states the individual stones making up the building, and "C" when in combination together adding up to something symbolically architectural was exemplified by another case in early American history. By 1819, the legalistic niceties surrounding the creation of new provinces had been put to the test nine times, and the twenty-two state federation now stretched as far west as the Mississippi.[121]. The river no longer formed a barrier to westward expansion but rather a blessing, for it greatly aided access to Louisiana, which, apart from the long settled area south of the thirty-third parallel that became the State of the same name[122] still hadn't began the metamorphosis into states. A cursory and contemporary look at the map and the frontier marching across it would therefore have led any contemporary observer to conclude, quite rightly, the Louisiana Purchase and beyond was where virtually all new states would be born.

Even so, although over eighty years had passed since James Oglethorpe's day, there was still work to do finishing the political line up facing the Atlantic. This task was specifically about what to do with lands at the extremities of the "Arch": the Spanish owned province of Florida to the south and the uppermost portion of Massachusetts, known as Maine, to the north. The tale starts fourteen years after the Louisiana Purchase, in the December of 1817, during the administration of America's fifth President, James Monroe, who, like George Washington, was another Virginia planter and Freemason[123].

---

121 By 1819, the following states had been added to the original thirteen: Vermont (1791), Kentucky (1792), Tennessee (1796), Ohio (1803), Louisiana (1812), Indiana (1816), Mississippi, (1817), Illinois (1818), and Alabama (1819).

122 The State of Louisiana was special in it was the only part of the Louisiana Purchase that had a sizable population of European origin in 1803, hence its statehood in 1812 ahead of the more easterly Alabama and Mississippi. The French had settled around the Mississippi Delta and its environs from the late seventeenth century onwards.

123 Monroe was a member of Williamsburg Lodge No.6 at Williamsburg, Virginia, and was initiated on November 9, 1775. Although there are records of his taking any further degrees, the records of Cumberland Lodge No.8 in

As a slaveholder and someone quite rightly concerned with the integrity of the republic's borders, Monroe was exasperated with the situation on America's frontier with Spanish Florida. The boundary was fast becoming a major nuisance, with slaves fleeing south to sanctuary, and Creek and Seminole Indians heading in the opposite direction to cause chaos in southern Georgia. Something had to be done, and to this end, he called on his fellow plantation owner and Mason[124], the Tennessean Andrew Jackson, to "terminate the conflict".

For someone who'd participated in at least thirteen duels — one of which ended in a fatality — Jackson took a typically bullish view of how to cure Monroe's embarrassment, namely the annexation of all of Spanish Florida into the United States. This was a rather controversial way of thinking considering America wasn't formally at War with Spain, although it was an argument he was quite happy to share with Monroe, who would pay the price if anything went wrong:

> Let it be signified through any channel ....that the possession of the Florida's would be desirable to the United States, and in sixty days it will be accomplished.

In many respects however, Jackson was the ideal man for the job. Born in 1767 in a log cabin in the backwoods of North Carolina, he encountered the violence of warfare as a nine year old, when an English redcoat slashed his forehead with his saber. Armed with a permanent scar, fearlessness, and an intimate knowledge of the frontier, Jackson moved westwards to Tennessee, where he not only married a woman by the name of Rachel Donelson, but built up a huge plantation, the Hermitage, and then entered the public eye when he became a hero in the 1812 war, which in turn ensured his election to United States Senate.

"Spectacular" might therefore be the best way to describe the man destined to become America's seventh President, and his military adventure

---

Tennessee, June 8, 1819, show a reception for Monroe as "a Brother of the Craft."

124 Jackson's original Lodge is unknown but he is said to have attended at Clover Bottom Lodge under the Grand Lodge of Kentucky. He was present in lodge at Greenville in 1801 and acted as Senior Warden pro tem. The records of St. Tammany Lodge No.29 at Nashville, which became Harmony Lodge No.1 under the Grand Lodge of Tennessee, show that Jackson was a member. He was also Grand Master of Tennessee 1822–1823

to capture Florida for the United States. Jackson and his men battered their way through the province, burning Seminole Indian villages (earning himself a further nickname, "Sharpknife," in the process), executing two British spies, Ambrister and Arbuthnot, and capturing the town of Pensacola with little more than warning shots. Bravado on such a scale wasn't without a price though, and the executions, plus Jackson's invasion of territory belonging to Spain, a country the US was not at war with, created an international incident.

Although some in Monroe's circle called for Jackson to be censured, his *tour de force* was defended by Secretary of State John Quincy Adams, an early believer in the idea of American territorial expansion. Responding to the Spanish minister in Washington, who had demanded a "suitable punishment" for Jackson, Adams bluntly replied that "Spain must immediately [decide] either to place a force in Florida adequate at once to the protection of her territory...or cede to the United States a province, of which she retains nothing but the nominal possession, but which is, in fact...a post of annoyance to them". Forced to deal with the issue of Florida's sovereignty, Spain, recognizing the hopelessness of its position, as well as the unsettling effect of Andrew Jackson firing on all cylinders, conceded to Adams's demands and sold the territory to America via the Adams-Onis Treaty during the following year.

Whilst "Sharpknife's" naughtiness had incurred the ire of the Washington elite, it went down well with ordinary Americans, in much the same way the Louisiana Purchase had for Jefferson fourteen years earlier. Building on his legendary exploits in the 1812 war, and his well crafted "Man-of-the-people" persona, the way was now open for Old Hickory to ride all the way to the White House. Meanwhile, with Florida now under his belt, James Monroe could straighten out the nuisances on his Southern frontier with no more ado, although it was also obvious, that with suitable settlement, Florida was odds on to become another state at some point in the future.

This frantic activity at one end of the "arch" was mirrored by changes at the other, although, by contrast, the birth of Maine in the far north east was far more straightforward. Unlike Florida, Maine in 1819 was already part of an existing state, Massachusetts, although "part" may be the wrong way of describing it, for Maine was actually an *exclave*, meaning that whilst it was technically a chunk of Massachusetts, it was also territorially separate, due to the south eastern corner of New Hampshire touching on the Atlantic coast. Relative isolation was therefore, alongside Maine's rapidly growing population, a reason why, publicly, the new state quickly came into being, although the creation of a new state in the north east suited Washington too, for the reason it balanced out the impending entry into the Union of Missouri, a state permitting slavery.

Although the need for political balance over slavery was crucial to who-joined-the-union-and-when, one unrecognized side effect was that it also underpinned America's evolution as a building. Architects throughout all ages and places would've laughed at the idea of one side being raised while the other stood neglected, and it was therefore serendipitous that the political situation in America prior to 1861 meant the same concept was applicable to the creation of new states. Of course, local conditions played a major role too. In the west, plenty of land, combined with a frontier that ran at a rough right angle to the lines of latitude crossing the continent meant it was relatively easy to create pairs of states north and south. On the Atlantic coast however, acquisition of Florida meant the "symbolic arch" was, potentially, looking at another "stone" to the south, and without a corresponding "stone" to the north, Florida's potential statehood risked leaving the eastern side of the building looking decidedly cock eyed.

Hence a secondary reason why Maine became a state less than a year after the annexation of Florida: architectural balance. Whilst America's most northeasterly state was historically paired with Missouri for the sake of politics, architecturally it complemented the territory — and future state — of Florida, north and south of the Arch made up of the original thirteen. This isn't to say Maine and Florida again represent the successful culmination of another section of Masonic ritual, for nowhere in the *Explanation,* or the rest of the ceremonial for that matter, are stones to the north and south of the Royal Arch, or the parameters laid down by the north east and south east corners ever referred to. What is more likely is that their creation was a contemporary, and practical, recognition of an unavoidable on the map, namely the absorption of Spanish Florida, rendering its inclusion not only harmless, but complementing the rest of the structure, in that it, along with the state of Maine, completed the frontage of the building.

What better way therefore to celebrate their addition to the Temple, replete with symbolism representing *achievement* and *completion*, than to have the congressional decrees authorizing their respective accession to statehood signed by Presidents who were Masons? For the first one to sign was indeed James Monroe, who "through any channel" had cunningly worked with his fellow "brother" Andrew Jackson to bring the territory of Florida into the fold, thus setting the whole process off. It was Monroe's signature that graced the decree granting Maine Union status, which duly took effect on March 15th, 1820.

The second was the eleventh President, the Tennessee lawyer James K. Polk[125], who followed Monroe's example and signed the State of Florida into existence on March 3rd, 1845. Bearing in mind the regularity of "thirteen" combined with "thirty-third" in the history of America, it stands to reason the two numbers should have again put in an appearance on these dates, but individually they didn't, for neither Florida nor Maine's statehood days added up to, or had any meaningful association with the numbers thirty-three or thirteen. This didn't mean they weren't there though, for accession to the Union by the two states led to a single architectural feature — stones either side of the arch — and it was within this conjunction the two numbers can be seen.

For the thirteenth year *after* Maine became a state fell between March 15th, 1832 and March 15th 1833, the thirty-third year of the nineteenth century. Likewise, the thirteenth year *before* Florida achieved statehood fell between 3rd March, 1833 and the 3rd March, 1832. This not only brought Maine and Florida's statehoods together at equal thirteen year time spans from 1833, but each also overlapped the other by nearly a full year, with periods of singularity either side of this year lasting for thirteen days. Even more important was their effect on America as a whole, for the setting of these specific stones in place also meant the continental landmass behind the fifteen states facing the Atlantic Ocean, the Temple

---

125 James K. Polk Masonic activities started and continued within Columbia Lodge No.31, Columbia, Tennessee. He was exalted a Royal Arch Mason in La Fayette Chapter No. 4 at Columbia in 1825.

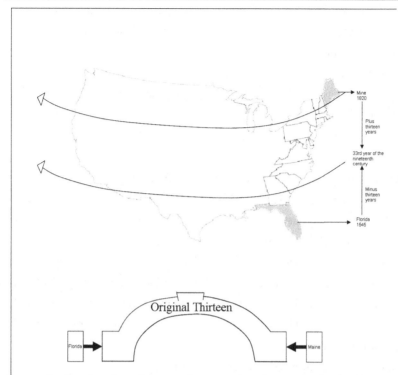

floor, which, when bought, seized, mapped and measured, was destined to be divided into a total of thirty-three states during the thirteen decades following the Constitutional Convention of 1787.

Florida – Minus Thirteen Years	Maine – Plus Thirteen Years

Florida – Minus Thirteen Years   Maine – Plus Thirteen Years

⟶   33rd Year   ⟵

3rd March 1845   of the   *15th March 1820*

Nineteenth Century

Fig. 20: *BALANCE:* The Statehoods of Maine and Florida were used to retain architectural balance on the East Coast

CHAPTER 8. "THE LENGTH THEREOF WAS THREESCORE CUBITS,
AND THE BREADTH THEREOF TWENTY CUBITS"

> The far-reaching, the boundless future will be the era
> of American greatness. In its magnificent domain of space
> and time, the nation...is destined to manifest to mankind
> the excellence of divine principles; to establish on earth
> the noblest temple ever dedicated to the worship of the
> Most High — the Sacred and the True. Its floor shall be a
> hemisphere — its roof the firmament of the star-studded
> heavens, and its congregation an Union...comprising
> hundreds of happy millions...governed by God's natural law
> of equality, the law of brotherhood...
>
> — John L. O'Sullivan, *The Great Nation of Futurity*, in *The
> American Democrat*, 1839

I

Whilst Livingston and Monroe were negotiating with alleged "Brother" Bonaparte over the future of the American mid west, all three would
have been familiar with their symbolic Temples being rectangular in
shape, and, to be fair, there were powerful historical and religious precedents for this. Starting with the allegorical foundation of the Order —
the building site — it was logical that a design be adopted that was not
only geometric, but universal throughout *global* construction never mind
that dominant in the Anglo-Saxon tradition. Even taking account of the
fact that there had been some experimentation in Lodge shape during

the first half of the eighteenth century[126], by the time Livingston and Monroe had been "made" Masons, the standard Masonic Lodge had not only assumed the rectangular shape that continues until the present day, but also its final relationship with the points of the compass:

> Our Lodges are situated due East and West...

Like its shape, the orientation of the standard Lodge, "due east and west", also drew on precedents originating deep in the English religious tradition. For centuries Church authorities in Britain — both Catholic and Anglican — had determined their Churches and Cathedrals be laid out this way, with the altar in the east, figuratively to represent the direction of the Holy Land. It was only with the rise of more dissenting denominations, such as Methodism, that the issue of orientation within ecclesiastical architecture began to be challenged — or ignored — although significantly, the vast majority of non-conformist chapels were only built after the Masonic ritual had undergone its most significant alterations.

The territory that had in ancient times been the Kingdom of Israel was, of course, home to the most famous inspirational building of all: the Temple of Solomon. According to *Kings* and *Chronicles*, this edifice was again a rectangular structure orientated east and west; though, in contrast to English Church habits, some of its most important characteristics were reversed, in so much as the entrance was in the east, and the altar in the west. It was therefore hardly surprising that as the idea of the Mason's Lodge developed from the Middle Ages through to the eighteenth century, it would again follow the east-west precedent, as well as the biblical directives regarding the entrance and altar.

Deliberate imitation of the shape and orientation of the Temple in their conventional meeting places was a clear indication that given their way, the Freemasons would also duplicate the dimensions of the build-

---

126 Nevertheless, it would be remiss not to mention the relatively experimental period during the eighteenth century, when other lodge shapes were tried for a while. Bernard Jones, in the *Freemason's Guide* mentions two specific examples of 'unusual' (i.e., square or hexagonal) lodges: that of the Old Dundee lodge, Wapping, London, founded in 1723, and the Three Golden Swords Lodge in Dresden during the 1740s, as being laid out these ways. (Jones, *The Freemason's Guide*, p.350)

ing for their ultimate symbolic structure. Of course, by the start of the nineteenth century America's Masons still had a model to work to, albeit one that was for normal diplomatic purposes technically defunct: the quasi-architectural boundaries that, until a quarter of a century earlier had defined British aspirations in North America, the forty-fifth and thirty-third parallel lines of latitude. These conveniently enclosed a rough rectangle of one thousand miles by three thousand, therefore neatly imitating the ratio of the original Temple in the Books of *Kings* and *Chronicles*:

> the house which King Solomon built for the LORD, the length thereof was threescore cubits, and the breadth thereof twenty cubits...[127]

So by the time Thomas Jefferson was walking to his inauguration as America's third President, the Masons of the world — or at least those in a position to influence the building of the symbolic Temple — had clear precedents of how its floor should look: as rectangular as possible, on a strict east-west axis and laid out as close as could be achieved to the ratio of one to three. The "one", the "breadth thereof twenty cubits" — a thirteen state symbolic Arch along the eastern seaboard — was already in place; meaning the challenge was to somehow accrue sufficient territory to the west to duplicate the "threescore cubits" defining the buildings length.

---

127   Obviously the idea of measuring the building's proportions in cubits, traditionally defined as 'a forearm's length' was hopelessly inadequate for a structure whose entrance alone spanned a thousand miles. It was therefore hardy surprising that any mention of a cubit or cubits was purged from the Masonic ceremonial — even if it had ever been included — during the changes of the eighteenth century. There was a certain inevitability here, for the men rewriting the ritual had already illustrated a willingness to bend the rules when expediency demanded it, the classic example being new ritual written around the idea of the Royal Arch, which, whilst adhering to the idea of an entrance at the east, departed from the Biblical script in that an entire Masonic degree was built around this non-existent feature. What the ritual writers were therefore stating was that the long term strategy was one of only using sections of the Temple story that could be made to fit conditions on the ground in North America. This was rational enough considering the task in hand, although it did dictate that some definitions described in *Kings* and *Chronicles* would be dropped, and this included the use of a cubit as a measurement.

To put it bluntly, this directive demanded, at a minimum, the accumulation of all lands within the two parallel lines as far as the Pacific Ocean: meaning the "west" side of the building would eventually be characterized by modern day California and Oregon. At the time, neither the name nor location of either would have meant much — if anything — to the average American, situated as these future states were at the extremities of the unexplored west. Conversely however, for those who knew America to be an architectural work in progress, and its States the stones making up the building, both California and Oregon naturally assumed a huge symbolic importance, in that they alone would eventually emerge as the cornerstones dominating the western aspect of the building.

So the *aim* was clear enough, but what of the *methodology* to achieve it? Well, as Jefferson's first term as President drew to a close in late 1804, the appearance of *completion* and *achievement* with regard to the absorbing of lands between the "two grand parallel lines" had already occurred twice in American history. The first was, of course, when Oglethorpe created the province of Georgia on the thirty-third parallel back in 1733, thus completing Great Britain's colonial adventure between that parallel line and the forty-fifth; whilst the second took place during Jefferson's Presidency, when the purchase of the Louisiana Territory again added a huge swath of land between the same two parallel lines.

Both of these events shared much in common, not least the symbolic appearance of the term "thirty-third" at the southern point of either expansion: In 1733 illustrated by the colonies being pushed south to the thirty-third parallel; whilst after 1803 the Louisiana Purchase was split along the same into the territory of Louisiana to the south, and the district of Louisiana to the north. The question was, was this a pattern? And if so, would the same feature appear again and again as America clawed its way to the Pacific?

Regardless of how architecturally accurate the enterprise was intended to be, the notion that America could storm across the Continent grabbing land hither and thither was highly dangerous too, and in all likelihood would have sent chills down the spine of Thomas Jefferson had he been aware of it. Nobody needed reminding that seventy years earlier in 1733, all that influential English Masons had to contend with when crafting the "Arch" were the Creek Indians, led by their obliging Chief, Tomochichi.; but that now, in 1804, the situation was reversed, insomuch as a small nation was set on a course putting it in direct conflict with the big beasts of the Old World, for the empires of Britain, France and Spain, and latterly Mexico all had prior — and legitimate — claims to the territory between the forty fifth and thirty-third parallel lines of latitude. If this section of the Temple's construction was to be brought to a successful conclusion, a far greater level of guile and surefootedness would be called for, because it was ridiculous to assume the major powers of Europe would simply settle for a worthless treaty in the same way as the Creeks.

On the plus side, one certainty in 1804 was that the workmen to carry out such an expansive project were already in place, and would continue to be so. This was due, in part, not only to the Masonic Order's collecting of men of influence and potential throughout America, but also sympathetic and influential individuals in other countries[128]. Ensconced in positions of power and influence in both Europe and the United States, many of these men would not only live long enough to see the American republic assume its rectangular shape, but would also be aware it was done in accordance with the Conformal Conic, the map making projection first devised by Lambert back in 1772.

II

For someone with as volcanic a temper as Andrew Jackson, hearing that his inauguration in March, 1829 was being laughed at as a "Saturnalia...of Mud and filth[129]" might, at one time, have had the lanky ex-frontiersman reaching for his pistol. The day had started off well enough, with an overcast sky giving way to sunshine; but then turned to farce when a rag-tag army of supporters, numbering twenty thousand plus, descended on genteel Washington, determined to cheer their beloved "Old Hickory". Being loud wasn't however the totality of the crowd's participation in the democratic process. Unaccustomed to Washington DC's habits, thousands proceeded to guzzle and gorge their way through the

---

128 Washington, Lafayette etc.
129 Quoted in *Liberty, Equality, Power: A History of the American People*, p.429

free refreshments provided, a bonanza that got the better of some hardy souls, who went on to invade, and then wreck, the White House itself.

The Mob's wheeze wasn't universally admired, however. "Ladies and gentlemen, only had been expected at this Levee, not the people en masse," spluttered one exasperated matron, a certain Mrs. Margaret Smith, in a letter written a few days later; an opinion doubtlessly shared by many across Washington society. Mrs. Smith and her compatriots must certainly have drawn comparisons with the rather more sedate inaugurations of Messrs Jefferson, Madison and Monroe, and shuddered inwardly as to what future indignities Andrew Jackson, the perceived roughneck from the wild country west of the Appalachians, was to inflict next on them and their wonderful city.

"King Mob" as one Washington insider tartly named him, was in all probability, sniggering slyly at the fuss, for the condescension of Mrs. Smith and other "city slickers" merely drove home the point that his election signaled a hugely important change in American politics: namely, that from now on, the people — or representatives in their image — would begin to proliferate across the political offices of the Republic. No longer would the nation be led by Virginian 'aristocrats' like Washington, Jefferson or Monroe; but rather men who had started life in far more humble circumstances. This was the start of the 'log cabin to white house' chief executive, a change indeed noted by Mrs. Smith, who ended her letter with the observation that "...it was the People's day, and the People's President and the People would rule"[130].

"The People's President" almost certainly recognized the shift that had taken place — or what it could lead to — for at least one contemporary newspaper, the Baltimore *Niles' Weekly Register*[131], noted "It is a favorite saying of the new president that 'the tree is known by its fruit'" and it would be three of these fruit of the hickory — all Freemasons and allies of Andrew Jackson — who would not only complete the symbolic stonework Jackson and Monroe had started on the east coast, but would go

---

130   Margaret Bayard Smith's account appears in: Smith, Margaret Bayard, The First Forty Years of Washington Society (1906); Leish, Kenneth, (ed.) The American Heritage Pictorial History of the Presidents of the United States; Seale, William, The President's House vol. 1 (1986).

131   Edition of 7th May, 1829

on to dominate the next stage of America's evolution into a fully worked out architectural phenomenon.

"Imitation is the sincerest form of flattery," goes the old saying, and never was it more true than in the relationship between Old Hickory and the eleventh President of the United States, James Knox Polk. Although a good twenty eight years younger, the course of Polk's life shadowed the older man's to an uncanny degree, and even predating his birth, for Polk's roots again lay in people of Scots-Irish stock who had first settled in the western borderlands of North Carolina, and then migrated to Tennessee. Samuel Polk, James's father, had moved west in 1803, to take advantage of the better soil and commercial advantages Tennessee had to offer, and over the next twenty years, the family emulated "Old Hickory's" rise into the plantation class, the revenues from which enabled James to ape Jackson yet again, by following a legal career and latterly public office, where, by early 1836, he was proving useful to "the People's President" as Speaker of the United States House of Representatives.

Being related solely on the grounds of background, experience and location didn't of course mean Jackson and Polk strode the Earth bearing a similar character. "Young Hickory" as he came to be known, was never to share Jackson's well-earned reputation as a man's man: whether it be for horse racing, dueling or battering assailants with a walking stick, though this was something that could be explained by Polk's chronic sickliness, which the eleventh president fought with a Presbyterian determination and dourness of character that eventually earned him the far more disparaging nickname of "Polk the Plodder".

Nevertheless, all was not lost for the plodder; for traits Polk did indeed share with the country-boy-made-good Jackson included a keen intelligence and look-you-straight-in-the-eye attitude. These attributes would be found to be absolutely essential during the four years this particular President and Mason sat and eyed the west from the Oval office, for what none of his detractors realized about James K. Polk, was he was not only destined to garner more territory for the USA than any President except Jefferson, but, more importantly, to do it in a manner, and in accordance, with an architectural *rationale* that last made its presence felt on the map of America when he was still an eight year old schoolboy in the backwoods of North Carolina.

By the time Young Hickory became president in March, 1845, the process of westward expansion even had a particular name: Manifest Destiny. The term first appeared in an article in *The Democratic Review* written by John L. O'Sullivan, the journalist who had already wrote several articles calling for expansion to the West. Whilst in some ways a rehash of the centuries old Coast-to-Coast theme, Sullivan's "Manifest Destiny" had two important differences, namely that the idea was now invested with a semi-religious feel, which fell in with the idea held by many Americans that they were a chosen people; and, more importantly, was coined by the journalist at precisely the right moment in history when it was possible to achieve. With the hand of history on his shoulder, Polk wasn't about to disappoint either the American people or John L. Sullivan, though in some respects what happened next was thrust upon "Young Hickory" rather than at his command.

At the heart of the South West, the Republic of Texas had been an independent nation since 1836, but as 1844 was drawing to a close requested annexation to the United States. By February of the next year, President John Tyler urged Congress to pass a Joint resolution admitting Texas to the Union; to which the Congress complied readily. The incoming President, Polk, along with many other Southerners, was broadly in favor of admission, as Texas was, and would continue to be, a state permitting slavery.

Admitting Texas as the twenty-eighth state did, however, have massive implications for both Polk's domestic and foreign policies. Mexico, still reeling from the loss of the "Lone Star" nine years earlier, and realizing its absorption into the United States meant Texas was gone forever, was furious over the arrangement, a resentment in turn stoked by Polk when he sent an envoy to Mexico City with a request to purchase California, an area Mexico had largely ignored, without a corresponding offer of compensation for Texas. If having the Mexicans on his back wasn't bad enough, trouble was brewing for Polk in the Congress too. Texas statehood inevitably tipped the "balance" of the states heavily in favor of the South; something that had to be addressed urgently, if the specter of succession, or even war, was to be avoided.

One solution, for Polk's domestic audience at least, was to finally settle the question of the Oregon Territory in the far northwest. For the previous twenty-seven years, this region, stretching up the West coast from California into what is now British Columbia, had been under the joint occupation and control of Great Britain and the United States. Intervening American administrations had offered to divide Oregon along the 49th Parallel, but this was unacceptable to the British, who claimed commercial interests south of this line. Polk was in a quandary; he needed a deal, and fast, and not only to recalibrate the 'balance' affecting the entire country, but also to placate his supporters, to whom he'd promised the whole of the Oregon territory less than two years earlier.

Boxed in on all sides, Young Hickory again offered the British a compromise — the 49th parallel — to which they again gave the thumbs down. Polk, exasperated, threatened war in the face of this intransigence, a remarkable act of bravado bearing in mind Mexican anger to the south, but one which worked, for England eventually caved in, and with the negotiations conducted by the son of a previous Masonic Grand Master, Lord Aberdeen, agreed to the 49th parallel as the border with Canada, via the Oregon Treaty of 1846.

The loss of Texas, the California offer, and now possible further encroachment from the direction of Oregon, pushed Mexico into rebuffing Polk's envoy Slidell, who returned empty handed to Washington in May 1846, though the President, armed with a secure northern flank, used his envoy's rejection as a reason to go to war. The conflict turned out to be a disaster for Mexico, and by the summer of 1846, New Mexico, Northern California as well as other parts of the country had already fallen under American control. Even Santa Anna, who had conned the Americans into believing he would persuade the Mexican government to sell California and New Mexico to the United States, couldn't stop the rot. Declaring himself President, his attempts to stop the Americans came to naught, and by September, 1847 General Winfield Scott[132] had captured Mexico

---

132 Scott was a member of Dinwiddie Union Lodge, No.23. Taylor and Santa Anna's membership is unconfirmed.

City, complementing a series of victories in northern Mexico by General Zachary Taylor. The writing was on the wall for America's southern neighbor, but the war, on paper at least, dragged on until the next year — 1848 — when an exhausted Mexico finally threw in the towel, and acceded to American demands set out in the treaty of Guadalupe Hidalgo.

Fig. 21 Territory gained by the USA during the Polk Presidency

Through sheer chutzpah, James Knox Polk had increased American territory by roughly a third, and in what was less than a full lifespan for some people, the Republic had traded in its fragile hold on the Atlantic seaboard for a solid grip across the continent, a rectangular shape it would exhibit for all time. Many people had played a part in this process, but none more so than the members of one particular fraternal society that had first arrived on American soil twelve decades earlier. These men — Livingston, Monroe, Jackson, Polk, and scores of others — had, at considerable professional and public risk, transformed the map, in the Florida swamps, the battlefields of the south-west and the staterooms of Paris and Washington. All that needed to be asked of this as this specific construction as it approached its thirteenth decade was how architecturally accurate the whole affair of territorial expansion had been; how close was it to the 'parallel lines' model long ago laid down by the British?

III

The outcome of the Mexican war had left a bad taste in many American mouths, and worst of all, deepened the growing tensions between North and South over slavery. Both sides knew that in the opening up of the west, an opportunity lay existed to expand their respective systems to the Pacific, and both realized their ambitions could only be achieved at the expense of the other. Speed was of the essence, and like there Romans two thousand years earlier, what were soon to be called the Union and Confederacy understood eventual dominance and subservience within America was dependent on effective communications, especially railroads.

One man who already recognized the powerful weapon railroads could was a sixty-one year old southerner by the name of James Gadsden[133], although such concerns wouldn't have meant anything in the World he was born into. A grandson of the Revolutionary war hero who created the "Don't tread on me" flag, James grew up amongst what passed for aristocracy in the South at the beginning of the nineteenth century, the classic plantation owner class of old. It was this environment that molded Gadsden's outlook for the rest of his life, and sure enough, after graduating from Yale in 1806, he did indeed try his hand as a planter of rice and cotton. Gadsden's attempts at agriculture must have been mixed at best though, for he soon changed tack and joined the Army, where he earned a commission, and first encountered Andrew Jackson when serving as the latter's *aide de camp* during the 1812 war with Britain.

Gadsden was also privy to all of Jackson's adventures in Florida, impressing the older man enough for a real friendship to develop, though it is also possible Old Hickory saw in the Charleston man something of the swashbuckler so evident in his own character. Certainly, Jackson had great faith in Gadsden's abilities, for he turned to the Carolinian several times during the eighteen twenties and thirties, with tricky missions to perform in pursuit of American interests. The first of these occurred in the May of 1821, when Jackson needed $3,000 worth of Government

---

133 James Gadsden was a member of Jackson Lodge Number 23, of Tallahassee, Florida which was then under the Grand Lodge of Alabama. It is now No. 1 of Florida jurisdiction.

Bills selling in New Orleans; a mission which, although a failure, enabled Gadsden do some spying on the side, reporting back to the General on Spanish Troop movements, and efforts to facilitate the transfer of Florida to the United States.

Far more controversially, Jackson felt comfortable enough to keep Gadsden informed by letter of one of his most unpleasant policies, namely the removal of thousands of Native Americans off their lands in the South East towards more inhospitable regions west of the Mississippi:

> You may rest assured that I shall adhere to the just and humane policy towards the Indians which I have commenced. In this spirit I have, recommended them to quit their possessions on this side the Mississippi, and go to a country in the west where there is every probability that they will always be free from the mercenary influence of White men, and undisturbed by the local authority of the states: Under such circumstances the General Government can exercise a parental control over their interests and possibly perpetuate their race[134].

James Gadsden almost certainly viewed this policy with indifference at best, or enthusiasm at worst, for he himself already had form in this early kind of ethnic cleansing, having removed the Seminole Indian tribe to the southern part of Florida under a commission from James Monroe. The unpleasant truth was that this particular Mason, alongside "brothers" Monroe, Jackson and Polk, was burdened with the characteristic blind spot of many "gentlemen" of the antebellum south, namely, that whilst they felt duty bound to behave in a courageous and courteous manner towards their own kind, to others they thought nothing of acting in direct opposition to the idea of "brotherly love" when it came to others of a different race, something Gadsden carried with him to the grave, as witnessed in this advert from the *Charleston Mercury* dated 6 Dec 1859:

A Very Prime Gang of 235 Negros belonging to the
Estate of the Late General James Gadsden.
BY SHINGLER BROTHERS,
7 BROAD-STREET
At Private Sale, a remarkably prime gang of two hundred and thirty-five (235) NEGROS, belonging to the Estate of the late General James Gadsden. They are accustomed to the culture of Rice and Provisions.

---

134 From: John Spencer Bassett, Ph.D. *The Correspondence of Andrew Jackson*, Vol IV, 1929.

Terms—one-half(1/2)cash;balanceinoneyear,withapprovedsecurity. New Orleans Picayune and Delta, Eagle and Enquirer of Memphis; Register, Mobile; News of Galveston — each will insert three times, and send bills to Shingler Brothers.

Even though the humanity of this particular character may have left a lot to be desired, what cannot be dismissed lightly was his contribution to American political geography, specifically its symbolic whole. For by the late 1840s, Gadsden, now President of the South Carolina Canal and Rail Road Company, was pondering the two main railroad challenges facing the South: the integration of all lines across the region into a single network, which could operate independently of the North, and the ultimate ambition: the construction of a Southern railroad — and by extension, slavery — all the way to California. Tooled up with the right engineering credentials, and relying on map projections like Lambert's Conformal Conic, Gadsden was indeed destined to drive two parallel lines across America, but they weren't to be the kind the South needed so desperately.

The most obvious route at Gadsden's ambition should follow was a line from El Paso through to San Diego, across territory recently won from Mexico. The catch with this plan was the line would not only have to curve around Mexico, but also be laid through unsuitable mountainous country too. The only other alternative, a line through Mexico, was also out of the question because of the diplomatic complications this would entail. Boxed in by these difficulties, the railroad man hit on a far more radical idea: the purchase of a strip of land from Mexico, on which a straight railroad could be built, and which, as a double bonus, tidy up some of the territorial vagueness left over after the Guadalupe Hidalgo Treaty, and placate the American public, some of whom felt Mexico had got a rough deal over the recent War.

The territory that Gadsden and his men concentrated on was south of the Gila River, in what is today Southern Arizona and South western New Mexico. At the time, it was considered fairly worthless semi-desert, and prone to Indian raids, though in the light of this, Mexico's President Santa Anna, favored the sale, as it would raise much needed capital for his tottering regime. President Franklin Pierce concurred with this opinion, for he realized the deal placated Mexico and The South too, and dispatched Gadsden to Mexico City to negotiate the purchase. In doing so, the President had repeated Jefferson's move of nearly fifty years earlier, when the third President sent Monroe to Paris to buy Louisiana, so for the second time in American history, a Mason was now negotiating with a foreign head of state reputed to be a "brother" an extension of American territory.

There was, therefore, a certain inevitability surrounding the appearance of 'thirty-third' and thirty-three' around the Gadsden Purchase. An area the size of Scotland, the proposed site of Gadsden's railroad had been bought for the United States for thirty-three cents an acre, and what was more, had brought the whole of the thirty-third parallel under American jurisdiction for the first time. The territory of the contiguous United States was, once agreed by Congress — the thirty-third — thus completed, in the thirteenth decade since the Freemasons had first arrived on American soil.

Fig. 22 The Gadsden Purchase

What was also remarkable was how Gadsden's addition again strengthened the Union architecturally, for Polk's establishment of America's shape, whilst rectangular, wasn't entirely accurate. Back in

1850, those with eyes to see realized a further, smaller addition was needed too, to re-emphasize something on the map of North America that, in law, had ceased to mean anything eighty years earlier. To summarize, as a railroad engineer, Gadsden was familiar with Lambert's work, especially the Conformal Conic, and would have used it had his dream of a Southern railroad ever taken shape. Failure to drive a conventional set of parallel lines across America was however, compensated by the successful alignment of the United States with lines of far greater importance, for Gadsden had successfully pulled off a great coup, the re-establishment of something "exact" that had last defined America back in British times, specifically from 1733 onwards, the prominence of the thirty-third and forty-fifth parallels, which, when combined with the conformal conic, approximated exactly with the territory of the United States, as noted in Wilford's book *The Mapmakers*:

> It was more than a century before cartographers fully appreciated the value of the Lambert projection. But now it is considered a preferred map for showing broad areas in the middle latitudes — the United States being a perfect example. Applying the Lambert projection to the United States, which extends from 49 to 25 degrees north, the tip of Florida, the standard parallels usually chosen are 45 degrees and 33 degrees. On these two parallels, scale is exact. Between them, scale is no more than 11 twentieths of 1 percent too small. On the Canadian border the scale is only 1 and one twenty fifth percent too large. At Key West the scale is at its most distorted — 2 and a half percent too large.[135]

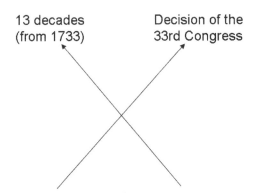

13 decades
(from 1733)

Decision of the
33rd Congress

Fig.23: The Mathematical formula underpinning the "Floor"

---

135 *The Mapmakers*, p.97

IV

One remarkable feature of territorial America in 1853 was how neatly its international borders fulfilled — by proxy — the theoretical empire the Duke of Newcastle and his colleagues at the Southern Department had unilaterally, and illegally, laid claim to 120 years earlier in 1733. Through planning based on Biblical precedent, the eighteenth-century British aspiration had succeeded in becoming a nineteenth-century American fact, in that the lands between and around the forty-fifth and thirty-third parallel lines of latitude, with the exception of Southern Ontario, were, thanks to an adherence to Lambert's projection, now part of a single jurisdiction.

American territory did, however, resemble its theoretical predecessor in yet another way that would have been recognizable to the bewigged functionaries of Newcastle's Office. Wave after wave of European immigration had increased America's population ten-fold on the figure estimated for the late colonial era, and by 1850, according to that year's Census, the number of American residents stood at twenty three millions, only two million more than contemporary Great Britain[136], an island one thirty-third the size. Americans were, however, still overwhelmingly concentrated east of the Mississippi, especially those regions that once swore allegiance to English kings, meaning that even though the settled area was far greater thirteen decades on, America, especially its western portion, was still in the main a territorial phenomenon, just as it was in Thomas Pelham-Holles day.

The map of the states was changing at breakneck speed, however, as the tide of settlement continued its inexorable westward march. As early as 1849, the Union already had a membership of thirty, in a checkerboard stretching from the Atlantic to the Great Plains. The origins of many settlers — Europe and the east — and stupendous fertility of the region east of the Mississippi were instrumental here, and during the sixty years following the Union of the original thirteen in 1790, all bar one new State had an already existing State bordering it to the East[137].

---

136   From the United Kingdom Census of 1851, excluding Ireland.

137   The sole exception was Louisiana, which for the five years following its admission to the Union in 1812, had been surrounded by Territories until the statehood of Mississippi in 1817.

During the 1840s however, a different pattern began to emerge. Although the settlement of the Great Plains was destined to fit in with tradition and expediency, thousands of migrants tramped and rode across the "west" to head straight for the Pacific coast, and specifically Oregon. The reasons why so many people risked the "Oregon Trail", rather than settle the plains were, of course, numerous, although a central one was a collective belief in the imagined fertility of the Pacific Coast compared to the Midwest. Newspapers and books published in the East and Europe, plus puffed up descriptions promoted by land speculators, portrayed the new American territories bordering the Pacific as one long Garden of Eden, whilst large stretches of country between the Mississippi and the Rockies were dismissed as worthless.

This misconception even permeated the government, for Jefferson himself had described the plains as "immense and trackless deserts", a comment reinforced by Zebulon Pike's boast they would one day be "equally celebrated as the sandy deserts of Africa", and later, government surveyor Stephen Long's term "the Great American Desert". To be fair to Long, he was probably using "desert" in the older sense of the word — a place devoid of woodlands and water — rather than in its modern sandy interpretation. Nevertheless, the name was to stick, especially as Edwin James, Long's geographer on his 1823 expedition around the west, wrote:

> I do not hesitate in giving the opinion, that it is almost wholly unfit for cultivation, and of course, uninhabitable by a people depending upon agriculture for their subsistence. Although tracts of fertile land considerably extensive are occasionally to be met with, yet the scarcity of wood and water, almost universally prevalent, will prove an insuperable obstacle in the way of settling the country.[138]

But as time wore on, some recognized how grossly misunderstood the true nature of the High Plains were, such as the writer Henry David Thoreau, who, in 1848, noted: "we have advanced by leaps to the Pacific, and left many a lesser Oregon and California unexplored behind us[139]," an opinion gradually accepted by more and more people as the nineteenth century passed its halfway mark. Armed with the science of effective irrigation, railroad transportation, and barbed wire, the west would indeed

---

138 Cited in D.W.Meinig's *The Shaping of America: A Geographical Perspective on 500 Years of History, Volume 2: Continental America, 1800–1867*
139 *Ktaadu*, (1848) published in *The Maine Woods* (1864)

be tamed, but the die had already been cast, and the prairies would wait until after the settlement of the Pacific coast.

More importantly for the underlying national architecture, it also meant the points on the map where the forty fifth and thirty-third parallels met the Western Ocean were likely to achieve statehood before much of the ground east of the Rockies. After nearly a thirteen decade wait, and with the rectangle in place and properly aligned, the stage was now set for the positioning of the western cornerstones of the Temple in line with those in the East.

One man who knew well the importance of correctly aligned cornerstones was James Polk's Secretary of State, James Buchanan.[140] Although not recognized for having a particularly forthright manner in the style of, say, Andrew Jackson, Buchanan had however started life in a similar way to the seventh president, in that he was again born in a log cabin, the second of ten children of James Buchanan senior and his wife Elizabeth. This was the Pennsylvania border country in the year 1790: hardly the most fruitful environment for a potential scholar part of a large poor family, but Buchanan fought against the odds to educate himself and eventually graduate from the Keystone State's Dickinson College in law by his early twenties.

By this time, the 1812 war was raging between England and America, and Buchanan although skeptical about the conflict initially, was incensed enough by Britain's invasion of neighboring Maryland to fight in the defense of Baltimore as part of a volunteer light dragoon unit. Once the war was over, Buchanan, like Polk, opted for a political career, firstly in Pennsylvania, and the Washington, from where Andrew Jackson appointed him Ambassador to the Russian Tsar. Armed with this valuable diplomatic experience, upon his return Buchanan was elected to Senate, and from 1845 onwards, the office of Secretary of State, where he:

> "...had the initiation of those measures which he had hitherto defended as Chairman of the Committee on Foreign Relations of the Senate. England and America both claimed the whole Northwestern Territory. The protocol between Mr. Buchanan and Mr. Packenham induced England to ac-

---

140 Buchanan became a Mason on December 11, 1816, in Lancaster Lodge No.43 of Lancaster, Pennsylvania. He was later the Deputy Grand Master of the Grand Lodge of Pennsylvania.

cept the compromise line of lat. 49 N... Buchanan also directed the negotiations that led to the termination of the war with Mexico[141].

Few in America therefore knew the political subtleties of the Western side of this particular construction as well as Brother Buchanan. He
was familiar with its boundaries, rivers, mountain ranges and legal status; its flora, fauna, climate and soils; and its human history. Armed with
such knowledge, he would've realized Oregon and California were likely
to be the sole provinces to emerge within the thirty-third and forty-fifth
parallels in the west; but what he didn't know was which of these states
would be founded before the other.

This wasn't the first time a Mason had hesitated over the "west" side
of something, for a century earlier Buchanan's Masonic predecessors in
London had also agonized over how the western side of their "Palace"
would eventually look, and so intractable was the problem, the finished
ceremonial illustrated their indecision and lack of knowledge for all time.
This was because whilst the construction elements of the "new" rituals
of the First and Second Degrees detailed how the eastern cornerstones
should be laid, and the Arch ceremonial defined the entrance at the East,
a shroud of silence obscured the west, in that nowhere in the Masonic
ritual was this aspect of the building ever mentioned.

So why could this be? It was inconceivable ceremonial written around
the construction of a rectangular structure, which put such great store
by correctly defining North, South and East, would leave out "West"
accidentally. Even if the nature of the building was left open to question, or extended to include the concept of an allegorical structure, the
answer still wasn't straightforward, for the "western" discrepancy was
even more illogical applied to a symbolic edifice as to a physical, on the
grounds that the rise of the Freemasons "Palace" would happen in a manner and time convenient to the writers alone.

Even bearing in mind these qualifications, all is not lost with regard
to the west, for some extrapolations on its role in Masonic lore can still
be made, worked out from other sections of ritual, as well as the oldest
source used in Masonic symbolism: the Bible. Firstly, the west would
naturally be bound north and south by the same "Grand Parallel Lines"

---

141 Obituary, *New York Times*, 2 June, 1868.

marking out the northern and southern limits of the east, for it states the whole building is bound by them, east to west; Secondly, the two eastern cornerstones would be joined by two in the west to complete the rectangular nature of the Temple, meaning the western side of the structure had to be made up of a minimum of two stones or more; and thirdly, the sequence in which the two eastern stones were laid — north east followed by the south east — suggested the western stones be set in a clockwise manner: the third cornerstone in the south-west, the fourth in the north-west.

To be fair to the ritual writers, nobody expected them to prophesize the future, just to take it into account. It was therefore understandable that the west side was left out, for the situation on the ground — the West Coast in the 1730s — was not only a good two thousand miles west of British and by extension Masonic influence, but also in the formal possession of France and Spain, Catholic empires unlikely to encourage an Anglo-Saxon secret society onto their territory, especially after Pope Clement XII's 1738 pronouncement *In Eminenti* threatened Catholics involved in Freemasonry with excommunication.

Because of this, a complete negation of the eastern experience took place in the West, in that the ritual was long completed by the time the region came within the orbit of the United States. Even so, by the year 1848, with all lands within the "Two Grand Parallel Lines" either under American control, or, in the case of California, about to be, it was possible to lay the western cornerstones parallel to the eastern. Only two questions remained: which was to be the third cornerstone and which the fourth? And did the indicators of *completion* and *achievement* — "thirteen" and "thirty-third" — make their usual appearance in the numerical symbolism of the west?

In January 1848, both questions remained unanswerable, though the signs pointed to Oregon being the third cornerstone, for not only had it had been a formal US territory since 1839, but the attractions of the "Oregon Country", natural and invented, meant America's window on the Pacific could boast a far higher number of white residents than its neighbor to the south, which, for good measure, was still a part of Mexico. This was the picture Secretary of State Buchanan had to work with —

even though he knew California was soon to fall into American hands — the possibility of the northwest corner being laid before he southwest; all very neat and tidy, but at the same time at odds with Henry Price's clockwise approach of nearly thirteen decades earlier.

Like any politician though, Buchanan was, however, at the mercy of events, and on 24th January, 1848, a workman cutting a ditch at Sutter's Mill in California noticed something glittering in the gravel, thus setting the scene for the California gold rush. This discovery transformed the population picture of the west coast, and in the next two years, California completely outstripped its northern neighbor in numbers of residents, to become a state first, in September 1850.

No-one could have foreseen this, or how yet again it reinforced America's architectural credentials. This was because, with Oregon relegated to second place as a west coast state numerically, from the moment it joined the Union in 1859, four fully fledged states, laid out clockwise, now covered the north east, south east, south west and north west points of North America where the thirty-third and forty-fifth parallel lines crossed the east and west coasts. This particular statehood therefore completed the "corners" of North America long before claimed by Great Britain and, additionally, the Masonic numerical symbolism constant on the American map for the previous thirteen decades.

All that was needed therefore was for *Completion and Achievement*, to come together again in the 'mark', and indeed they did. 'Thirteen' was obvious enough in that California followed Oregon to statehood and cemented in place the thirteen degrees between the two 'parallel lines' in a northerly sequence. This was something that was to be repeated with *achievement* too, for when Oregon, the fourth cornerstone on the huge rectangular floor, was signed into existence in late 1858 by President and Brother James Buchanan, it became the thirty-third state of the Union.

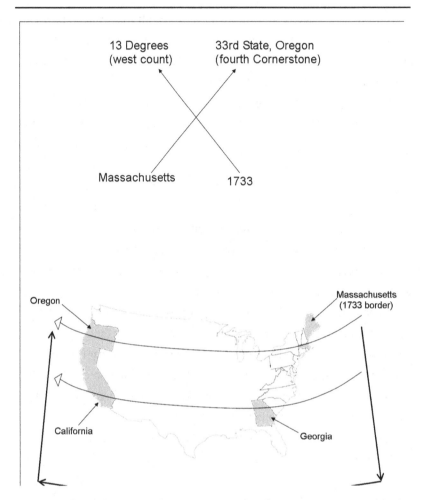

13 Degrees
(west count)

33rd State, Oregon
(fourth Cornerstone)

Massachusetts

1733

Oregon

Massachusetts
(1733 border)

California

Georgia

Figures 24 and 25: The accession of Oregon, the 33rd State, in 1859 meant that the four cornerstones were now in place, bound by the *Two Grand Parallel Lines*, the 33rd and 45th parallels.

CHAPTER 9. "THEY LIE OPEN AND IMMOVABLE IN THE LODGE"

Question: "What form is your Lodge?" *Answer:* "An Oblong Square." — Masonic exposure, 1762

I

By 1860, the political cartography of the United States clearly illus-trated how dimensions of a Masonic Temple could be engraved onto the map of America via surveying technology, willpower, and a westward moving frontier. There were, of course, many reasons to explain the success of this venture, though one was, undoubtedly, the design was of such immense size, minor fluctuations in the physical background — such as a range of hills or water features — had been excluded from the ritual a century earlier on the grounds they wouldn't affect the overall picture. This tactic — let's call it *un*description — had already proved its worth in the case of the "east" and "west" sides of the building — the two coastlines — and could therefore be called upon to account for terrain irregularities like the Edwards Plateau, Mississippi river or Ozark hills.

Nevertheless, for those Freemasons penning the ceremonial to dis-miss the physical background entirely would have been naïve. The USA was hardly the floor of the *Goose and Gridiron*, where symbolic lines were drawn with scant regard to topography; and it was in keeping with the rest of their approach that the ritual writers were canny enough to know no builder worth his salt would begin to raise a structure without first reconnoitering, and then assimilating the limitations of the ground to be built on. This 'operative' outlook was now revisited when drawing up their plans for their greatest symbolic structure, because there were natural features — the Great Lakes and the Appalachian and Rocky mountain ranges in particular — that covered such huge areas and affected the landscape so fundamentally, it would damage the descriptiveness of the ritual pretending they didn't exist. Somehow, and in a style complimenting the remainder of the ceremonial, the topographical background of America, or at least some of it, had to be included.

Serendipity again played a part in the Fraternity's fortunes, for in the same way that the Order appeared when Architectural science was scaling new heights, by the 1730s enough geographical knowledge existed for men like Desaguliers and Senex to pen an accurate picture of American topography, albeit filtered through the allegorical story of the construction site. This awareness came primarily from recent discoveries in North America, for even though a mere forty years had passed since John Sellar's *The English Pilot, Fourth Book*, with its fuzzy attitude to the interior, by the time Price and Oglethorpe crossed the Atlantic all bar one of the major physical features of the continent, if not their detail, were known in Europe. Of course, the Appalachian mountain range, running spine like against the eastern seaboard, was already familiar because it abutted territory long settled by the British. The Appalachians were, in turn, joined by the Great Lakes, where French penetration west of Quebec was so comprehensive by the third decade of the eighteenth century that Erie, Superior *et al.* were already being portrayed on European maps like John Senex's 1722 *North America according to the latest observations* with a great deal of accuracy.

For Senex, along with the rest of Europe, the great unknown was the western mountain range: the Rockies. Rising up two thousand miles west of British and French settlement, the Rocky Mountains' existence wasn't officially confirmed in 1730, and what was known was unsubstantiated and anecdotal. Nevertheless, the desire to explore the west was already intense enough to encourage at least four French adventurers to reach the eastern approaches of the range in the years that followed. These four, two pairs of brothers — the fur traders Paul and Pierre Mallet and Louis-Joseph and Francois la Verendrye — were exploring independently of each other, but both sent back similar reports back east, and by extension Paris and London, that they had seen the snowy peaks of the Rockies in the distance whilst wandering through the region in 1741 and 1743 respectively[142].

By doing this, the Frenchmen had filled in the last piece of the puzzle with regard to the major physical features of America, information that was invaluable to the land hungry powers of the Old World. This didn't mean, of course, that Europe was suddenly set ablaze by the news, for at the time the overwhelming majority of British and French citizens were unlikely to have ever heard of the Rockies, or for that matter were even capable of recognizing North America on a globe. This was information only of interest to the few, and greater understanding and knowledge was the preserve of academics, and crucially, personages responsible for national defense and interests abroad.

However, following 1743, those mapping the continent in Europe could now include the Rockies in their calculations, even if only in an abstract sense. This privileged set certainly included someone like John Senex, the map maker and publisher of Anderson's *Constitutions* who had to keep abreast of discoveries from overseas for the sake of his livelihood, along with many of his Masonic "brothers" too, such as Oglethorpe, Montague, Pelham-Holles and the Prime Minister, Sir Robert Walpole. All of these Freemasons would have been familiar with — or at least had easy access to — maps and reports accumulated by the Royal Society, Colonial Office or Admiralty, and the constant stream of additions ad updates to such collections.

It is therefore logical to assume that the above — and others — influential enough in terms of both Government policy and the recalibration of Masonic ritual were in pole position to include newly discovered American topography into the gradually evolving ceremonial of the fraternity, in particular the description of the layout of the Temple, the *Explanation of the First Degree Tracing Board*. The question is which physical characteristics of North America made it into the ritual and Lodge lay-

---

142   The Mallets were fur traders who saw the Mountains whilst on a 2000-mile trek through the interior during 1741. The la Verendrye brothers saw them from what would become western Wyoming on New Year's Day, 1743.

out? And more importantly, which when metamorphosed by the symbolism of the construction trade, came full circle to be etched onto the map of America in the shape of States?

Fig. 26: This map from 1744 shows the Appalachians and the Great Lakes but not the Rockies.

II

> ...the Rough Ashlar for the Entered Apprentice to work, mark, and indent on; and the Perfect Ashlar for the experienced craftsman to try and adjust his jewels on. They are called immovable Jewels, because they lie open and immovable in the Lodge... The Rough Ashlar is a stone, rough and unhewn as taken from the quarry, until by the industry and ingenuity of the workman, it is modelled, wrought into due form, and rendered fit for the intended structure;... The Perfect Ashlar is a stone of a true die or square, fit only to be tried by the Square and Compasses;[143]

The above extract from *The Explanation* outlines another two characteristics of a standard Masonic Lodge: the stone ashlars lying on the

---

143 *The Perfect Ceremonies, p.54*

floor. The ashlars (old English for cut stone) are unique in they are the sole features of the Lodge where emphasis is placed on their underlying physical makeup, in this case, stone. Like other oddities in Masonic lore, why such an exemption was made to allow something so fundamentally "physical" into the description of the symbolic structure is again unexplained, for the ashlars' presence contradicts the whole ethos of the Lodge as it developed during the first half of the eighteenth century: a temporary structure, who's equipment could be hauled easily from one London tavern to another.

Despite this quirk, what is ascertainable about these "immovable" features is they are clearly some form of ornamentation, and a Masonic decoration too, for like the 'Royal Arch', they are again part of the abrupt departure from the interior ornamentation of the Temple as cataloged in *Kings* and *Chronicles*. Biblical precedence being closed off for all practical purposes, and far from the "cherubim", Sephardim' and "moulten sea" of Schott's 1730 model, the ashlars most likely origin is therefore either in the operative tradition Freemasonry emerged from during the seventeenth century, or conversely part of the invented Masonic imagery so characteristic of its successor, dating from the eighteenth.

Superficially, it is indeed possible the origin of the ashlars lies within the older, operative tradition. Why this is so rests not with the availability of evidence, but within the sphere of common sense, for what is instantly noticeable about the ashlars' and their role within the structure of Freemasonry is the stone they are formed from isn't defined. The vagueness of the men who created the concept of the "Ashlars" is understandable here, in that many kinds of stone can, and have been, adaptable enough to be cut for use in building, The same rationale underpins their place in the Lodge, for it again stands to reason that meetings of medieval stoneworkers could possibly have included an elementary technical instruction, whereby two stones, one illustrating "before" and the other "after" could be employed by experienced masons to instruct junior colleagues in the correct way to ply their trade.

Nevertheless, it is also plausible, due to the lack of any kind of precedent, that the symbolism of the "ashlars" — or at least part of it — could simply be a further example of "speculative" eighteenth century Freemasons like Doctor Desaguliers again embellishing "modern" ritual with another totally fictitious feature. Certainly, Samuel Pritchard only ever mentioned the rough, uncut stone on the floor of the Lodge in *Dissected*; and whilst it is possible he was ignorant of the "perfect" ashlar, on the grounds he was a con man in possession of an incomplete ritual, the alternative argument has to be that the well cut stone cube was added to the ceremonial for some reason at a later date.

If the latter is true, and to be fair the evidence doesn't contradict it, then the invention and inclusion of the "perfect ashlar" didn't take long, for just over a decade after Pritchard's *expose*, the cubical stone made its debut in not one, but two fresh exposures. The first of these was *Le Secret des Francs -Macons*, published in Paris during 1742 by the Prior of the Paris Sorbonne, one Abbe Gabriel Louis Calabre Perau[144], whilst two years later, the French connection was maintained by the journalist Louis Travenol's 1744 *Catechisme des Francs-Macons*[145]. Within ten years, the well cut ashlar had migrated across the English Channel as well, to take root within Masonic symbolism in Britain, an example of which can be seen in a satirical cartoon of 1754, by a certain Slade, which, apart from other symbolism, clearly shows a stone in the shape of a cube at the bottom left hand corner[146].

With respect to America, the French exposures date to the perfect ashlar's invention to within a year of the Mallet's and the La Verendrye brothers discovering the Rocky Mountains: 1742 or 1743. Such temporal tightness inevitably suggests a question, and that is could the creation of the "perfect" stone to balance the rough be an allegorical nod in the direction of how the addition of the Rockies to the topographical map of America complimented the Appalachians? Certainly, one definite was confirmation of the existence of a hitherto unknown mountain range would reach the eyes and ears of the Masonic Fraternity very quickly indeed, even in 1743. Take, for example, the cartographer Senex, Senior

---

144 Perau stated Lodge floor drawings were in Crayon, and that the Rough Ashlar was drawn for the 1st degree, the Perfect Ashlar was drawn for the 2nd.
145 Both the exposures of 1742 and 1744 are from *Three Distinct Knocks*, published in 1760.
146 Cited in *The Freemason's Guide*, page 384.

Grand Warden of the Grand Lodge of England. Until his death in 1740, Senex was savvy enough to advertise many of his maps with the powerful imprimatur that they had been "corrected from the observations communicated to the Royal Society at London, and the Royal Academy at Paris." Apart from the obvious financial benefit such a move generated, Senex's blurb was also indicative of how speedily parties in government, scientific societies and fraternities with a vested interest could digest news of new discoveries.

Even though the second "immovable" stone fixture within a Masonic Lodge was invented at precisely the same time another "immovable" stone mountain range appeared on European maps of America, there is still one bone of contention with regard to identification of the "perfect" rock in Freemasonry: and that is there may have been, centuries ago, some confusion about whether it started out as either a cube or a rectangular brick shape. This discrepancy didn't simply lie with the early Masonic fraternity's apparent unfamiliarity with the word "rectangle", which they preferred to call an "oblong square", but also because of the relative uselessness of a cubical stone in building.

The inadequacy of cubes in construction was certainly recognized by 1733, if not millennia earlier, and inevitably in the face of such powerful precedents, rectangular building blocks — of stone, or the stone-cutters' nemesis, brick — have been central to building worldwide, for the obvious reason they bond together far more effectively than cubes. Such blatant practicality therefore suggests that if the "modern" rewritten ritual really did mean business in terms of emphasizing an operative connection, then the "perfect" ashlar, far from being cubical, should actually have been rectangular in its original incarnation. The ritual itself certainly isn't much help, as it doesn't say whether the well cut stone was cubical or a "long square", although Bernard Jones in the *Freemason's Guide*, has tried to clear up the issue by arguing that the word "perfect" is actually a corruption of another term:

> An ashlar is any wall building stone whose main angles are right angles, but the speculative's ashlar is a cubical stone, although the "perfect" ashlar originally was probably not cubical but perpend, by which name it was known by our early Brethren, who at times called it the "perpent" or "perpin" ashlar or achillar," the "perpendester" etc. What the operatives

know as a perpend ashlar is a stone much longer than it is wide or deep, and having its ends finished. The stone goes through the wall from face to face (otherwise it is not "perpend") and both of its ends are in view and "perpend"-icular, or vertical. It follows that the perpend ashlar can very seldom be a cubical stone, because its purpose is to lie across the underneath stones and bind them, or key them, together; but probably as a result of confusion between the terms "perpend" and "perfect," the use of cubic stones has become customary in Lodges, and accordingly the old idea of the perpend ashlar must disappear, which is a pity, as it taught the principal of bonding, without which any wall must fail".[147]

So if the "perfect" ashlar was in its original form perpendicular, and the designers of America were following the ritual to the letter, then the identification of both stones' location and character on the map should be straightforward enough: one will be rectangular, and the other, irregular. The tiny fragment of ceremonial, "they lie open and immovable in the Lodge," also provides further clues: firstly, the ashlars would be solidly within the interior, ideally equidistant between the "two grand parallel lines", and secondly, "open and *immovable*" meaning they represent something not only geometrically higher than the surrounding Temple floor, but also features which, for some reason, couldn't be shifted in any way whatsoever.

III

As discussed in chapter seven, two key determinants in the establishment of a political boundary are the presence and aspirations of a local populace, combined with the quirks of a physical background. It scarcely needs emphasizing that people always desire to be lumped together geographically with those they feel kinship, and at one extreme, societies where the population suffers from intractable division — Northern Ireland or Israel and Palestine for example — the nature and position of an administrative boundary can be a decisive hindrance to political and social harmony. On the other hand, for those portions of the globe free from discord, home to small, scattered or homogeneous communities, or people happy to acquiesce to the desires of the authorities, the creation of political divisions can have little or no importance whatsoever.

147　*The Freemason's Guide*, page 411.

It stands to reason therefore the more a border is a matter of indifference, those creating boundaries — governments, cartographers and surveyors — have a correspondingly greater freedom of action to design as they see fit. Better still — from the point of view of the designers — are environments where the population is either negligible or none existent, where the will of the authorities — or a group within them — can become all pervasive.

Likewise the physical background: European cartography had, during the era when the concept of nation states was emerging, been bogged down not only by the above human considerations, but also by the lack of a proper scientific method. The result was a mish mash of borders often following the course of river and mountain ranges, though, by contrast, as the same European powers plus America moved outwards centuries later, surveying science had, and would continue to develop, to such a point that more and more natural topography could be ignored, to be replaced by the greater and greater use of geometry in the design of nations and colonies. It was a long, continuous, but upward learning curve, though the emergence of the geometrical method in the sixteenth century, the lack of an resident population of European origin, combined with the new science of surveying, created a revolution in the mapping of empire, and by the mid nineteenth century, Australia, Canada and soon Africa were home to a large number of increasingly geometric provinces.

Naturally, another place that succumbed to this revolution was America, where a great many territories were highly mathematical because they were mapped prior to large scale white settlement, combined with an absence of rivers and the preponderance of generally level forest areas, plains and deserts, especially to the west. Even the one huge feature which might have been seen as a problem — the Rockies — was constantly ignored by surveyors and map makers plotting the outlines of what would become the western states during the second half of the nineteenth century, in that Mountain contours were only used to mark one large scale state line, between Idaho and Montana, and some minor partitions, such as the stretch of border at the north western corner of America's second most rectangular state, Wyoming.

Nobody has ever suggested that there was competition between the above nations and empires in the creation of geometric provinces, for practicality was far more important. Nevertheless, had it been a race, America would have been the winner, because at that moment in time when the east started to be convulsed by civil war, the fusion of geometry and political cartography reached its apogee in the geographical definition of a new US territory: Colorado, which was named after the Spanish word for "red", on account of the soil color explorers from that country had encountered there,

By 1860 though, it wasn't so much the soil, but what could lay under it that was attracting attention, for by this time Colorado was home to a miniscule two thousand white Americans, many of whom had arrived in the area to take advantage of a gold rush centered in the region a year before. These "Coloradoans" were almost to a man and woman, migrants from the East or Europe, and were, quite naturally, more concerned with establishing themselves during the early years, rather than worrying about abstract concepts like the geographical limits of local administration. For the Government surveyors responsible for drawing up the borders therefore, this local indifference meant near ideal laboratory conditions existed for mapping Colorado's boundaries according to their will and specification, though this was also an experiment whose value was underscored by a whiff of urgency too, thanks to the Union's desire to solidify control over a mineral rich region in the thick of the secessions in the South.

But what was unusual was what happened next to the "red soil" territory, for urgency combined with simplicity combined with science affected the alignment of this particular state line in a manner not seen before, in that it came closer to a specific geometric shape, not only amongst any former or future state, but of anywhere else on Earth. Even more important was the origins of this particular design, because far from the miners and speculators of embryonic Colorado, its definitions were planned and mapped in the corridors of power of Washington DC, as the Government itself stated publicly in the November 30 1861 *Report of the Commissioner of the General Land Office*:

> The new Territory of Colorado was organized by the act of Congress approved February 28, 1861. It is situate between the 37th and 41st degrees of north latitude, and 25th and 32nd degrees west of the Washington meridian, embracing an area of 104,500 square miles, or 66,880,00 acres, of which 8,960,000 acres were formerly included within the Territory of New Mexico[148]

So someone in Washington had ordained Colorado would take the shape of a rectangle. Certainly, the ability of surveyors to ignore the physical background, with the exception of height above sea level, testified to their skill and the supremacy of their science — and geometry — over nature, something that must have occurred to the Government at some point in the process. What better way was there therefore, than to emphasize this triumph by taking the one physical fact that couldn't be controlled — elevation — and turning it to advantage? For mountainous Colorado, was, at an average height of 6,800 feet above sea level, destined to overlook all other states on the floor of the Union. Crucially, and unbeknown to nearly everyone in America, what was to become "the Mountain State" had, thanks to the United States Government, identical form, height and relationship to all other states the "stone of true die or square" had to the rest of the floor of a Masonic Lodge, when it first appeared in 1742-43, the years when the Rockies were first sighted.

America's well cut 'stone' was also aligned in precisely the location it should be. It was important that this particular rock lay in a central position on the floor, not just because it may have had some educational value to the operative Mason's of centuries earlier, but also insomuch as it represented the Masons ultimate symbolic achievement of taking something natural — stone — and converting it into something of use: a rectangle. Thus Colorado's position with regard to the boundaries of the Temple to the North and South, the "two grand parallel lines" long ago defined by the British, was also symbolic too, for, as the Government report stated, Colorado was to lie between the thirty-seventh and forty-first parallel lines north, thus equidistant — and "open and immovable" — between the forty-fifth and thirty-third parallels.

It is therefore inevitable, with a plan in place, that this four degree band is also where the highest state in the Appalachians, the eastern

---

148   General Land Office, 30th November, 1861.

range, is also situated. The state in question is West Virginia, which has a mean elevation of 1500 feet above sea level, though, apart from height and position in a north — south sense, West Virginia does however share a further common denominator with Colorado, and that is its borders were again drawn up during the Civil War. This was a point that was to have important consequences for its eventual shape, for, by recognizing how sophisticated surveying science had become by this time, and the general tendency towards geometry across the states, it could be assumed science could have been brought to bear to mold West Virginia into something geometrical as well. But this wasn't to be the case, for even though West Virginia paralleled Colorado in an east west sense, and enjoyed a specific relationship with the future highest state in the west in that it had a corresponding role as the highest State east of the Mississippi, it's borders were destined to become the most irregular man made state lines of the entire Union, and the reason for this was, paradoxically, the same crucial element behind Colorado's regularity: people.

Unlike Colorado, which only began to experience white immigration in the 1860s, the north western third of Virginia had been settled for decades. This was due, in part, to the region's proximity to England's first settlements on the Eastern seaboard, for the rich soil of lowland Virginia had attracted migrants from the day Captain John Smith had first stepped ashore back in 1607. The English found that the natural fecundity was ideal for the cultivation of these most excellent of cash crops, Cotton and Tobacco, and oiled by money from an enthusiastic City of London, plus a static workforce in the shape of indentured white laborers and, after 1619, slaves imported from Africa, by the late seventeenth century the Virginia colony had already emerged as a jewel in the imperial crown.

There was, however, a price to pay for this success, and part of it lay in the sense of disadvantage felt by many of Virginia's poorer white residents. An economy dominated by large scale plantations meant Virginia began to resemble the estate ridden English countryside, in that a small number of families held title over a disproportionate portion of the best land and labor. Combined with a constant demand for new ground to clear because of exhausted soil, this arrangement may have been acceptable to the great Virginia dynasties — the Washington's, Jefferson's, and Madison's for instance — but for those further down the pecking order, forced to eke out a living on small plots or worn out soil, further migration, even deeper into the interior, was the only alternative.

Thus the dynamic behind the settlement of the region destined one day to become West Virginia. During the late eighteenth century, and into the nineteenth, thousands of poor Virginians and others trekked north-west hoping for a better deal than they had got further east in the state. Even so, history wasn't about to repeat itself, for if the settlers thought they would be running plantations of their own, their hopes were soon dashed, for though cotton and tobacco cultivation took root further west, in Kentucky and Tennessee, the planting of such crops failed to take off in West Virginia, for the simple reason the Appalachians were a landscape of forests, hills, and poor soil.

From the first days of settlement therefore, nature dictated the economy of the north-west part of Virginia was pre-ordained to evolve differently to that in the eastern part of the state. Trades like mining and small scale farming were to become far more common than cotton and tobacco plantations, leading to a different economic and political culture from the rest of Virginia, which in turn manifested itself in a variety of ways, none so more than the absence of the "peculiar institution" that had long characterized Virginia and the rest of the South, slavery.

Such a fundamental difference could be ignored until 1861, but once the civil war got underway, it was clear differing attitudes to the issue of bonded labor was tearing the state apart, and Virginia, half slave, half free, couldn't endure. Both the Union and Confederacy legitimately laid claim to the loyalty of *all* Virginians, a conflict of interest inherent even as the opening shots of the civil war were being fired, when only nine out of forty six delegates to a secession convention held in the city of Wheeling[149] voted "yes" to leaving the United States and joining the Confederacy.

Following Abraham Lincoln's advice that 'a house divided against itself cannot stand', on October 24th of the same year the voters of the western part of Virginia balloted to whether to separate from the rest

---

149 May 13th, 1861.

of the state — with an overwhelming 18,489 voting in favor, and a mere 781 against — and now all that was left was for the President to issue the proclamation of West Virginian statehood. Lincoln, with far more weightier things to consider, didn't move on the issue for eighteen months, but finally signed West Virginia into existence on 10th April, 1863, thus letting both sides go their separate ways.

Apart from the obvious implications West Virginia's birth had for the north/south conflict, one subsidiary complication was the course of the "state line" bounding the new province. Colorado's regularity had been due, in part, to the indifference (not to say non-existence) of a local population, fused with surveying technology sufficiently advanced to ignore the presence of the mountainous background. But here in West Virginia, right on the dividing line between the Union and the Confederacy, a completely different approach was needed, to ensure the best, and most harmonious outcome for both conflicting interests.

Common sense dictated that the first move was to devolve the decision whether to stay or leave Virginia down to the lowest levels of local administration: the parishes. Once these had made their minds up whether to stay or go, the map makers could use the "will of the people" to chart the division of Virginia, although more in keeping with European tradition than American, the men who drew the boundaries of the new state also made use of the mountainous backdrop and the large rivers in the vicinity, the Shenandoah, Potomac and Ohio. The resultant border — which has remained unchanged to the present day — was destined to be a highly irregular squiggle looking more old world than new; which, in itself, was a logical outcome considering the political pressure gnawing away at wartime Virginia, but simultaneously, was also a complete contrast to the perfect rectangle established to the west less than a year earlier.

IV

So, in less than two years from the spring of 1861, the boundaries of continental America's most geometrical and non-geometrical states showed their face on the map of the Union. Superficially, this meant nothing, or it could be argued, was simply the sum of nothing more than another curiosity of American political cartography. In an alternative sense however, and again in keeping with other features on the map, it also chimed with another set of features long existent within a standard Masonic Temple, and probably the most potent symbol of all with regard to the identity of the "buildings" designers. These, having taken the most ancient, yet basic, image of the Mason's art — that of the rough stone being set out ready to be cut to form a regular cube or rectangle — and then placing them on the "floor" straight after it had been completed, were also making a powerful statement about a host of other things: art, design, and the strength of science to transcend the most daunting of natural phenomena. From 1863 onwards, two stones, one rectangular, the other irregular, sat astride — and above — the rest of the Union of the States in exactly the same way the stone ashlars lay on the floor of a Masonic Lodge. .

Fig. 27: Colorado and West Virginia, the Ashlars. Both are equidistant between the 45th and 33rd parallels, and directly west of "the Master's place" Washington DC. One is the highest state in the east, and the other the highest in the west. Notice how "33rd" and "13" come to the fore: 33 degrees latitude from east to west, 33 different in terms of size west to east, thirteen years between statehood, and designed in the thirteenth decade of the Temple.

The symbolism was crystal clear, and nothing would have been amiss had there been no further Masonic symbolism or geometry on display with regard to Colorado and West Virginia. Nevertheless, the creation

of America's "Ashlars" also demanded their numerical symbolism as accurate too, though, like the rest of the architectural features already in
place, these too had already been built into the design.

"Thirty-Third" does indeed appear twice, and in ways that again
emphasizes *achievement* with regard to both states in conjunction. The
General Land Office report on Colorado had, as a side effect, neatly un-
derlined the point that, by the 1860s, Government surveyors could plot
positions on the map with ease, using degrees, minutes and meridians
with the upmost accuracy. What better way was there therefore to again
invest the map with "thirty-third" than to do so by using the number of
degrees covered by the rough and well trimmed stone on an east to west
basis? For by plotting the westward course from the most easterly point
of West Virginia — the confluence of the Shenandoah and Potomac rivers, which lies at seventy seven degrees longitude west of Greenwich, the
line does indeed reach a highly symbolic number once it has crossed the
states in between, and arrives at the western border of Colorado. This is
the one hundred and ninth degree line of latitude west of Greenwich, the
thirty-third degree west of the seventy-seventh.

The idea of a one-way "thirty-third" wouldn't work, however, because
it suggested Colorado alone marked the achievement, when in reality
both stones had equal value, a duality if you like, one as the raw material
and one as the finished product. It was therefore vital to have a further
indicator of *achievement* cemented into the two states' relationship going
west to east, and indeed by heading this way, thirty-third" again puts in
an appearance, although not in a way recognizable in the 1860s, because,
over time, Colorado has emerged as the eighth largest state in the country, and West Virginia the forty first.

Double use of "thirty-third" wasn't of much value unless it was again
paired with a corresponding appearance of *completion*, and it is noticeable that "thirteen" does again exist, and in a double, westerly and easterly progression. Going west, it is noticeable in the difference between
the years both states achieved statehood: West Virginia in 1863 and
Colorado, 1876, which could also be interpreted as a further example of
the 'thirteen years' concept that had carried symbolic weight since Bibli-

cal times, never mind its frequency throughout the history of post-1733 America.

This was something in turn replicated in terms of decades and west to east too, for the adoption of the two stones were also completed in relation to Henry Price's opening of the first Masonic Lodge in America at the "North East Corner" insomuch as the boundaries of both states, mapped out in 1862, and the first half of 1863 respectively, again took place during the thirteenth decade on from when America first started to have design thinking applied to its geography, the foundation of American Freemasonry, and the creation of the 'arch' by Oglethorpe. This decade, lasting from 1853 to 1863, had witnessed the completion of the territory of the Continental United States to a satisfactorily rectangular shape, the setting down of the fourth and final cornerstone, and the laying out of the stonecutter's basic materials across the floor of the building, and it ended neatly, a few weeks later, on June 30th 1863.

Part IV. Roof

Chapter 10. "So he was seven years in building it..."

'Perfection is attained by slow degrees; it requires the hand of time' — Voltaire

I

As he endured the arduous voyage home to Boston in 1733, Henry Price would, in all likelihood have found himself in need of something to read, if only to take his mind off the rough and tumble essential to a high seas journey during the in the eighteenth century. To be fair to history, the biographical details that still exist about this Anglo-American, who was destined to fell trees and father children well into is seventies, doesn't suggest a particularly bookish man. Even so, and regardless of whether or not he was a 'reader' or not, what is indisputable was that there were certainly enough new titles stacked up in London bookshops to catch his eye, and relieve him of a guinea or two, before embarkation. For the enlightenment had impacted on literature too, and 1733's output included Berkeley's *The Theory of Vision*, Bowden's *Poetical Essays, A Description of Bath*, Mary Chandler's take on part of the country Price was leaving behind, and, if he was in the mood to improve his understanding of the world by studying the opinions of a foreigner, Voltaire's *Letters Concerning the English Nation.*

To put it bluntly, Price was spoilt for choice, for the late seventeenth and early eighteenth centuries had already turned out to be a very fruitful period indeed for English literature. Works by a myriad of authors tumbled off the printing presses, ranging from great scientific works by the likes of Hooke and Newton, through to the more literary efforts of men such as Hammond and Alexander Pope. The Boston tailor therefore had no reason at all to while away his time twiddling his thumbs as he sat in his cabin, for all — or none — of the above would serve admirably to temporarily banish the dreary meandering across the North Atlantic, as he headed west to establish his great foundation.

There must have been times though, amongst the Oceanic swell, when Henry Price might have needed something stronger — a flight of fancy — to take his mind off seasickness or the awful food. Again, there were certainly enough novels around, so the founder of American Masonry could quite easily have turned his eye to some of the great fiction of the time, maybe his fellow "brother"[150] Jonathan Swift's classic *Gulliver's Travels*, or even, if he were lucky enough to come across it, one of the weirder titles to appear in 1733, albeit one with a particular resonance, Samuel Madden's *Memoirs of the Twentieth Century, Being original letters of state under George the Sixth.*[151]

One of the first works of science fiction, *Memoirs of the Twentieth Century* had been published anonymously by Madden, an Irish Anglican clergyman, who two years earlier had co-founded the Royal Dublin Society. Claimed by the author to have been "received and revealed in the year 1728", the Dubliner's work was laid out as a series of state papers purporting to describe relations between Great Britain and the rest of the globe during the late nineteen-nineties, though, in reality, it was yet another satire on George II's England, and Sir Robert Walpole's government in particular, reason enough for the unnerved Irishman to pulp as many copies he could lay his hands on post-publication, and for England's first Prime Minister to suppress Madden's efforts before too many susceptible minds got around to reading it.

Putting aside Madden's abilities as a visionary, which were non-existent, certainly one passage in *Memoirs* that wouldn't have robbed Walpole of too much sleep concerned the Irishman's views on relations be-

---

150 According to Denslow's *10,000 Famous Freemasons*, Swift was a member of Goat-at-the-foot-of- the Haymarket Lodge No. 16 (although unconfirmed).
151 Published by Osborn, et al, London, in 1733.

tween Britain and America two hundred and sixty-five years n the future. Madden clearly wasn't a great admirer of the colonists' or their abilities, seeing them 'in part made up of the filth and purgings of the nation', a rather bleak and negative analysis only mitigated by a more optimistic opinion of America on the cusp of the twenty-first century:

> The truth is, our colonies abroad have, and are likely to aquire still such an increase of hands and strength, that the greatest care will be necessary to keep the strongest of them dependent; and yet to provide that the weakest of them may not live on the blood and spirits of the mother nation, nor suck, if I may use the allusion, on her breast too long............but we all know *Rome* it self built up all its courage and virtue on no better a foundation: and after all, even such offenders have often such resolution, subtilty, strength, sharpness and activity as make their posterity, (by these qualities they derive from them,) sufficient amends for their decending from such evil ancestors[152].

Perhaps Walpole's approbation was a blessing in disguise, for it is unlikely Madden would've wanted the "evil ancestor" Benjamin Franklin to read such a passage, never mind anyone else amongst the colonies sizable reading public. This was a work clearly aimed at the British alone, not for perusal by foreigners, even related ones, and it could be argued that it marked the start of a dismissive attitude, which, when imbued by men of far greater power and influence, was to have serious implications forty years in the future. Such is life, that sometimes the truth is said in jest, though for the moment this particular entertainment must have provided at least some distraction for Georgian Londoners, who were constantly on the look-out for new diversions.

Against all odds, *Memoirs* does, however, have a value, and not simply because it was the first literary attempt at painting a picture of the far future. Until the early eighteenth century authors of fiction had traditionally confined their works to the here-and-now, meaning that Madden's work illustrates a change in direction, in that writers were now prepared to speculate on imaginary places they would never see and possible futures that would occur long after their demise. Alongside *Gulliver's Travels*, published seven years earlier in 1726, *Memoirs of the Twentieth Century* therefore carries within its pages something of great significance,

---

152 *Memoirs of the Twentieth Century*, pp. 374–375.

and that is its publication marked that moment in time when the Anglo-Saxon imagination started to look outward, and more pertinently, ahead.

Of course, to try to imagine the future, it would help to get some knowledge and understanding of the past. It was therefore again serendipitous that the intellectual curiosity so characteristic of the time was also applied to the study of history, which began to be treated as a serious academic subject, rather than as a dumping ground for the semi-comic musings traditionally churned out before. Of course, this change wasn't to mean many of the works hitting the shelves of early eighteenth century London suddenly began to exhibit the rigor that would be required today: Stukeley's *Itinerarium Curiosum* and his opinions on Stonehenge and Avebury were testament to that; but rather it was a declaration that, for all their fumbling, historians were now, at least, beginning to head in the right direction within their works.

Again conditions were right, for a real advantage enjoyed by eighteenth century British and American historians was that they could write and lecture in an environment that, compared to many parts of the world, was still relatively tolerant. Although not democratic in the modern sense, the United Kingdom and its Empire was in many respects free, in that the man and woman in the street could go about their business and express themselves with far greater assurance than their opposite numbers in Europe. This liberal atmosphere, when alloyed with the general tendency towards rational thinking, meant historians could respect objectivity far more than they could before.

One example immediately springing to mind was Bible history. After the religious tumult of the seventeenth century, scholars and commentators might have felt it a subject best left alone; but by the mid 1720s, intelligent people felt on safe enough ground to apply a more rigorous analysis to theology than had ever been seen before. Joseph Addison's *The Evidence of the Christian Religion*, Matthew Tindal's *Christianity as Old as Creation* and William Wotton's *A Discourse Concerning the Confusion of Languages at Babel* — all published in 1730 — sat on bookshelves alongside works covering more contemporary religious issues, such as Daniel Neal's 1732 *The History of the Puritans or Protestant Non-Conformists* and

William Sewel's 1724 *The History of the Rise, Increase, and Progress of the Christian People Called Quakers.*

There were studies exploring specific events and epochs in another contentious area: British history. Again, everything was up for grabs, as accounts of events long before vied for attention with works covering some of the more traumatic events of recent times. The informed reader circa Seventeen twenty two was free to thumb through not one, but two new titles by the great Daniel Defoe: his classic *Moll Flanders* and study of the epidemic that hit London in 1665, *A Journal of the Plague Year.* Two years later saw the publication of Thomas Hearne's *Robert of Gloucester's Chronicle,* Edward Hyde's *An Appendix to the History of the Grand Rebellion,* the Frenchman Paul de Rapin's *L'Histoire d'Angleterre* and, throwing a little excitement and novelty to the mix, Captain Charles Johnson's *A General History of the Pyrates.*

The fact that history was starting to be treated as a science was also exemplified by a public spat between two of its practitioners, Zacherey Grey and John Oldmixon. In 1725, Grey wrote *A Defence of Our Antient and Modern Historians* aimed at Oldmixon, who, in the previous year, had churned out his *The Critical History of England, Ecclesiastical and Civil* replied, in the same year with *A Review of Dr. Zachary Grey's Defence.* Oldmixon, fresh from his quarrel with Grey, published *The History of England, During the Reigns of the Royal House of Stuart* in 1729, followed by John Horsley's *Britannia Romana, or The Roman Antiquities of Britain* three years later. All in all, for the enlightened Anglo-Saxon circa 1733, there was no excuse for an all-embracing ignorance of the past. As tome after tome was stacked on library shelves throughout Britain and its Empire, men of leisure and purpose could digest, analyze, and then apply with confidence, the historical precedent therein.

Four hundred years earlier, a comprehensive perusal of Horsley's *Britannia Romana* or anything like would have been the last thing on the minds of William of Sens and his men. These were far tougher times, and the Frenchman and his stonecutters didn't have the luxury of studying previous eras in construction; to them, and any other builders prior to the eighteenth century, Britain's ruins — Roman or not — were good for one thing only, and that was as a source of cheap and accessible stone.

By 1733, however, William of Sens' operative successors were gradually starting to realize their work had merits that could be looked upon favorably by future generations. For the building trade, or at least that part of it devoted to structures of some interest, was itself becoming infected by the burgeoning historical *zeitgeist*. This movement exhibited itself in so many ways: a trend towards the ornate, new materials and styles, and the adoption of classical influences; although one manifestation, in everyday architecture, was the growing habit of physically dating ordinary buildings by labeling them with the year of construction for all to see.

This again wasn't a particularly new idea for great buildings such as castles and cathedrals had had their commencement recorded even prior to the arrival of William the Conqueror. Nevertheless, this innovation was rarely applied to more humble structures prior to 1600, due in part to the fact that the farms, barns, cottages and town houses of England were originally raised for functionality alone, rather than the aesthetic, and were only looked upon as a temporary necessity, destined for demolition at some later date. The lack of any paperwork, in the shape of title deeds, for example, was another cause behind a failure to date many man-made structures, for England was still a place where most land was owned by a few people, meaning transference of property was a rarity, and generally due to heredity or marriage causes.

By the late sixteenth century, however, things began to change. A growing population, merchant class, and towns, all overlaid the decay of the older agricultural England, leading to more and more property sales and purchases across the country. Naturally, lawyers — who needed tighter property definitions including the date buildings were started — were some of the first to benefit from this, although builders could also earn a fortune too, meaning that some constructions, recognized as something to be proud of, began to exhibit, in both Roman and modern numerals, the year they were commenced.

Little wonder therefore that by 1733 Freemasons co-opted this phenomenon for their ultimate structure, by commencing work on a highly symbolic date. Nevertheless, this wasn't some house that could be knocked up in under a year; but an edifice that was obviously going to take centuries to finish, and the question was, with symbolism the aim, could the entire building be raised and completed during and at a point in time again emphasizing its connection to King Solomon's Temple? Of course, at the time, Masons like Price and Oglethorpe had no more idea about what the future would hold than the Clergyman Samuel Madden, and the course of the next quarter-millennium was as much a mystery to them as anyone else. Even so, armed with the historical and geographical awareness characteristic of their era, and a wealth of both Biblical and mathematical symbolism to draw on, they could indeed plan for the future with a far greater assurance than the author of *Memoirs of the Twentieth Century*.

II

The idea that men ago could establish a timetable for the construction of something as large as America three hundred years ago is, of course, absurd. Franklin, Washington *et al* may as well have initiated Madden or some other 'seer' into their Order, for all the use he and they were at prophesying events. An inability to foresee the future didn't of course mean that thinking people even then couldn't discern at least a few *general* trends. Projections based on common sense, reinforced by the huge arsenal of knowledge, both historical and geographical, could indeed be applied to the (possible) future of an undeveloped area, and a basic outline plotted, though as an indicator of a schedule to be met, such assumptions were well near useless.

Looking specifically at America, the first and most obvious idea was that white settlement was likely to continue to role westward from the thirteen colonies, especially if unchecked by powers to the north and south. This concept even existed publically, in the charters of the individual colonies, which unilaterally stretched British power all the way to the Pacific. A second likelihood was that this potential result would again continue to use at least some characteristics inherent in English civilization, because America in 1733 again illustrated how a predominantly Anglo-Saxon culture had the knack of absorbing people of different nationalities, whilst the sheer size and fertility of the country also hinted at something else to look out for: that at some time its people and economy were likely outstrip those of the older country, leading to a fundamental realignment in their relationship.

The above — coupled with that great unknown, scientific and technological advance — would almost certainly earned nods of agreement if presented to people in the know, like the former Governor of Pennsylvania, Sir William Keith, or Thomas Pelham-Holles and his staff at the Southern Department. But with regard to the specific details of whether and when America would one day have a presence on the Pacific, or for that matter rearrange its relationship with the English and their language, these were questions nobody on Earth could answer in 1733.

Lack of foresight didn't however rule out a timetable being applied retrospectively. Like builders of any age who were on top of the job, the closer the work was to completion the more likely it was that the men in charge could hazard a guess as to when the building would be finished. In the round though, for conventional Masons and builders, this could be a day of mixed blessings. In times when there was plenty of work about, signing the job off, with its promise of payment and opportunity to do something else, couldn't come fast enough,; though on days when work was hard to find, the hour of completion was something to be avoided at all costs.

For the medieval Masons working on Cathedrals, who knew the science of construction far better than their ecclesiastical clients, the temptation to stretch or contract the time the work took must have therefore been overwhelming. They were all aware of the power and sheer financial clout of the Roman Catholic Church, and the relatively luxurious conditions in which its priests and monks lived; so a cynical desire to squeeze their employers for as much as possible must have entered at least some builder's minds. If these thoughts filtered through to the collective consciousness, and were then executed with a great deal of cunning and subtlety, it would lead to an unspoken recognition about the nature of the builders efforts: that it was *them*, rather than the Church, who determined the exact date the great cathedrals were finished.

Timing was also critical to the medieval Masons' symbolic inheritors. The actions of James Oglethorpe alone had illustrated this, especially when he started putting Georgia together on the "second day of the second month" thus replicating, via the Julian calendar, the day King Solomon had started work on the Temple. This, in turn, lay within a defined time period, a retrospective timetable, for Oglethorpe had, of course, marked his symbolic stonework with a chronological take on "thirteen crossed with thirty-third" in terms of years too, with everything happening during the thirty-third year in the middle of the thirteenth decade of Britain's colonial adventures.

Once the Arch was completed however, the symbolic stonemasons' mark unsurprisingly ducked out of sight during what was left of the Colonial era. British Masons didn't have any new stonework to erect during the remainder of their time and influence in America, and between the mid-1730s and the 1770s there was no obvious deployment of the term, which reinforced the fact this particular formula was only ever used to underscore great events. Unbeknown to most however, one such "great event" lay just around the corner, as the dispute between King George III and his insurrectionary American subjects was reaching the point of no return.

By late 1775, the lack of any architectural action contrasted sharply with the contribution of Masons to the nascent American Revolution, a phenomenon that can never be underestimated. Whilst part of the reason for this involvement can be laid at the door of Masonry's appeal to individuals of influence and intellect, men who would be at the forefront of a movement against tyranny, another was that by the first half of the 1770s, the two Masonic Lodges founded by Henry Price and James Oglethorpe at the extremities of British America had been joined by scores of others, not only in Georgia and Massachusetts, but also in the other eleven colonies that lay in between as well. For some undefined reason, the Fraternity and its meetings formed a home from home for American Patriots and Loyalists, British soldiers, and even, with the initiation, in March 1775, of Prince Hall and fifteen other free blacks into the Order, ethnic minorities, who could meet together away from the conflicts of the war and society in general.

Out of these Lodges poured some of the great — and not so great — names of American independence. There was, of course, George Washington, who, as a twenty year old, had been initiated into Alexandria

Lodge No. 22, of Fredericksburg, Virginia, on the evening of 4ᵗʰ November, 1752[153]. Washington was, in turn, joined by the founder of the United States Navy, the Scotsman John Paul Jones, who had been a member[154] of a Lodge in Scotland, although special mention should be given to the membership of Saint Andrew's Lodge, Boston as a whole, and one member in particular, Paul Revere.

Like Washington and Franklin, Revere also followed a highly active Masonic career, not only becoming Master of Saint Andrew's in 1770, but also by following Henry Price's example of sixty years earlier to become Grand Master of Massachusetts Freemasonry between 1794 and 1797. Indeed, there is some evidence that Paul Revere lived within a nexus of revolutionary Masons, for legend has it that it was his fellow members of Saint Andrew's who, dressed up as Indians, headed down to the port one night in 1773, boarded the British Merchant Ship, *Dartmouth*, and tossed the cargo of tea overboard.

Even to those whose conduct left a lot to be desired, in American eyes at least, also had a role to play. These included not only officers and other ranks of the British Army stationed in America, but also one twenty four year old man who, having presumably joined Freemasonry in the West Indies, returned to New England to petition a Lodge for membership during 1765, which, once agreed, was recorded in the minutes of Hiram Lodge, New Haven, Connecticut, as saying:

> Brother Benedict Arnold is by Right Worshipful [Nathan Whiting] proposed to be made a member of the Right Worshipful Lodge and is accordingly made a member in this Lodge...[155]

The high visibility involvement of Freemasons in the Continental Army was mirrored by a comparable Masonic presence within the political machinations and intrigues leading to independence. Benjamin Franklin's role has already been mentioned; though according to one

---

153 Between 1775 and the Treaty of Paris in 1783, it has been estimated that there were 33 'Masonic' Generals in Washington's Army, forty six percent of the Total. Source:

154 Jones was a member of Saint Bernard Kilwinning Lodge number 122 in Kirkcudbright, Scotland from 1770.

155 The Empire State Mason Magazine, spring 2007, p.31 'Benedict Arnold and Solomon's Lodge No1' the meeting of Hiram Lodge No.1, New Haven, 10t April, 1765.

source, at least eight other signatories to the Declaration of Independence were proven Masons — William Ellery, the Rhode Island customs collector and attorney; John Hancock, the millionaire merchant and/or alleged smuggler, who was another member of Saint Andrews Lodge in Boston; Joseph Hewes, Quaker and first secretary of the US Navy; William Hooper, a member of Hanover Lodge, Masonborough, North Carolina; Tavern-keeper's son Thomas McKean; Mayflower descendant, lawyer and preacher Robert Treat Payne; George Washington's friend and New Jersey Mason Richard Stockton; George Walton; and last, but not least, William Whipple, the former ship's captain, who had been a Mason for a full twenty-four years when he signed the Declaration in the summer of 1776[156].

These individuals constituted a total of nine out of the fifty six who were destined to sign the Declaration — hardly evidence that Freemasons were instrumental in the founding of the Republic. Nevertheless, known or unknown to them, the mathematical symbol employed by James Oglethorpe of "thirteen crossed with thirty-third" was again about to make its appearance in conjunction with their actions. The story starts with a non-mason, Richard Henry Lee, who, as one of the Virginia delegates to the Congress, submitted a resolution for approval calling for outright independence from Great Britain. Although shortly to be outshone by the much more famous declaration, the Lee Resolution, once voted on and agreed, was reported on in the July 2 edition of the *Pennsylvania Evening Post* as saying:

> This day the Continental Congress declared the United Colonies Free and Independent States.

Independence having been voted for on July 2, it might therefore be supposed that that day would become the national birthday of the "Free and Independent States." Future President John Adams, who had been central to the passage of the resolution, certainly thought so, for he wrote to his wife Abigail a day later — July 3rd — offering the following prediction:

---

156   A further twenty-four others — including Elbridge Gerry and Thomas Jefferson — with a lot less certainty, have also been connected to the Order. Source: Knight, *The Brotherhood.*

> The second day of July, 1776, will be the most memorable epoch in the history of America. I am apt to believe that it will be celebrated by succeeding generations as the great anniversary festival. It ought to be commemorated as the day of deliverance, by solemn acts of devotion to God Almighty. It ought to be solemnized with pomp and parade, with shows, games, sports, guns, bells, bonfires, and illuminations, from one end of this continent to the other, from this time forward forever more.

Adams was out by two days. On July 3rd and into the 4th, the Congress tinkered with the text of the Declaration, making a number of alterations, including the addition of Lee's resolution to the conclusion. The final text was therefore approved on the 4th and sent off to be printed, meaning that it was this date, rather than 2nd July, that is remembered.

Although this looks like a mere quirk of American history, the emphasis laid on the 4th July at the expense of the 2nd again marked yet another occurrence of "thirteen crossed with thirty-third" cropping up around some 'great event.' There was a certain inevitability to this, as America's national birthday was strictly numerical and was coined when mathematics and symbolism were all the rage, though what was remarkable was the sheer scale of what the symbol encompassed, for it was the entire history of British America, and more importantly, its passing.

This basically, thirteen being recognizable in that 1776 marked the completion of British authority in the American colonies, one hundred and sixty-nine (thirteen times thirteen) years on from the first settlement at Jamestown in 1607, whilst "thirty-third" becomes more apparent by looking more closely at the date, and specifically the 4th's relationship with the 3rd and 5th July, 1776:[157]

---

157 Using dates from recent times, (i.e., in the last five hundred years) then the lowest number is January 1st 2000, $(1 + 1 + 2 + 0 + 0 + 0 = 4)$. Conversely, the highest number that could be reached using this method would be 29th September 1999, $(2 + 9 + 0 + 9 + 1 + 9 + 9 + 9 = 48)$. Of course, with such a narrow range of numbers to choose from as 4 to 48, it is obvious that during a five-hundred-year period that each number would reoccur on a fairly regular and random basis. Whilst classical numerology would recognize 4 as the number for the 1st January 2000, the same analysis wouldn't apply to 29th September 1999. Numerology requires that numbers are single digits only, between 1 and 9, and therefore 48 would be seen as a false number. To get the 'proper' number for 29-09-1999, further addition would take place until a single digit number had been achieved. So 29th September 1999 would be further analyzed thus: $4 + 8 = 12$ then finally: $1 + 2 = 3$. But this only occurs if numerological analysis is being applied. Where simple addition is the de-

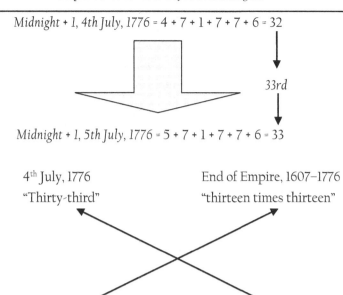

Fig. 28: *REVOLUTION*. The British Empire in America ended during its one hundred and sixty ninth year (thirteen times thirteen), on a date representing "33rd"

III

The above imagery shows that apart from an awareness of history, geography and science, one huge advantage eighteenth century Freemasons had with regards to their design was the recognition of the power of numbers. They were well aware of the adaptability of numerical symbols, and the ease in which they could be chiseled onto so many facets of the republic's imagery. Not coincidentally, the presence of so many mathematicians and architects within the Order had obviously played a large part in this, though an understanding of the idea was also something that's roots could be traced back — in England at least — to "operative"

---

sired method, then numbers in the higher range were especially pronounced when the years are made up of high digits, such as seven, eight and nine. This naturally results in the late eighteenth, nineteenth and twentieth centuries' being littered with them. By contrast, the first time the date will add up to 32 in the twenty-first century will be the 29th September 2019, and following that, only six more times in the next twenty years, due to the effect of two and zero. But two and a quarter centuries ago, the year 1776 was marked by the '32' effect occurring no less than 27 times — on average every 13 or so days — including July 4th 1776.

days, because even if King Edward II could only define an inch, clumsily, as "three grains of barley, dry and round, placed end to end, lengthwise" the average Medieval Mason, by contrast, knew well the importance of accuracy, and the effective use of numbers was the key to such accuracy.

The employment of numbers for definitions on a infinitely greater scale was a phenomenon if not unique to America, did mark it out far more than any other country. Some of this was because of the newness of the whole enterprise: for Europe — and the rest of the Old World — was awash with institutions and cultures the origins of which began long ago in the mists of antiquity, meaning it was difficult, if not impossible, to apply numerical definitions to them. Take for example, the British Monarchy, and King George II in particular. Whilst he was indeed the thirty-third monarch since William the Conqueror, in the larger spread of UK history he cannot really be identified as such, because the monarchy evolved out of the success or failure of various warring tribes, marriages of convenience, diplomacy and political intrigue rather than reliance on a distinct set of rules. The same applies to many other institutions across the old world: they emerged during times devoid of historical thinking or legal process, by peoples concerned with the struggles of the here-and-now, rather than a clear headed application of law or mathematics.

By contrast, by the time the United States came along, the above demands meant that institutions, offices, and political units not only had their powers tightly defined, but could, for the sake of identification, also be classified numerically. It was therefore logical that in an era of greater historical awareness, enlightened individuals could indeed assume that one day there would be a thirty-third State, Congress or President, and plan accordingly. What foresight based on logic didn't mean however was that any old numbers had potential symbolic value: figures for population, life expectancy, tire production or a million other things — statistics — were, and are, strictly temporary in nature, and wouldn't do. It was only those numbers that could stand the test of time that would be used, the ones that once engraved on something stayed engraved on it.

With regard to the stones making up the building, the states, any operative mason, would have again recognized the value of numbers being applied to them, especially numbers of a special symbolic importance.

This had already been illustrated by the listing of states joining the Union (Oregon) and relationship to one another (Florida and Maine) although it could be applied in other ways, some of which were still to happen. Of special importance, for the timing of the construction, was, of course, the date when each state joined the union, especially the last one. This day, which had to come sometime, wouldn't necessarily have to be a major turning point in the country's history: for what was always recognizable was that the politics, society and economy of America were, up to a point, bubbling away nicely regardless of the symbolic construction work going on around. To put it bluntly, all that was required was that territorial gains, once converted into states, should not only emphasize the fact that the country was being laid out to a design, but that it be completed, with the final state of the Union, at a time and date that was suitably symbolic.

Changes in the rhythm of working life would also help speed the formulation of an accurate completion date. Compared to now, the Builders and Masons of earlier times were used to a more leisurely pace, and cut their deals on the shake of a hand. By the late nineteenth century though, this cozy way of doing business was crumbling fast in the face of an all-pervasive contract culture, something that also be applied to the country as a whole. The census of 1890 noted that for all extents and purposes, the "frontier" had ceased to exist, and that America was now settled, in a European sense, from coast to coast, although there were still huge regions, especially in the West, that were only sparsely inhabited or not at all. East of the Mississippi, many areas had, and were, succumbing to a further stage of human occupation: urbanization, which in turn was driven by industrialization and the rise of the corporate culture.

This was the era of Standard Oil and US Steel, soon to be joined by other emblematic names such as Coca-Cola, Du Pont and the Ford Motor Company; each of whom owed some of their success to a far tighter approach to commerce. This hard-headedness demolished the old, more familiar ways of doing business meaning deals would no longer be done on the strength of a handshake. For a Freemason like Henry Ford[158], history might indeed be bunk, but when it came to negotiating with a con-

---

158 Ford joined Palestine Lodge, No. 357, at Detroit, Michigan in 1894.

tractor supplying nuts and bolts to Ford Motors, he now demanded that a strict deadline had to be met.

As Ford was starting to crank up the gears toward what would become Ford Motors, the time had also come when a final date could be set for the completion of the country as a whole. Until now, variables had existed that complicated matters: one was the constant addition of new territory, the other the need to find enough people to fill these empty spaces. By 1898, however, these drawbacks had effectively ceased to mean anything, insomuch that territorial growth that would one day be hammered into individual states ended at this time, and areas of the country still at "territorial" level (i.e., with insufficient population to become States) were shrinking rapidly.

Fig. 29: The States in 1912

Already, States crossed the country from East to West, and the territories that were scantily inhabited were more than likely to achieve Statehood before long. It was therefore now possible to introduce a timetable for the completion of the Temple into the equation. The question was, should one timetable be used, to give an exact date for completion, or should several? On one hand, the use of a single timetable, though dramatic, would however leave open the possibility of failure for some unknown reason. A more cautious approach would be to employ several timetables, each based on the use of 'thirteen' and 'thirty-third' to identify a more general period when *Completion* and *Achievement* would arrive. The establishment of a date when the job could come to an end was therefore on the cards by the turn of the twentieth century: when either Hawaii or Alaska became the fiftieth state, and it would be up to the skill of men like the Masons to imbue date with as much symbolism as possible.

IV

At the beginning of their great enterprise, the Freemasons involved had at least one realistic aim chronologically: that the Temple be completed at a time that not only chimed with their own particular brand of numerical symbolism, but with that of the Bible too. Oglethorpe himself had illustrated how seriously this idea was being taken when he had left London, crossed the Atlantic, and then arrived at Yamacra Bluff during the evening of 1st February, 1733 in order to commence work on the "second day of the second month". The MP's actions therefore hinted at one overriding temporal theme his fellow Masons should follow: and that was, to be true to the Old Testament, then whatever year was chosen for *completion*, the month had to be an August, thus harmonizing with a further statement from *Kings*:

> And in the eleventh year, in the month Bul, which is the eighth month, was the house finished throughout all the parts thereof, and according to all the fashion of it.

— Kings 6:38

Events around independence had already shown that the "start" and "end" of a specific era, in length more than two human lifetimes, could be arranged to emphasis something symbolic. If this methodology was revisited and reprised after 1776, then by adding a further one hundred and sixty nine years onto American chronology brings us to the year 1945, which, in itself, was a highly symbolic year for the country — and the world — in that it marks the United States' emergence as a superpower and the leading nation of the "West".

Birth: The Colonial Era	From 1607 to 1776	*One Hundred and Sixty Nine years, the square root of which is thirteen*
Growth: The National Era	From 1776 to 1945	*One Hundred and Sixty Nine years, the square root of which is thirteen*
Maturity: The Superpower Era	From 1945 to the Present	?

However, the year that America first gained superpower status still didn't mark the completion of the United States as a building. Two territories were still to join, and both on the western extremities of the structure. These — Alaska and Hawaii respectively — were unique in that not only were they physically disconnected from the contiguous USA, but as an Island group and the largest territory of all, were destined to impact on the countries underlying geometry too. As their populations expanded, the day would come when they had every right to join the Union, with status equal to the other forty eight states, but with an economic downturn to tackle however, and internal and external forces opposed to their respective statehood powerful enough to thwart the process in the short run, by 1940 the idea of statehood still seemed a far way off.

But more recent events, concocted thousands of miles away, had raised the issue like never before. A measure of vulnerability mixed with strategic importance had characterized Hawaii and Alaska's role during the recent war with Japan, something that stayed in the minds of military planners as they balefully plotted the moves of another superpower across the Pacific, the Soviet Union, and the potential possibility of a third, Red China. The Communist threat — as well as the demands of the local population and burgeoning local economies — was to have a significant effect on the completion of the Union of fifty states, though what was virtually no-one was to know was that it was also to be done in accordance with words that were probably written nearly three thousand years earlier.

For a further timetable existed that harmonized perfectly with of all of the inspirational imagery and scientific, architectural precedent be they Biblical, Masonic or Mathematical in nature. The Key to this chronology actually lay in the oldest source of all, the Old Testament, where the *Book of Kings* states that the original Temple took Seven years to build, starting in the "the month Zif, which is the second month" and ending in "the month Bul, which is the eighth month". Obviously, a building program lasting seven years in total couldn't be repeated in 1733, simply because of the scale of the project, which was going to take centuries to complete. Something new had to be called for — a combination of "symbolisms" if you like — but still based on the imagery so far.

On this occasion the Mason's ritual couldn't help, because as a specification solely determining the geometry underpinning the structure, it didn't concern itself with the actual date or time of building: that was for the men on the ground to work out. This avenue being closed off therefore, there was only one other source that could be called on: the Biblical description of the construction in *Kings* and *Chronicles*, which, as already mentioned, did offer a guide where it states:

> And in the eleventh year, in the month Bul, which is the eighth month, was the house finished throughout all the parts thereof, and according to all the fashion of it. So he was seven years in building it. — Kings 6:38

Whilst "he was seven years in building it" offers up a specific time, the usage of such a chronological entity does require some clarification. Firstly, taking the timescale from *Zif*, the second month, to *Bul*, the eighth, suggests that the original Temple actually took seven *and a half* years to build rather than a straight seven. As a rule however, the Bible routinely makes a habit of rounding years up or down, rather than a more exact description. It therefore follows that for anyone hoping to emulate Biblical precedent, sticking to "seven" would be the more accurate way of doing things. The second point is that the time it took to build the original Temple wasn't any kind of deadline — or described as such in the *King James* Version — but merely a statement of what transpired. So, in theory, there was no real reason why anyone should stick to this timescale anyway. To be true to this "seven years" directive, the new Temple would either have to be built in that time, or a multiple of it.

Obviously, seven alone wasn't used for the straightforward reason the Temple would have had to be completed sometime around August, 1740, when Patrick Tailfer and the other Georgia dissidents were cooling their heels in Charleston. Neither was seven times thirteen acceptable, for this would dictate the building be raised and finished sometime around the year 1824, an era when Andrew Jackson and James Monroe were still applying the finishing touches to the Eastern seaboard.

The most sensible and obvious mathematical formula that existed was, therefore, the multiplication of "seven years" by the symbol of achievement, "thirty-three", which added up to a grand total of two hundred and thirty one. This may appear to be an odd number, but when conjoined with the foundation year, 1733, totals up to the following:

$$1733 + 33 \times 7 = 1964$$

Of course, "thirty-third" couldn't really be applied without its partner, and it was again symbolically significant that when the figure of two hundred and thirty one was divided by thirteen, then a numeral highly iconic in American history came to the fore:

$$231 \text{ divided by } 13 = 17.76$$

Throughout the construction, the builders had of course, traditionally favored "thirty-third" over "thirty-three" in their mark, just in case some flexibility was needed. This meant that it was during the last seven years of the "thirty three ties seven" cycle where, to achieve maximum impact, the final date of completion should be secreted, or to put it another way, between 1957 and 1964. The pinning down of the end into a seven year window didn't inevitably mean that an even tighter timescale couldn't be drawn up. An industrialist like Henry Ford would have understood and worked on the principle, that the more ruthless he could be with his deadlines, the better it would be for business, and it therefore follows that for men determined to make their building as symbolically as tight a construction as possible, they would squeeze as much out of the possibilities they still had to play with. So it was that the ideal time would be an "eight month" — an August — to chime correctly with Biblical imagery, and again, everything fell into place, for there was one August in the seven years between 1957 and 1964 that could indeed be "worked" as a symbolic representation of "thirty-third":

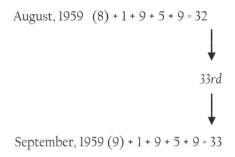

August, 1959 (8) + 1 + 9 + 5 + 9 = 32

33rd

September, 1959 (9) + 1 + 9 + 5 + 9 = 33

And what of the actual date itself? The Book of Kings had been oddly vague about this point, in contrast to the "second day of the second month" precision applied to the start of construction; but which, in essence, conversely gave the men charged with completion *carte blanche* to pick a day loaded with maximum significance. And this they did, for there was indeed one day in the eighth month of the non-leap year of 1959 that bore — in part — the signature "thirty-third", and this was the two hundred and thirty third day of the year: 21st August, 1959.

Chapter 11. "...And Covered the House with Beams and Boards of Cedar..."

> "I've got every degree in the Masons that there is." —
> Harry S Truman, thirty-third President of the United States

I

Mrs. Frances Cleveland had supreme confidence in the political abilities of her husband, the twenty-second president, Grover Cleveland. Indeed so much, that, in the aftermath of Cleveland's defeat in the election of 1888, she instructed the White House staff to take good care of the ornaments and furniture, "for we are coming back just four years from today". Mrs. Cleveland's optimism and ability to predict the future was fortuitous, for the incoming administration — that of twenty-third President Benjamin Harrison — was doomed to go down in American history as a monumental non-event. Four years on, and frustrated beyond measure, the people were again looking for change, and a canny Democratic party was astute enough to re-nominate Cleveland, who returned triumphant to 1600 Pennsylvania Avenue at the following election.

Of course, there was nothing particularly odd about Grover Cleveland's political comeback, taking place as it did in a mature democracy like America. As the first Democratic candidate to be elected to the Presidency since the Civil War, Cleveland had worked to distinguish himself during his first term especially as an opponent of political corruption, and his fall from office in 1888, even though he had won the popular vote, only happened because he found himself on the wrong side of an argument over tariffs. Due to his personal honesty and Harrison's mediocrity, there was no reason why Grover Cleveland could not reverse the 1888 result four years later.

The Constitution was sympathetic to the idea of a comeback as well. The law as it stood in 1892 didn't say how many — or in what order — a sitting or former President should serve his terms, and even when amended following Franklin D. Roosevelt's historic four election victories in a row, future holders — now reduced to a maximum of two terms — still weren't obliged to serve consecutively. Even so, for Grover Cleveland, victory, defeat, and victory again meant he was destined to became one of those American Presidents of whom it is said "The only President to...", for like Andrew Jackson's cows grazing on the White House lawn, or James Buchanan's bachelor status, Grover Cleveland was — until now — the only president to return to the White House having lost it in a previous election.

Apart from its role as a political curio, one side effect of Cleveland's non consecutive terms was that he was not only the twenty second president, but the twenty fourth too. For a society founded on the basis of numbers, this was indeed a curious state of affairs, and one with implications for every President since, because the sitting President always numbers one less in terms of being the *person* in Office. This has been the case since 1892, and will continue as long as the Republic in its present form exists; though it also meant, for good measure, that the thirty-third President would in turn be followed by the thirty-third person in Office.

How apt then that the Office effective from that moment in March 1789 when George Washington swore the oath of allegiance on the Bible belonging to Saint John's Masonic Lodge[159], New York, should, during the thirteenth period of thirteen years of its existence — 1945 to 1958 — be occupied by Harry S. Truman and Dwight D. Eisenhower, thirty-third president and thirty-third person to be president respectively. *Completion* and *Achievement* had permeated into America's imagery as far as the

---

159 The same Bible has been used by several presidents, namely Harding, Eisenhower, Carter and George Bush Sr.

numerical symbolism of the head of state, although for the record, only Truman was a "brother", albeit a prominent one, having got, in his own words, "every degree in the Masons that there is".[160]

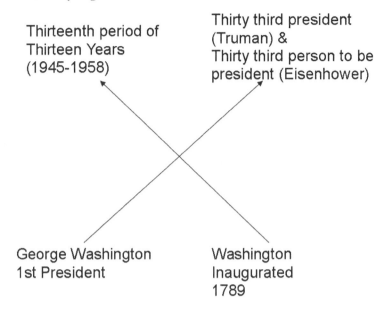

Fig. 30. The Presidency.

For the thirty-third President, the decision to drop the atomic bomb on Japan was probably the hardest one he ever had to make. Superficially it made sense, in that it delivered a knockout blow to an empire which through its use of Kamikaze pilots had already shown the American military it wasn't going to surrender the Japanese mainland without a colossal fight. Then there were wider strategic considerations to think about as well, for Harry S Truman and his administration were painfully aware that British and American troops, though victorious in Western Europe, now faced a battle-hardened Army three times their size in the Eastern Zone of Germany. It wouldn't do any harm to remind Stalin, via Hiroshima and Nagasaki, that America not only had a card up its sleeve that couldn't be trumped in conventional terms but a President who was prepared to use it, too.

---

160 Truman was a thirty-three degree Mason.

Truman probably recognized that the Atomic bomb, or more specifically its detonation in an offensive sense, carried within it an enormous symbolic value too. This wasn't just because it illustrated in no uncertain terms, that for the first time America was ahead of the curve when it came to technology, but in other, more subtle ways as well. One obvious example of this was that it showed everybody, and not just Stalin, that the science of destruction had taken a quantum leap forward, when compared to what gone before, and the very future of civilization was at stake; whilst another was it was a clear example of how a political decision taken in the modern, more complex, World often had more than one meaning, each subtly attuned to the audience it was meant for.

Regardless of who was symbolizing what to whom, the post-war years were certainly a period of *completion* and *achievement* for America. Truman inherited from FDR in 1945 a country far stronger and more influential than it had been a mere five years earlier, and unlike Great Britain or France, both battered and practically bankrupt, the USA not only came out of World War II virtually unscathed but had also watched its industrial output double in the process of doing so. This was quite a reversal of fortunes, for back in 1940, the economy had still been technically depressed; and, for all its great size, the United States was still a relatively small player in international affairs. Now, five years later, and due to its role as "the arsenal of democracy" and overall contribution to the War effort, America had usurped Britain to become the most important element in the Western alliance.

A renewed confidence also led to a reversal of the isolationist foreign policy that sufficed until the war. Whilst Britain's empire was beginning to fall apart, Truman, following Teddy Roosevelt's advice to speak softly and carry a big stick, started to flex American muscle in pursuit of global interests. The "speaking softly" came in the guise of a far greater willingness to engage with the rest of the world, primarily through US membership of institutions like the United Nations and in other, more direct ways, such as the Marshall Plan, which provided money to rebuild the shattered economies of Western Europe. The "stick" loomed large in the background too — primarily in the shape of the military's new toy, the atomic bomb — but also in more assertive policies as well, such as the

1947 Truman Doctrine, which had been designed to contain America's newest, and most persistent bogeyman, Soviet Communism.

Ten years later, and still free of invasion by either the Russians or flying saucers, the United States, now Presided over by Dwight D. Eisenhower, was apparently at the zenith of its power and influence. The undisputed leader in the West, Eisenhower's administration was powerful enough to bang Britain and France's heads together over the Suez crisis and keep the Russians pinned down behind the Iron Curtain at the same time. At home, meanwhile, a deeply conservative political culture was at least relieved by a year-on-year rise in the standard of living. By 1957, the United States found itself setting the standard for the rest of the world when it came to consumerism: American incomes, car ownership, and a thousand or more other things were leaving everyone else, especially the older powers of Western Europe, struggling to catch up. This was a society completely at ease with itself, confident, conservative — and complacent.

A political decision that again fused symbolism and science reared its head when, on the 4th October, 1957, the Soviet Union launched *Sputnik 1* into space. This achievement by the world's other superpower came as a terrible shock to the American public, who had long fallen for the cozy but naive assumption that their technology was pre-eminent across the globe. Traumatized by the sudden loss of prestige as well as the possibility of nuclear destruction raining down from above, a shaken Eisenhower, refusing to believe *Sputnik*'s success was down to "their Germans being better than our Germans", countered by pumping unprecedented amounts of cash and support towards scientific research, development and education across the board, and creating new agencies such as NASA in an attempt to "catch up" with the supposed Soviet menace.

Urgency was also permeating other unresolved issues facing the Republic. Whilst American TV circa 1957 had fallen into the habit of dishing out to its audience a vision of life free from major controversy, Eisenhower's administration couldn't escape the matter of the Union's greatest embarrassment: race relations. The President, amiable and well meaning, had signed into law a half-hearted Civil Rights Bill in September; but also had a taste of how toxic this issue could be when, two weeks later, he was forced to call out the 101st Airborne Division to ensure that nine black students enrolled at the Central High School in Little Rock, Arkansas, and if this wasn't bad enough, race also took on an international dimension when, a few days after *Sputnik*, Eisenhower had to apologize to Ghana's Finance Minister, Komla Agbeli Gbdemah, after the latter was refused service in a Delaware restaurant.

The need to court representatives of newly independent nations in the face of Soviet scientific prowess also turned the administration's attention to an issue unresolved since Eisenhower was a twenty-one year old student at West Point. For the country *Sputnik* flew over unmolested was itself an edifice needing further work to finish it architecturally. This was a task now invested with some urgency too, seeing that one of the unused "stones" actually abutted Soviet territory, and alongside America's sudden zeal to roll up its sleeves and get on with the job of screwing the nuts and bolts of its own space program into place, the time had now come for the last two territories, Alaska and Hawaii, to accede to the Union.

II

Just over ninety years earlier, the end of the Civil War had removed two of the last obstacles to Union expansion. Every politician in the land knew that the constant political compromise characterizing the creation of new states — the "one for one" deal between north and south — was defunct now that Ulysses S. Grant and the rest of the Union army had secured victory over the Confederacy, whilst the other, strategic considerations, was also largely irrelevant, because the need to ward off Mexican and British-Canadian aspirations in the West — important as recently as the statehood of Texas and California — was again redundant now that the United States had showed through force, it was, by far, the largest military power on the western side of the Atlantic.

States could now be laid like tiles across a concrete floor, and by the last third of the nineteenth century, apart from scattered and uncoordinated resistance from Native American tribes, only time and settlement stood between the dream of Franklin, Jefferson and John L. Sullivan and its eventual realization. Certainly, the raw material behind settlement, people, existed in abundance, and would increase year on year. Americans numbered something like thirty million[161] around 1865, and even though this was an impressive increase on the 1850 figure, it would, in turn, pale into insignificance compared to what occurred during the next thirty years, when the census takers would begin to calculate numbers approaching ninety million.

Whilst some of this explosion was due to natural causes common to Western societies in the second half of the nineteenth century, plus, for the first time, the recognition by the census of the correct number of African Americans, by far the greatest contribution to growth was from people seeking entry into the country. Up until 1860, immigration was still characterized by people hailing from north-west Europe, but afterwards began to be complimented by others, in ever increasing numbers, from further afield, such as Southern and Eastern Europe, Africa, Asia, and Latin America, until, by 1907, over one million people a year were entering the United States.

Naturally, most immigrants would be soaked up by the giant sponge that was Industry and Commerce; but a significant number of people — newcomers and native born, black and white — headed west to try their luck in the "Wild West." Such adventurism didn't even entail the hassle of carting a covered wagon halfway across the continent any more, for where James Gadsden had failed, others succeeded in building the first trans-continental railway, linking San Francisco with the east from 1864 onwards. Now, with no major cities more than a few days away from one another, the West was quickly tied together with the east as a single, cohesive whole; and by 1890, the Surveyor General of the United States could, with authority, state the frontier was "closed"

It was therefore inevitable that 1890 was also the year it first became possible to cross America from coast to coast by way of fully fledged states. The honor for making this possible fell to Idaho, whose own accession that year also finalized the line up along the border with Canada. In itself, Idaho statehood was part of a process that had again been gathering speed since the closing days of the civil war, for between 1864 and

---

161 Taken as an average between the 1860 and 1870 US censuses.

1890, the West was carved up into the political map familiar to the present day. Nevada got off to an early start, becoming a state in 1864, in turn followed by Nebraska in 1867, Colorado in 1876, North and South Dakota, Montana and Washington, all in 1889, and Idaho and Wyoming, 1890, Utah 1896, Oklahoma 1907, with New Mexico and Arizona being slotted into place to complete the map of the contiguous Union in 1912.

Thanks to the density of population[162] and the requirements of the Constitution, the result was an emerging checkerboard of provinces from the Atlantic to the Pacific, aligned between, and around, the thirty-third and forty-fifth parallels. By the time Arizona took the plunge and became a state on the 14th February, 1912, nowhere else on the surface of the Earth resembled as closely a tiled floor, and specifically another section of the *Explanation*, the description of a Masonic Lodge written at least a century earlier:

> The Mosaic Pavement may justly be deemed the beautiful flooring of a Freemason's Lodge, by reason of its being variegated and chequered[163].

With an alignment based east–west along parallels 33 and 45, it stands to reason that the North-South halfway mark of this particular floor — the 39th degree line of latitude — should in itself illustrate some form of architectural symbolism related to the whole structure: but it

---

162 It is noticeable that comparable sized nations with much smaller populations — such as Canada and Australia — are broken up into a much smaller number, but far larger, states and provinces.

163 *The Perfect Ceremonies of Craft Freemasonry.* Bernard Jones gives an extensive summary of the possible origins for this feature where he says: "In the absence of all the links of evidence, we are left to conclude that, with the passing of the painted floor cloth or even much earlier, the need arose of a carpet, and this was ultimately met by the mosaic patterned or chequered carpet, woven with its own tessellated border, with which we are all familiar, and which traditionally, but hardly historically, represents the pavement of King Solomon's Temple. The black and white alternating squares are said to symbolise the chequered life of man. The tessellated pavement of square dies, or tesserae, of tile or stone, was common in ancient buildings. The remains of Roman buildings provide many beautiful examples, in some of which the tesserae were arranged to form geometric figures. Pavements of this design were much in vogue in Damascus. We read in the Book of Esther that "the couches were of gold and silver, upon a pavement of red, and white, and yellow, and black marble. These were a feature of some English Churches (Glastonbury)" Source: *The Freemasons' Encyclopedia, pp.398-399*

doesn't. Part of the reason for this is that whilst the thirty-third and forty-fifth parallel lines define the contiguous United States according to Lambert's theorem, they are in fact an *average*, for the geographical extremities of the forty-eight states collective differ quite considerably over the three thousand miles from the east to the west coasts.

Starting on the Atlantic seaboard, the southernmost point of the Florida Keys rests at twenty-four degrees twenty-seven minutes north; whilst at Maine in the northeast, the northernmost point lies at forty-seven degrees twenty-eight minutes. In the east, therefore, the halfway mark between these extremities falls just south of the thirty sixth parallel; whilst on the Pacific, the political boundaries of the United States start and finish further north: from the southernmost point of California (thirty-two degrees and thirty-two minutes) to the border with Canada (the forty-ninth degree line) the half way mark is the forty-first degree: a full five degrees difference from the east.

Being a skewed structure, this meant that whatever the center of gravity was across the contiguous United States, it wasn't the thirty-ninth parallel. Nevertheless, there still had to be one, for this was indeed a man-made, designed construction. Too much time and effort had been spent in getting it right over the previous one hundred and twenty odd years too allow the building to be off center, and indeed a center of gravity did exist, again illustrated by a symbolic interpretation of a construction technique thousands of years old.

Throughout the history of Architecture, the tried and tested method of finding the gravitational center of an irregular shape has been by use of a plumb line or plumb bob. At its most straightforward, this device is simply a length of string with a weight attached, that when suspended from some high point in a structure, gives a true reading of the point of gravity at ground level. For increased accuracy, the weight is usually pointed, like a pencil; and was, originally, made of lead, hence its name, derived from the Latin for that metal, *Plumbum*, and which in turn has given rise to other phrases and words in English, such as "to plumb the depths", and plummet.

Although the name of the "bob" probably first appeared in Britain thanks to the importation of the Norman French word *Plomb*, this simple but effective vertical reference line has been an architectural tool since the days of ancient Egypt. Ptolemy understood its principles, as did Roman and Arab architects; whilst in slightly more modern times, William of Sens almost certainly used it at the rebuilding of Canterbury Cathedral; as did Sir Christopher Wren, when he was busy constructing new churches in the aftermath of the Great Fire of 1666.

Wren, of course, made his greatest use of the plumb-line when building Saint Paul's Cathedral. This edifice, with its soaring arches and dome, *had* to be raised in a true relationship with the center of gravity. The plumb bob was therefore the ideal tool to achieve this; for it, by its nature, was perfect for measuring the center of a feature incorporating an open space beneath it, such as stonework above an arch.

When it comes to finding the gravitational center of the Contiguous United States, the tools of the surveying trade, rather than bits of lead and string, are called for. Here, the Theodolite is the instrument of choice, for it had long proved its worth in providing tight geographical definitions. Although the dimensions Wren would have had to master: height, depth and gravity are redundant in this scenario, they are replaced with others of a more cartographical kind: size, space, and position in relation to east and west. This wasn't to mean that some kind of symbolic string had to be extended across the country: rather it suggested the recognition of a specific architectural feature in the east, and its successful alignment with a further feature in the west.

Logically speaking, the only place a symbolic plumb-line could realistically be seen to run from was America's west coast. The east had to be ruled out because the fifteen state line-up represents the beginning of the building — its lowest level, so to speak — and is grafted onto a natural feature stretching all the way from Key West to the northernmost tip of Maine. By contrast, that region of the United States covered by the states of California, Oregon and Washington was the end result of the treaties of Oregon and Guadalupe Hidalgo, signed between Polk and Buchanan on one hand and representatives of the British and Mexican governments on the other. For all extents and purposes, therefore, the west is the only coastal strip that can be employed as a point to define the center of gravity, for, unlike the east, its limits are man-made.

The obvious point to run a line from would be equidistant from the northern and southern boundaries of the Pacific coast: at equal distance from the borders with Mexico and Canada. This is the 41ˢᵗ parallel, which, when run directly east, cuts through the following states:

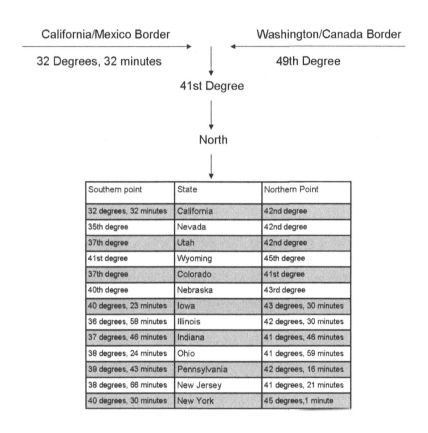

Southern point	State	Northern Point
32 degrees, 32 minutes	California	42nd degree
35th degree	Nevada	42nd degree
37th degree	Utah	42nd degree
41st degree	Wyoming	45th degree
37th degree	Colorado	41st degree
40th degree	Nebraska	43rd degree
40 degrees, 23 minutes	Iowa	43 degrees, 30 minutes
36 degrees, 58 minutes	Illinois	42 degrees, 30 minutes
37 degrees, 46 minutes	Indiana	41 degrees, 46 minutes
38 degrees, 24 minutes	Ohio	41 degrees, 59 minutes
39 degrees, 43 minutes	Pennsylvania	42 degrees, 16 minutes
38 degrees, 66 minutes	New Jersey	41 degrees, 21 minutes
40 degrees, 30 minutes	New York	45 degrees,1 minute

Fig. 31 The geometrical center of the contiguous USA.

The importance of this symbolic "plumb line" wasn't simply that it cut through thirteen political sub-divisions from west to east, but how neatly it bisected one state in particular: Pennsylvania. Situated between thirty nine degrees forty three minutes north and forty two degrees sixteen minutes — two degrees and thirty-three minutes wide — the 41ˢᵗ parallel plumb line runs straight through the middle of the Keystone, and by extension, the symbolic arch across the eastern seaboard too. Polk and Buchanan, aided by the surveyors who divided the 41st parallel into thirteen states, had therefore correctly identified the center of gravity of the building and acted accordingly, by aligning it with the arch in the east.

Even so, with the correct center of gravity now identified, running from the "top" of the structure, the west coast, straight through the center of Pennsylvania at the bottom, the Keystone still didn't exhibit the usual signature "thirty-third" marking the *achievement* of successfully completing another section of the overall work. This apparent omission was however, exactly in keeping with the emerging architectural *rationale* underpinning the whole United States, for, as Christopher Wren, Inigo Jones or any other architect well knew, the Keystone would only come into its own when the whole structure was finished. Occupied by people of "all nations" by 1912, and its entrance and floor completed and correctly aligned, the time was fast approaching for the roof to be put onto the Temple.

III

Six weeks after the *Ann* and her motley cargo of adventurers, farmers and "broken shopkeepers" landed in Georgia, an expedition struck out from Saint Petersburg that would mark the first European contact with the future America's most north westerly state, Alaska. The expedition was led by Vitus Bering, a Dane who, back in 1703, had opted to spend his life working for the navy of the Russian Tsar, Peter the Great. Working for Europe's foremost autocrat wasn't such an extreme step as it might first appear, for Bering was entering the service of a ruler who would not be remembered as "the Great" for nothing. Peter had travelled across Europe as a youth, and had seen with his own eyes how progressive the continent was in comparison with his own domains. Returning home determined to drag Russia into the enlightenment transforming the west, Peter the Great was therefore a keen advocate of importing ideas, and people with ideas, into Russia to shake up his moribund Empire.

Although some aspects of the Tsar's modernization program, such as the mandatory shaving off of beards, encountered resistance, no one quarreled with the idea of, for the first time, a proper accounting of Russia's lands to the East. To this end, he had already sent a German scientist, Daniel Gottlieb Messerschmidt, to roam around western and central Siberia from 1720 onwards, and whilst the expedition was a success, in that Messerschmitt brought home a great deal of information regarding the natural and human characteristics of the region, it still didn't answer the question of how far the Empire extended. Well aware that other European powers were starting to poke around in the Pacific, especially regions he could call his dominions, Peter the Great realized it was imperative that Russia joined in as well.

Just before his death in February, 1725, Peter signed an order creating the basis for an expedition to map the reach of the Empire to the east. Apart from obvious military overtones, this expedition again had a scientific twist: specifically the mapping of Russia's Arctic and Pacific coastlines. This was a particular Russian ambition a long time in the planning, because even as early as 1575 rumors began circulating about a channel between the Eurasian and North American landmasses, something still not confirmed one hundred and fifty years later, despite knowledge of the explorations of Semyon Dezhnev, who had actually sailed through this passage of water back in 1648. The reconnoitering of this channel was therefore essential to Peter the Great, for not only would it define Russia to the east, but also confirm whether a northern trade route to the Pacific was possible.

On this occasion, it was the Dane, Vitus Bering who led the expedition supported by his able deputy, Alexei Chirikov. The mission was another great success: Between 1728 and 1729, the two plotted the Pacific coastline from the deck of the *Saint Gabriel*, a ship especially built for the purpose. Their findings indeed pinpointed the limits of Siberia — East Cape — as well as the stretch of water destined to separate Russia from the United States along the one hundred and sixty ninth parallel line of longitude: the Bering Strait. Returning to Saint Petersburg by 1730, Bering was ennobled by the new Tsarina, Anna, who, impressed with Bering's discoveries, ordered a second expedition. The "Great Northern Expedition" as it would come to be called, was to be a far larger affair, with over three thousand individuals involved in its execution at one point or another. An idea of its size — and how effectively the autocratic Russian state could marshal resources — is indicated by the sums of money involved in its execution, for the government spent something like one and a half million rubles on the project, equating to approximately one sixth of the entire state budget for 1724.

Bering divided his team into three groups: the first was charged with mapping the coastline of Siberia, in order to test the viability of a sea route to the Far East; the second was to assess the effectiveness of trading links with Japan, whilst the third, led by the Dane himself, was to explore the coastline of Kamchatka and the Ocean to the east. Each of these missions also had further roles to play: a number of European academics, lured to Russia by Peter's enthusiasm for the sciences, were called upon to provide information on the human, animal, plant and mineral features of the region, as well as an overall aim: the tying in of Siberia to the rest of the Empire.

This expedition wasn't destined to move with the speed of *Sputnik*, however. Bering arrived on the Pacific coast in 1735; and like the *St. Gabriel* seven years earlier, ships had again to be custom built at Okhotsk. These were the *St. Peter* and the *St. Paul*, and it was from the deck of the latter that Bering's deputy, Alexei Chirikov, first sighted Alaska on July 15th 1741, on what is today probably the west side of Prince of Wales Island. Several Russian parties landed on Alaska, taking back botanical and mineral examples to Saint Petersburg, as well as the otter pelts that, for the next century and a half, would be Alaska's main contribution to the world economy.

Vitus Bering wasn't to survive the journey home, but back in Saint Petersburg, his and Chirikov's discoveries created a sensation. Chirikov, as the sole survivor, took part in creating the first accurate map of Russia's eastern extremities, in the 1746 *Pacific Ocean*. The publication of this map and other discoveries were then disseminated in the manner usual for the time, and by the 1750s, they were being printed as *Russian Discoveries* by the London mapmaker and "Geographer to King George III", Thomas Jefferys. Thus, a further part of the jigsaw with respect to the North American Continent was fitted into place, making information on Alaska, and its position, available to any parties who may be interested.

A century later, the excitement that had greeted Bering and Chirikov's discoveries had curdled into disinterest on the part of Russia's attitude to its possessions in America. The Tsarist government, despite attempts at settlement, still hadn't achieved much in their province across the Bering Strait, with the possible exception of the destruction of the native Aleuts, and if truth be told Alaska was proving to be a bit of a nuisance. Like any European empire, some efforts had been made to exploit the natural resources found there — specifically sea otter pelts — but even at its height, Russian settlement only ever totaled a mere 700 people, hardly a match for the far more dynamic British style of imperialism, just over the border in Canada.

The British were a problem in more ways than one. Alexander II, Tsar from 1855 onward, had been rudely awakened to the weakness of his empire thanks to its mediocre performance during the Crimean War. Like Peter the Great before him, Alexander realized radical reform was needed, and new measures promoting industry and commerce, a proposed railway network, reform of the army, and the abolition of serfdom were all enacted within a few years.

The Tsar also recognized the vulnerability of Alaska. Afraid of losing it to the British through conflict, Alexander decided to sell the province to raise money for his domestic reform program instead. The Tsar tried to start a bidding war between the imperialist British and the Americans, who had already shown three times before they would buy their country if necessary. In 1859, however, the British weren't that interested, and neither was the United States Government, who probably reasoned that the purchase of such a large area would exacerbate the growing tensions between the north and south.

A world away from Alaska, and thirty years before Alexander II reform program a "runaway" by the name of Andrew Johnson made his escape from his master in South Carolina. On this occasion the enterprise was successful, for the escapee got right across the state line into Tennessee, where, after a legal challenge, he was free to remain, prosper, and eventually rise up the political ladder to become the seventeenth President of the United States. This was an adventure more akin to *Huckleberry Finn* than *Roots* though, for the future president was only running from an indentured apprenticeship to a tailor; and he was to remain a life-long supporter of the south and slavery.

Johnson's brief acquaintance with bonded labor had come about because of family tragedy rather than purchase. Born in 1809, the traumatic event of his childhood was the death of his father, Jacob, a stableman employed at *Casso's Inn* in the town of Raleigh, North Carolina. The expiration of Johnson senior left the family in highly straightened circumstances, and Jacob's widow, Mary, left with three young children to feed, was forced to eke out a meager living as a seamstress and weaver. Inevitably for a family living on the edge, the young Andrew Johnson was apprenticed to a tailor, in Laurens, South Carolina, from where he soon made his break for Tennessee.

Settling in Greeneville, Johnson took up the trade to which he had been apprenticed and married Eliza McCardle, the daughter of a local shoe maker. Eliza patiently taught her eighteen-year-old husband to read and write, and her efforts in turn helped to unlock his genetic inheritance, for Johnson's father. Jacob was not only the son of a preacher who hailed from the British Isles, but had also been heavily involved in public service in Raleigh, serving as a sexton and constable. It was in Greeneville therefore where Andrew's father and grandfather's influence started to assert itself, and when combined with the example set by fellow poor-boys-made-good Jackson and Polk, opened the door for Johnson to rise through political offices of the state and nation.

By 1857, Johnson was in Washington as one of Tennessee's two Senators, and though in many ways an archetypal Southerner, he still believed in the sanctity of the Union. This was a tricky position to be in as the Civil War approached, something Johnson's 'brother' James Buchanan knew only too well. It was, however, a point of view Johnson held fast to, and siding with Lincoln throughout the conflict, an unusual opportunity arose for the former tailor during 1864, because, as the only Southern senator to stay onside, Johnson was ideally placed to share the ticket with Lincoln as the vice presidential candidate. Duly elected in November, he found himself in the top job when, in the following April, John Wilkes Booth assassinated Lincoln at Ford's Theatre.

Whatever Johnson's presidency was going to be like, he was doomed to live in the shadow of his predecessor. Nonetheless, Johnson really didn't go out of his way to help himself, either, for many of his policies ran counter to what had been decided prior to Lincoln's death. Rather than helping the freed black population, he placed greater priority on bringing former Confederate opponents, and their attitudes towards race, back into public life with no strings attached. Like many administrations with internal troubles, Johnson therefore looked for achievement abroad, and here he met with some success, for the Johnson administration, and in particular the efforts of Secretary of State William H Seward, were not only instrumental in removing Napoleon III's phony empire from Mexico City, but more importantly for America's underlying architecture, he negotiated during 1867 with the Russian minister to the US, Eduard de Stoekl, the purchase of Alaska for $7,200,000.

Fig. 32 Russian territory in North America, 1860.

Seward, who had kick-started his own political career as a candidate for the short lived Anti-Masonic party[164], may have had cause to regret his contribution to America's territorial spending spree, because even though the acquisition of Alaska was generally well received, unlike Jefferson, Monroe and Gadsden's highly popular purchases, it became a subject of popular ridicule. "Seward's folly" "Seward's Icebox" and "Seward's Polar Bear Garden" were some of the kinder epithets applied by the press at the reputation of the future 49th state, for like the Russian tsars, nobody quite knew what to do with this isolated, frozen mass. Between 1867 and 1884 its management was tossed between the Army, Treasury and Navy respectively and even after it became the District of Alaska, Washington DC and nearly everyone else in America ignored it. Gold rushes in nearby Yukon in Canada (1896) and Nome three years later stirred some interest, but unlike the California rush fifty years earlier, temporary hunts for this precious metal failed to translate into permanent economic success.

Doubtless part of the problem was that for Americans, there was still plenty of land to be had in the "lower forty-eight states". Who would want an icy wasteland when you could have a decent-sized farm in, say, Wisconsin or Iowa, instead? And like any sensible people, most Americans preferred to stay inside the house, rather than camp out on the roof. Nevertheless, by 1900 some settlement and industry — in the form of fisheries, canning and copper mining — started to take root and with this the population slowly started to rise. But even after it passed the magic 50,000 figure around the start of World War I, statehood still wasn't on the cards, for when a statehood bill was introduced during 1916, it was treated with indifference by virtually everyone, soon sinking without trace.

There was even hostility to the idea of statehood for Alaska. In 1920, commercial interests in Seattle led by Senator Wesley L. Jones, pushed through the Jones act, which demanded that American goods could only

---

164 William Morgan was a Freemason from Batavia, New York who, in 1826, published *Illustrations of Masonry*, which purported to probably give away the secrets of the Order. Rumors of his subsequent murder sparked a huge anti-Masonic movement across America, knocking the organization back for decades, although in all probability Morgan ending up living in Canada.

be delivered from one American port to another in American built ships owned by Americans. Even though this looked highly patriotic, it did, as a side effect, tie Alaskan produce to Seattle merchants and ship-owners, who soon started to raise the cost of carriage, much to the consternation of Alaskans, who saw their wealth disappearing into Seattle's pockets. Twenty years on, Alaska was still the Cinderella of the United States, uninvited to the ball; though it was to be the intervention of some highly unlikely Prince Charmings who were to make the rest of America sit up and start to take Alaskan statehood seriously.

On June 3rd 1942, the Japanese launched an air raid on Dutch harbor, a US Naval base on Unalaska Island. The attack was repulsed, but a few days later three of the outer Aleutian Islands — Attu, Agattu and Kiska — were temporarily occupied by the invader. The first proper compromise of American territory since the war of 1812 outraged the rest of the country, and realizing Alaska's frontline status, the Roosevelt administration began to build military bases, highways and other infrastructural necessities. The population of places like Anchorage nearly doubled, and in the post war years the profile of Alaska continued to improve, especially when Oil was discovered on the Swanson River. There was now no further excuse for Alaska not to become a state, and faced with Russian satellites, if not bombers flying overhead, Dwight D. Eisenhower signed the Alaska statehood bill on the 7th July, 1958, which took effect on January 3rd of the following year.

IV

Like any formularized learning curve, basic craft Freemasonry breaks its teachings down into its component parts: the degrees of the Order. The first degree, Entered Apprentice, quite rightly concerns itself with the new initiate. The second, Fellow Craft, with the progress of the student, whilst the third, Master Mason, in one sense, "completes" an individual's learning, an achievement that has even entered the colloquialisms of the English language, as in "given the third degree."

Regardless of the changes wrought since the early eighteenth century, what titles they bear actually show is that for all extent and purposes, the "symbolic" Masons of King George II's England were again conscious of the need to imbue their ceremonial with as much "operative" imagery as possible. To them, the actual names of the degrees were just another surface to be "worked" to perfection, and in this endeavor they were largely successful, for the idea of a new member starting off as Apprentice, then Fellow, then Master, would have been as obvious to William of Sens as it would to Inigo Jones, Sir Christopher Wren, or for that matter, Frank Lloyd Wright.

Back in the 1730s, the creation of new names for degrees — at least with respect to the first few — wasn't too onerous, for all available evidence points to the first two having existed from a time long before the foundation of the Grand Lodge of England. Again, this makes sense, for in more straightforward operative times, all that was required was a classification that delineated that when an individual was still in training, he was an "apprentice" and when qualified, a "fellow". The creation of the third degree, Master Mason, closely follows this precedent, with the proviso that the learning curved is made up of three specific areas of knowledge, rather than the original two.

At this point there comes an abrupt departure from this pattern, for the next degree encountered by the ascendant Mason isn't named to indicate a specific level of knowledge, but rather a defined section of work incorporated into the Temple: the Royal Arch. So why should this be? In any conventional construction setting, especially a large job, titles like overseer, surveyor, architect or superintendant would, even three hundred years ago, indicated where a specific individual fitted into the great scheme of things, so an orderly progression through those titles would, theoretically, have been a rational course of action.

Naturally, one obvious and correct analysis of why the "Arch" degree comes fourth is that this may be a simple recognition of the historical chronology in which the Degrees were written and developed. As mentioned previously, available evidence points to rudimentary versions of the Entered Apprentice and Fellow Craft degrees existing prior to, and cotemporary with Prichard's *Masonry Dissected* in 1730, whilst the Master Mason degree started the process of emerging from the Fellow Craft around the same time. These in turn were followed by the Royal Arch, which first appeared at Montague's party sometime over the Christmas and New Year of 1734/35, making it the last in the sequence.

Desaguliers, as the chief symbolist and ritual writer of the Order, may of course have created the Royal Arch to emphasis the fact that the "new" degrees were organized in a manner — a cycle so to speak — that in itself represents a straightforward journey of a new stonecutter from initiation, through learning, to being fully qualified to work on the Temple. Here, the student Mason is introduced to the various aspects of the trade in the first three degrees: its correct application, and desire for geometry, regularity and beauty, until he reaches a level of knowledge that confirms he is now fit to start work on the Temple itself, and naturally, this work should normally commence at the entrance.

Desaguliers was, of course, also well aware that the ideal symbol was one that carried within it multiple meanings, with each facet showing itself depending on how one looked at it. The former refugee had already shown he meant business in this area by cramming the three degrees existent by 1734 with as much symbolism as possible; so it would be logical to assume the name of the Royal Arch, and its place in the Degree structure, also contains a deeper, more revelatory meaning. As a mathematician, religious scholar and lecturer in experimental philosophy, Desaguliers would have understood and concurred with the mystical idea of an arch acting as a gateway to a new life, though as a scientist, especially one writing Masonic ritual through the focus of the science of architecture, there is possibly a secondary reason why the Royal Arch came last: its role in architectural practice.

In this scenario, what the sequence of Masonic ceremonial basically says is that the value of the Arch cannot be truly appreciated until the building — the learning curve inherent in the first three degrees — is, to all intents and purposes, completed. By following this course of action, Desaguliers and his fellow ritual writers would be falling into line with the accepted thinking of the time with regard to the role of arches within architecture, something they couldn't really avoid considering the number of professional architects who were fellow "brethren" around 1730. Such men would've advised that the arch could only be tested with the full weight of symbolism bearing down on it, illustrating its true strength to the world, in the same way the weight of bricks and mortar would rest on a conventional Arch, though Desaguliers' architect brethren could've also added, for good measure, that in the case of the Palladian arch and its variants, one stone in particular would be required to take the strain: the Keystone.

Although the timing of Alaska's admittance to the Union points to it being the roof of this particular edifice, is this replicated where it really matters, in the geometry of the States? The answer lies, naturally, in the *impact* this section of the "Symbolic Building" had on the rest of the structure, and in a conventional "Physical" building, impact would of course, be measured in one straightforward way: weight. A roof that was too light would render the construction weak, in that sufficient pressure was absent over the "lower" sections, whilst at the other end of the scale, a roof too heavy would be liable, in time, to crash down on the rest of the structure with disastrous results. One only has to look at the ingenious methods employed by Sir Christopher Wren into getting the cupola of Saint Paul's Cathedral just right to see how important the correct weighting of the roof has been throughout Architectural history, so getting it right this time was again important, though the question remains, could such an important architectural principle, filtered through the prism of North American political geography, be recognizable in a symbolic form?

Of course, "weight" in its traditional, physical sense was meaningless, so it therefore fell to the nearest equivalent geometry could offer as a comparison, and of all the characteristics inherent in the mathematics of design, this could only be size. With square miles substituting for tons, hundredweights or pounds, Alaskan statehood provided the requisite gravity to hold the structure together, for weighing in at over half million square miles, *size* was one thing this particular territory had in abundance. This weight naturally exerted a downward pressure on the rest of its partners in the union: passing through the intermediate stonework, and coming to rest at the lowest level of the structure: the Arch at the entrance.

As mentioned before, mystical systems assign an arch two qualities. One of these is strength, in that this element of the structure bears the responsibility for holding up the building work above. The Keystone is obviously vital, as an arch — especially one in the "modern" Palladian style — cannot maximize its effectiveness without it. Substitute state size for stone, and look again at Pennsylvania. When in January 1959 the huge Alaska territory finally gained statehood, it automatically became the largest state. This meant that the running order in terms of size was now changed for the last time, and the USA was more or less (tiny Hawaii was still to join) in its final form. Texas, for over a hundred years the giant of the United States, was now pushed into second place and California into third. It also meant that Pennsylvania, the "Keystone State" sitting astride the "center of gravity" the forty-first parallel, now became the thirty-third largest state in the Union.

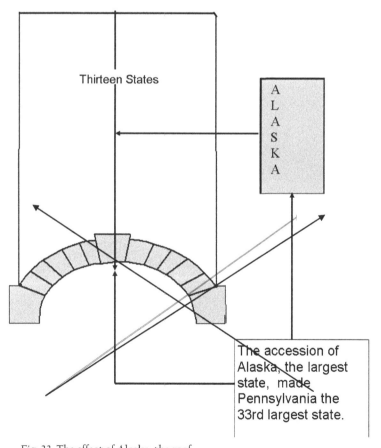

Fig. 33. The effect of Alaska, the roof

CHAPTER 12. "IN THE MONTH BUL, WHICH IS THE EIGHTH MONTH..."

> The Sphere with the parts of the Earth delineated on its Surface is called the Terrestrial Globe; and that with the Constellations and other Heavenly bodies the Celestial Globe Their principal use besides serving as Maps to distinguish the outward parts of the Earth and the Situation of the fixed Stars is to illustrate and explain the Phenomenon arising from the Annual revolution and the diurnal rotation of the Earth round it own Axis...but are also induced to apply with more diligence and Attention to Astronomy, Geography, Navigation and all sciences dependent on them which are equally useful to Society.

> — Fragment of (defunct) second degree lecture Masonic Ritual from Redruth, Cornwall, 1815 describing the two Globes that form part of the Ornamentation of a Masonic Lodge.

I

"When a man is tired of London, he is tired of life," observed Doctor Johnson, and with good reason. The City that had begun life as the Roman *Londonium* and seen out the Dark Ages as the Saxon *Londonwic* had by the year 1733, blossomed into a metropolis second to none. From here, a benign George II ruled an empire that already counted exotic places like Barbados, New York and Gibraltar amongst its dominions, and would rise, in less than a century and a half, to control a quarter of the Earth's surface, an Empire larger in area than that of Rome.

Under a skyline dominated by the soaring cupola of Wren's recently completed Saint Paul's Cathedral, there hummed a kaleidoscope of human activity: from the coffee shops through to the "men of fashion" through to John Senex, toiling to turn out another *Globe* for the inexhaustible curiosity of those with money to burn; where the satirist, painter and Mason William Hogarth was putting the finishing touches to *A Rake's Progress, a* series of eight engravings that charted the decline and fall of the fictional Tom Rakewell from rich merchant's son through marriage to a wealthy old crone, to debtor's prison, and eventually insanity in bedlam. This and other works by Hogarth illuminated the other London that lurked in the shadow of Christopher Wren's masterpiece: a place of gin-soaked old women, sewage in the streets, cut throats, whores and swindlers, a city where, on at least one occasion, the King himself was beaten up and robbed.

London in 1733 was also the home to the Reverend Desaguliers and his esteemed colleagues in the Royal Society. For the previous twenty-two years the "RS" had met in their own Offices in Crane Court, an alleyway just off the Strand and adjacent to Fleet Street. Unlike the previous meeting place at Gresham College in Oxford, the Society owned these premises, thanks to the initiative of the Royal Society's president in 1710, the great Isaac Newton, who had negotiated a price of £1,450 for the building from the previous owner, a Doctor Brown. Crane Court included a room "25½ foot long and 16 foot broad," a Wren designed Repository, other rooms, a small garden, coach-house and stables.

It was to this august location that Doctor Desaguliers made his way on two consecutive Wednesdays, the 21st and 28th of February, 1733. In all probability, he walked, for the distance from his home in Channel Row in Westminster to Crane Court was less than a mile. Nevertheless, he still would have to circumnavigate the booze soaked and the desperate, the detritus of night-time London, though if approaching from the direction of Fleet Street, he would have at least seen the welcome glow of the lamp hung over the courtyard entrance, which, when lit, indicated that the Society was in session.

On these last two Wednesdays in February 1733, it was Desaguliers himself who was penciled in to give the lecture. The Doctor was an old hand at this: from 1715, when he had presented a translation of the Frenchman Gauger's treatise *Fires improved: or, a new method of building chimnies*, he had stood before the fellows of the Society on many occasions. The Huguenot refugee was happy to conduct several experiments a year for the benefit of his colleagues, and English science in general, which included, amongst others, ideas to measure the elasticity of steel balls, the depth of the sea, and "a machine to draw damp or foul air out of mines".

The lecture Desaguliers had prepared for the February meetings aimed at an explanation of something higher than mines, namely the orbits of the planets of the known solar system, via a new invention of his, the Planetarium. The lecture was entitled "A Description of the Planetarium", which was destined to be included in volume one of his *A Course of Experimental Philosophy* published the following year. In this, the Doctor's style is highly evocative of the era, a kind of microcosm of what was happening all around, in that it was again an amalgam of science and superstition, although the quickening change of pace is also noticeable, as in Desaguliers use of both the Julian and Gregorian calendars on his invention, which the scientist also said was:

> Is fix'd in a Frame of Ebony about 6 Inches high, and 3 Foot in diameter, contain'd by 12 vertical Planes, on which are represented the 12 Signs of the Zodiac. The upper Surface is flat of polish'd Brass, on whose outward Circumference are screw'd in six Brass Pillars, which support a large flat silver'd Ring representing the Ecliptick, with several circles drawn upon it. The three innermost are divided into 12 Parts for the Signs of the Zodiac, each of which is divided into 30 Degrees; and among those Degrees are grav'd in their proper Places, the *Nodes, Aphelia,* and greatest North and South Latitudes of the Planets. Between the next two Circles are mark'd the Cardinal Points. The next three Circles have the Months and Days of three Months, according to the *Julian* Account; and the three last have them likewise engrav'd, according to the *Gregorian* Account...Upon the Brass Surface of the Machine , are graduated Silver Circles, which carry the Planets (represented by silver'd balls) upon Arbors or Stems, that raise them up to the Height of the Plane of the Ecliptick; and by turning about the Handle or Winch of the *Planetarium*, all the Planets move at their proportional Distances from a little gilt Ball in the middle, which

represents the Sun, and perform their Revolutions according to their periodical Times.

To be fair, Desaguliers' "Planetarium" wasn't an entirely new idea, because from Archimedes onwards devices existed that were engineered to mimic the movements of planetary bodies, and as time wore on, these mechanical models normally took the shape of a vertical pole with metal rods of different lengths projecting from its sides like spokes from a wheel. Atop each rod was an imitation planetary body, whilst the vertical pole was topped off with a model of the Sun. By the early eighteenth century, these mechanical models even had a particular name: *Orreries*, which were named after the Irish Peer, the Earl of Orrery, who had one built by a certain George Graham around 1704.

Mention is made of Graham at this point because one important fact about Desaguliers and his fellow enlightenment scientists was they were perfectly happy to share their discoveries with the rest of the World. Unlike later ages, where new inventions would become jealously guarded secrets until a patent had been agreed, the transcripts of the Royal Society were published for all to see, and such men were also conscientious when giving credit for any possible influence on their work. Desaguliers bookmarked George Graham in his *Description*; and even devoted a large part of the preface to *A Course of Experimental Philosophy* to another more famous personage:

> It is to sir ISAAC NEWTON's Application of Geometry to Philosophy that we owe the routing of this Army of Goths and Vandals in the philosophical World; which he has enrich'd with more and greater Discoveries, than all the Philosophers that went before him: And has laid such Foundations for future Acquisitions; that even after his Death, his Works still promote natural Knowledge. Before Sir Isaac, we had but wild Guesses at the Cause of the Motion of the Comets and Planets round the Sun; but now he has deduce'd them from the universal Laws of Attraction (the Existence of which he has prov'd beyond Contradiction) and has shewn that the seeming Irregularities of the Moon, which Astronomers were unable to express in Numbers, are but the just Consequences of the Actions of the Sun and Earth upon it, according to their different positions.

Whilst Desaguliers was happy to socialize with and name drop the great and the good, he also realized that the true value of his science lay in the number of people it could be brought to the attention of. As shown by the public lectures he had pioneered, he understood that knowledge shouldn't be the preserve of a few, and he felt it important to include a statement in *A Course of Experimental Philosophy* underlining that fact:

> By Help of such Machines, a great many Persons, who have not time to apply themselves to the Study of Astronomy, yet are desirous to be acquainted with the celestial Appearances, in a few Days may get a competent Knowledge of several Phaenomena, especially be cured of the common Predjudices against the Motion of the Earth.'[165]

Today, Desaguliers Planetarium would be viewed as a prime example of the inventiveness and ethos of the enlightenment, for the free sharing of ideas, in this case between Graham, Newton and the Doctor, had led to a scientific innovation that could indeed lead the masses towards a speedier and more accurate analysis of the night sky. Nevertheless, its use was limited by time, because, unbeknown to him, there were further planets to be spotted in the Solar System, the first of which wouldn't be found until thirty seven years after Desaguliers death, when, in 1781, Uranus was discovered by the German-born astronomer, Sir William Herschel, who, coincidentally, was elected to the Royal Society and awarded its Copley medal for his efforts.

II

With Desaguliers and possibly John Senex in the vanguard of recalibrating the Masons ritual and symbolism, it was inevitable that the ceiling of a Freemason's Lodge also came to exhibit a clearly defined images of the sky, at both day and night. In the center of the Lodge was a Star, which, according to the new ritual:

> ...refers us to the Sun, which enlightens the Earth, and by its benign influence dispenses its blessings to mankind in general...

What this symbol reinforces is the idea of the Masonic Lodge as the *Templum*, the sacred space open to the elements, which in itself is a further confirmation that the Temple being built by Speculative Freemasonry was again to be an open air phenomenon. This, which must have represented a Sunburst of some kind, was possibly a tapestry, or ornament fashioned from Copper or Brass. According to Bernard Jones, at one time the "Blazing Star" must have formed part of the Lodge floor, which makes sense when taking into account how lodges met at the time,

---

165 *A Course of Experimental Philosophy*, p.448

though the practice of marking out a tavern floor with chalk, and charcoal mentioned earlier, was gradually replaced (at least in some places) by the use of red tape and nails, giving a clue to the antiquity of this particular symbol:

> The change gave rise to ridicule, for we find a mocking advertisement of 1726 (quoted by Henry Sadler, the well-known Masonic historian) alluding to "*the innovations...introduced by the Doctor [probably Desaguliers, 3rd Grand Master] and some other of the Moderns, with their Tape, Jacks, Moveable Letters, Blazing Stars, etc. to the great indignity of the Mop and Pail.*[166]

The chronology of this — sometime in the 1720s — is also confirmed by another Masonic historian, Henry Coil, though he puts its addition a decade later:

> But whether the Blazing Star of Freemasonry refers to Saturn or the Sun or some other heavenly body is not ascertainable. The first mention of it in Masonic symbology occurred about 1735, when it was included in the furniture of the Lodge and occupied the center of the Mosaic Pavement forming the floor of the Lodge.[167]

The use of the "Sun" in this context isn't to say that Masonic ceilings didn't carry such decoration — or any other kind for that matter — prior to the eighteenth century overhaul of the Fraternity's symbolism. The problem about whether Lodge ceilings did, or did not, exhibit celestial imagery prior to 1717 is again down to the lack of evidence, not only because no "physical" Lodges from that era still exist, but also because early *exposes* — most noticeably Pritchard's *Masonry Dissected* — neglect to mention the concept of roof decoration anywhere. Everything points to the ceiling of the "Symbolic Temple" meaning little or nothing to the Masonic fraternity prior to the 1730s, which again contrasts sharply with the approach of the "new" Order, who saw in it another surface to be "worked", something again borne out by the Ritual, specifically the *Explanation, where it says:*

> The Heavens he has stretched forth as a canopy...the covering of a freemason's lodge is a celestial canopy of divers colors, even the heavens...the starry firmament, emblematically depicted here by seven stars...

"The starry firmament" illustrates a further celestial symbol: a depiction of the night sky, and again this makes sense, in that if the Lodge is

---

166 *The Freemasons' Guide*
167 *Coil's Masonic Encyclopedia*

indeed a *Templum*, then it should indeed represent the sky at night some-where in its imagery. The *Explanation*, written after the beginnings of the 1730s, does however, describes this feature in a far tighter way, as "seven stars" in total, a symbol that appears to have been adopted quite widely and quickly, as seen in the examples of eighteenth century Masonic im-agery shown below:

Fig.33 Examples of Masonic symbolism, showing the Moon and Seven Stars in conjunction.

Like so much Masonic imagery, there is again a plethora of theories as to the origins of his particular symbol. One of the more popular ideas has it that it represents the Pleiades group of stars, and their alignment on June 24th, 1717, the day of the founding of the Grand Lodge. This theory isn't particularly outrageous, considering Newton, assisted by the sym-bolism manufacturing Desaguliers, was working hard to tighten up As-tronomical data around this time. Even so, and accepting that it could indeed refer to another star group, the most obvious answer is that it is in reality a symbol of something far closer, and that is the subject of Desaguliers "Planetarium": the Solar System.

The invention of this particular device, its presentation to the Royal Society, and then inclusion in *A Course of Experimental Philosophy* was, of course, happening at precisely the same time Desaguliers and others were rewriting the ritual in the aftermath of Pritchard's *Masonry Dissected*. It stands to reason therefore that it may have been added — or refined — to again distance the Fraternity from what had gone before. Nevertheless, even if the "Seven Stars" is a depiction of the Solar System, it contains one monumental mistake that Desaguliers couldn't have been unaware of in 1733: and that was, until 1781, the known system of planets orbiting the Sun only contained *six* planets: Mercury, Venus, Earth, Mars, Jupiter and Saturn. This suggests that at some point in the future, and certainly after the discovery of Uranus in 1781, this specific item in a Masonic Lodge was altered to take account of the new line up in the night sky.

Apart from the chronology of its change from a "star spangled canopy" to "seven stars" in total, there are two further characteristics about the night sky element in Lodge symbolism that warrant attention: the feature it is always in conjunction with and its position within the Lodge. For the "seven stars" are always depicted next to, or surrounding the Moon. Superficially this is again logical — and bolsters the Fraternities claim to a scientific basis — in that it means the full solar system known about at the end of the eighteenth century features in the Lodge: the Sun, Moon and seven planets that were known about at the time, although this particular idea does again date the completion of this feature to sometime after 1781, and Herschel's discovery of Uranus. The second important point is this symbol's normal position within the Lodge: the West. This again, is logical, in that it is a representation of the night sky, which would occur as the sun set in the west, therefore acting as a balance so to speak, in that it indicates the Masonic lodge as being in existence during the night and day, as well as being a *Templum*, a consecrated place open to the sky.

Like so much of the "new" symbolism, the inspiration behind such a distinctive feature as a Seven Stars and Moon conjunction could again arise from a multiplicity of different origins. At its most superficial, the sky at night could have been added simply because of the craze for night sky ceilings that affected the interior design of British ceilings during the "Palladian" era. The first half of the eighteenth century was marked by the increasing use of star maps on the ceilings of many buildings in Britain, and whilst some of these were painted for purely decorative reasons, others were created for scientific purposes, a testament to the developments that had taken place in the science of astronomy during the previous one hundred and fifty years.

Even with the addition of Uranus, there is still one glaring discrepancy — or at least an alternative explanation — behind the Seven Stars symbol, and that is, when viewed from the Earth, the site of the symbolic Temple, again, only *six* planets would be in view after 1781, and they are Mercury, Venus, Mars, Jupiter, Saturn and Uranus, because the Earth was under the "brethrens" feet. The Seven Stars couldn't even represent the Solar System with the further addition of Neptune, for this planetary body wasn't discovered until 1846, a third of a century after the symbolism of the ritual and Lodge had been completed. This means that the idea of the 'seven stars' as a depiction of the solar system is fundamentally flawed, suggesting it must be an image of another system; unless its origin lies somewhere else entirely, and that the symbolism of one large cratered entity, accompanied by seven smaller ones, was, far from being a depiction of the sky at night, emblematic of something far more down to earth.

III

Three years before Herschel first spotted Uranus, on the morning of January 18th 1778, to be precise, Captain James Cook stood on the deck of HMS *Resolution*, and eyed the two most westerly of the Hawaiian Islands, Nihau and Kauai. The discovery was accidental, for Cook wasn't actually looking for islands or for that matter any other landmass in the vicinity, *Resolution* being en route for the Bering Strait, where Cook hoped to find the Holy Grail of North American exploration, the North West Passage. Like all great explorers, Cook fastidiously marked the position of the two islands, and then ordered *Resolution* to continue on its journey to the region first mapped and investigated by Vitus Behring and Alexei Chirikov thirty six years earlier.

Finding a passage between the Pacific and Atlantic above the North American landmass would have undoubtedly been another golden chapter in a career already boasting the formal discovery of both Australia and New Zealand amongst its achievements, but on this occasion Cook's touch deserted him, for his explorations above Alaska and Canada failed to add anything substantial to the earlier Russian discoveries. Gradually Realizing the futility of further searches, and the prospect of spending part of the oncoming winter within the Arctic circle, Cook turned southward in late 1778 to spend the winter charting the island group he had discovered earlier in the year. HMS *Resolution* arrived off the island of Maui on the morning of 26th November 1778, and Cook spent the next seven weeks mapping the coastline of Hawaii, and the seven smaller islands making up the rest of the archipelago.

By spending his time in this way, Cook was acting in strict accord with Admiralty policy. Ever since HMS *Porcupine* and *Raven* had sailed from England to look for military bases in the South Atlantic and Pacific Oceans during 1749, ships belonging to the Royal Navy had often found themselves seconded for voyages of discovery. This innovative approach to naval time and resources can be laid at the door of possibly the story's most interesting character, the First Lord of the Admiralty, Lord Sandwich. For not only was Sandwich to have the honor of having James Cook name the entire island group after him, but he was also the son of Viscount Montague, the Grand Master of the Masonic Order who had issued Henry Price with his deputation forty five years earlier.

Undoubtedly, Sandwich and other members of the Government looked forward to James Cook's return and the scientific knowledge that went with it. The Royal Society was always eager for information on native flora, fauna; new cultures and civilizations, plus maps that could be pored over by the learned of the day. Cook was certainly aware of this arrangement: witness his letter to the Royal Society describing in detail a solar eclipse off the Canadian coast, on August 5th 1766. This took place whilst Cook was charting the coast of Newfoundland as "The King's Surveyor", for Britain, in possession of Canada following the treaty of 1763, needed a detailed account of the coast for Admiralty charts.

Cook was, of course, destined never to return to England, dying of wounds incurred from an altercation with Hawaiian natives in 1779. Nevertheless, his journals, plants and charts did survive the journey back to Britain, arriving on board *Resolution* and *Discovery* early in 1781. As first Lord of the Admiralty, Sandwich convened and subsequently chaired a committee to edit Cook's Journal and maps upon their arrival in England. This was to be the last occasion that Sandwich was to chair such a committee, for he resigned as first Sea Lord later that year, and the Admiralty simultaneously dropped the policy of using Royal Navy vessels for voyages of exploration at the same time.

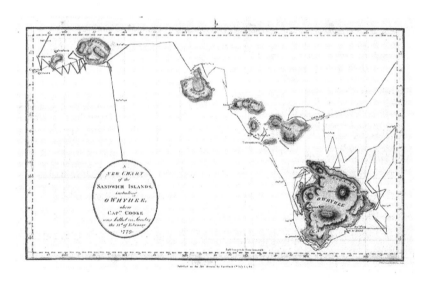

Fig.33: Harrison & Co. Map of the Hawaiian Archipelago, London, 1786

So the cartography of the Hawaiian archipelago in the shape of Cook's charts travelled the same path to the heart of the British establishment as all other natural features one day making up the United States. The maps, of one larger island studded with volcanic remains, accompanied by seven smaller ones, were duly added to the collections of the Admiralty, the Royal Society, and then published for anyone to see.

In some respects, the history of Hawaii after James Cook can be summarized as a gradual transfer for one English-speaking Empire to another. Nominally independent in the early days, the King, Kamehameha I, united the Islands for the time in 1810 with help from the English, assistance which the Islanders — or at least their chiefs — acknowledged by considering themselves a British protectorate, and still, in theory, independent. American influence began with the arrival of missionaries in 1820, who, though initially only allowed to stay for a year, were so successful in their proselytizing that they were allowed to carry on until, by the 1830s, Hawaii had been converted into a largely Christian nation. The importation of Western theology was complemented with Anglo-Saxon ideas of democracy, too. King Kamehameha III issued a Declaration of Rights in 1839, followed a year later by a Constitution, though the Hawaiian flirtation with Western ideas may have been moving too fast, for an 1848 law allowed Westerners to own land for the first time, leading to more and more of Hawaii being owned by Americans, British, and other nationalities.

The white man could own as much land as he wanted, but it wouldn't be much good unless Hawaii could be cajoled into a tighter trading relationship with one or the other of the nations with an interest in the Islands. By now — the 1870s — American power was clearly in the ascendant, for trading agreements signed between Hawaii and the United States between 1874 and 1875 allowed for the importation of duty-free sugar cane from the archipelago. Soon, bigger and bigger plantations started to appear, worked by Immigrants from Asian countries such as China and Japan. Although it was still an independent country, the cracks started to show, and fiscal and general incompetence shown by the King, David Kealakekua resulted in a *coup d'état* in 1887 which stripped the monarch of many of his powers and Asian immigrants of their right to vote.

Four years later, Kealakekua died and his sister Liliuokalani assumed the throne, from where she attempted to reverse the 1887 decision. In response, an alarmed group of European and American citizens resident in the Kingdom formed a "Committee of Safety" on January 14th 1893. The United States Ambassador, John L Stevens, colluded with the committee by claiming to be worried about possible threats to American lives and commercial interests, and went as far as to summon a company of uniformed US marines from the USS *Boston* and two companies of US sailors to land on the islands and take up positions on the afternoon of January 16th.

Besides the threatened loss of voting rights and concerns from business interests about the effect of the McKinley act, the Committee considered the idea of annexation to the United States, though for the mean time, realized a provisional government would suffice, and Liliuokalani, seeing the writing on the wall, abdicated in favor of the Committee of Public Safety. Although there was an inquiry into Stevens' and the military's intervention, resulting in Stevens' recall and the military commander's resignation, eventually the matter went the revolutionaries way, with a republic declared in 1894, under the Presidency of an American, Sanford Dole. With commercial opportunities hammering on the door of Dole's white businessman Republic, the time was fast approaching for Hawaii to be annexed to the United States.

The construction of the country had always been overseen by Masonic Presidents or their representatives, so it was inevitable this pattern would again occur during the annexation of Hawaii. The catalyst this time was America's twenty fifth President, William McKinley[168], who was a native of Ohio, and the last President to have served in the war between north and south. McKinley's time in office was marked on one hand, by a sympathetic attitude to the injustices being suffered by America's black population, whilst on the other there was the stirring of a new kind of imperialism, the American variety, especially after victory over Spain brought the Philippines, Guam and Puerto Rico under the direct control of Washington DC, and allowed for the American occupation of Cuba.

Oddly though, none of these territories would ever become states, but would exist in a sort of no-man's land as unincorporated territories, unable to make the move to full statehood. This wasn't to mean that Washington had finally gone off the idea of expanding its lands, or saw

---

168 McKinley became a Mason in Hiram Lodge No.21 of Winchester, Virginia in 1865. He was then a member of Lodges in Canton, Ohio.

too many difficulties in absorbing Pacific Island groups with largely Asiatic populations, for during McKinley's presidency, there would indeed be one new addition to the country's territorial portfolio, but it would be the last. This was independent Hawaii, which was annexed by the United States by a treaty signed on June 16, 1897, and after a few details were sorted out, like the prohibiting of Chinese laborers moving to the mainland, the group of one large island and seven smaller ones became an official US territory, and one step away from a full state, on April 30, 1900.

Like Alaska before it, Hawaii was another US territory that waited an inordinate amount of time for full statehood. Unlike Alaska however, where Seattle business interests and nationwide indifference were largely to blame, the reasons for delayed statehood for Hawaii was driven by factors peculiar to the Islands, rather than something external. With a near tropical climate, the future fiftieth state was ideal for the growing of products like sugar cane and coffee, and in the case of the latter, being the only US state to do so. Sugar was to be the mainstay of the Hawaiian economy, however, something that has traditionally been cultivated in a plantation environment, and by the beginning of the twentieth century the Hawaiian sugar industry had evolved to a point where it was dominated by five large companies: Castle & Cooke, Alexander & Baldwin, C. Brewer & Co., American Factors and Theo H. Davies & Co.

Statehood was the last thing these corporations wanted, for by ensuring Hawaii remained at the halfway house of territorial status, the "Big Five" as they came to be called, could take advantage of a whole host of commercial advantages denied to everyone else. One of these was the ease in which they could import workers from Asia, for the arrival of non-Europeans had already become an issue in many states on the mainland. It was therefore fortuitous for the sugar planters that territorial status meant there was no problem hiring cheap labor from Asia, and easy to hold onto them as well, as these laborers wouldn't find many job opportunities on the mainland. Having laborers drawn from countries as different as China, Japan, Korea, the Philippines and Puerto Rico also led to a further advantage for the sugar barons: and that was if one ethnic group went on strike, the others could be called on as strike breakers.

The Big Five were also able to take advantage of greater investment opportunities, for territorial status meant they could circumvent the high tariffs set by the Government on sugar brought in from non-US sources, like the Caribbean or Latin America. The above meant that by 1910, the "Big Five" had already vacuumed up political power on the islands, and would attempt to hold onto it. When fused with back scratching that was evident in mutually agreed prices for goods and services, what emerged was a *de facto* oligarchy that would dictate Hawaii's status until after World War II, leading the Attorney-General of the territory, former President Dole, to comment angrily in 1903 that:

> There is a government in this Territory which is centralized to an extent unknown in the United States, and probably as centralized as it was in France under Louis XIV.

One thing the "Big Five" couldn't however prevent was the number of people who were actually born on the islands. The children and grandchildren of the original immigrant plantation workers were, according to the law, full US Citizens, meaning that by 1945, a new militancy was abroad amongst the general population. In previous times, the "Big Five" could always count on the ethnic rivalry to sort their problems out, but this now began to fade, as more and more Hawaiian born realized they weren't leading the same kind of lives that their fellow citizens were on the mainland. Peaking in massive non-violent protests across the Islands in 1954, which broke the back of the sugar planter's ascendency, things were changing. Eisenhower, also mindful of covering his flank adequately in a theatre not too far away from Mao's China or the Soviet Naval base at Vladivostok, saw the writing on the wall for this territory that had always been so strongly Republican, and after an overwhelming referendum vote of ninety four percent in favor of statehood, signed a bill making Hawaii the fiftieth and final state on March 18th 1959, which took effect a few months later:

> Proclamation No.3309: the admittance of Hawaii into the Union

> WHEREAS the Congress of the United States by the act approved on March 18, 1959 (73 Stat. 4), accepted, ratified, and confirmed the constitution adopted by a vote of the people of Hawaii in an election held on November 7, 1950, and provided for the admission of the State of Hawaii

into the Union on an equal footing with the other States upon compliance with certain procedural requirements specified in that act; and

WHEREAS it appears from the information before me that a majority of the legal votes cast at an election on June 27, 1959, were in favor of each of the propositions required to be submitted to the people of Hawaii by section 7(b) of the act of March 18, 1959; and

WHEREAS it further appears from information before me that a general election was held on July 28, 1959, and that the returns of the general election were made and certified as provided in the act of March 18, 1959; and

WHEREAS the Governor of Hawaii has certified to me the results of the submission to the people of Hawaii of the three propositions set forth in section 7(b) of the act of March 18, 1959, and the results of the general election; and

WHEREAS I find and announce that the people of Hawaii have duly adopted the propositions required to be submitted to them by the act of March 18, 1959, and have duly elected the officers required to be elected by that act:

NOW, THEREFORE, I, DWIGHT D. EISENHOWER, President of the United States of America, do hereby declare and proclaim that the procedural requirements imposed by the Congress on the State of Hawaii to entitle that State to admission into the Union have been complied with in all respects and that admission of the State of Hawaii into the Union on an equal footing with the other States of the Union is now accomplished.

IN WITNESS WHEREOF, I have hereunto set my hand and caused the Seal of the United States of America to be affixed.

DONE at the City of Washington at four p.m. E.D.T. on this twenty-first day of August in the year of our Lord nineteen hundred and fifty-nine, and of the Independence of the United States of America the one hundred and eighty-fourth.

IV

Whilst there were some local, small scale celebrations, the accession of Hawaii to the rest of the Union didn't create much of a fanfare. The event, like virtually every other statehood before it, went largely unnoticed by the rest of the country, and there were no tickertape parades, tanks rolling through Washington streets or fly-bys by the USAF to mark the birth of this, the fiftieth, and last, state of the union. No doubt, the minimalist nature of this particular alteration to the United States' internal architecture was crucial to the level of indifference stirred up, because, as a formal US territory for nearly sixty years, the people of the Islands — at least those that were born there — had long enjoyed full American citizenship, with an economy and strategic position that had long been hard wired into the national whole. Hardly anyone could remember a time when the stars and stripes didn't flutter over public buildings in Honolulu; or that Dollars and Cents weren't the official currency; meaning the real change was taking place in the boardrooms of the "Big Five" and five thousand miles away in the corridors of Washington DC.

Internationally, the accession of the fiftieth state was again greeted with total indifference, partly because the world's eyes were focused on countries and provinces that were going, or trying to go, in the opposite direction. The late fifties was the time when European imperialism finally found itself on life support, as one colony after another asserted its right to self determination, and though there was the occasional twitch of life in the old dogs yet, like when Britain and France meddled in Egypt over the ownership of the Suez Canal, the game was up for the old world powers.

There was also a new type of nation that was drawing the world's attention: those that had got themselves tangled up in the rivalry between the two superpowers. Whilst the USA and USSR eyed each other warily like Floyd Patterson and Ingemar Johansson from behind the hair-trigger safety of their respective nuclear arsenals, places like Korea, Vietnam and Hungary found themselves grabbing the limelight, albeit as pawns in a deadly chess game. The T-44 tank and B-52 bomber were Russia and America's weapons of choice by the late 1950s, though their effectiveness was limited when faced with something that would cost both dearly in the 1960s and 1980s: guerrilla warfare.

It was the outcome of one such guerrilla campaign on an island sixty times closer to the United States mainland than Hawaii that grabbed the world's attention as 1959 started, and the year would be remembered primarily because of Fidel Castro, and his seizure of power in Cuba. Against such a backdrop, and the Cold War in general, Hawaiian statehood paled into insignificance, and if most people were asked today to name a specific historical or contemporary event associated with the Islands, would probably answer Pearl Harbor or maybe the death of James Cook.

Statehood hardly registered on the radar; after all, there had been forty nine accessions to the union already, so what was different about this particular one?

Well, one great difference was this particular states geographical position and its physical shape. At two thousand five hundred miles off the California coast, Hawaii was actually further away from the American mainland than places like Iceland or Jamaica, and though in earlier times this might have meant something, by 1959 the sophistication of communications was fast reducing this isolation to an irrelevance. Then there was the new state's shape to consider, for as islands, Hawaii's boundaries were of course natural in origin rather than the result of man-made processes. The fiftieth state was therefore unique, for every other state in the union had at least some geometry in the makeup of its boundaries; although this uniqueness also posed a further question, for how could this particular archipelago fit into a construction where mathematics and geometry had played such an important part?

Like Pennsylvania and Oregon, the answer to this question again came in the relationship of Hawaii with all of the other states in the Union, for one key characteristic of this particular building had been the lack of any mention of walls. On a three dimensional and conventional level, this was logical, in that from the time the "symbolic temple" was first marked in chalk and clay across the floors of London ale-houses it had been one dimensional, all the better to harmonize with the ancient idea of the *Templum*, the "open, or consecrated space". This wasn't to mean that specific architectural features normally associated with the vertical couldn't be included: Desaguliers, Newcastle and Montague had seen to that with the inclusion of the Arch into Masonic ritual at Ditton back in 1735; so it was highly likely that something numerically symbolic would also emerge out of the statehood of Hawaii, the fiftieth and final state.

Well, for a start, the *timing* of everything was highly symbolic. Back in 1733 James Oglethorpe had been conscientious enough to make sure the construction of the "Arch" was commenced on the "second day of the second month" thus emulating the directive laid down in the Book of *Kings*. With Hawaii's statehood becoming effective from August 21st, 1959, involved Freemasons were again illustrating how tightly they were following precedent; for not only did the two hundred and thirty-third day of 1959 fall in the thirty-third week of the year, but it also meant the Temple was completed during the thirty-third cycle of seven years since the arrival of the *Ann* at Yamacra bluff. Even more importantly, Completion at this time had succeeded in emulating Biblical precedent in another way, for Oglethorpe's use of the modern equivalent of the Hebrew month Ziv, February, was also repeated at the end of the buildings construction, when the final stone, Hawaii, was slid into place in the "Eighth Month" August:

> The foundation of the temple was laid in the second month, the month of Ziv, in the fourth year of Solomon's reign.

> In the eighth month, the month of Bul, in the eleventh year of Solomon's reign, the Temple was completely finished exactly as it had been planned. It had taken Solomon seven years to finish it. — Kings, 6:37–38

Hawaii's role in the overall architecture of the United States was highly symbolic too. The key to the stonework of all fifty states was, of course, the concept of statehood, rather than the creation of a British colony. The first thirteen of these had taken place during the Constitutional Convention of the late seventeen eighties, when the states making up the Arch finally came together in the Federation that, with thirty seven additions, survives until the present day. The last of the "original thirteen" to do so was Rhode Island, which only caved in after threats from the others that it would be treated as a foreign country if it didn't join, pressure to which it duly caved into, and ratified the Constitution, thus becoming a full member of the Union, on May 29 1790. Again, this was another example of *achievement* coming together with *completion*, for Rhode Island's acquiescence happened during the thirty-third month since the Constitutional Convention had first met, bringing all of the former colonies together in a thirteen state federation.

From George Washington to Dwight D. Eisenhower, thirty-three men had occupied the office of President. Over that time, the entrance, floor, features and ceiling of the symbolic, and new, Temple of Solomon had been rebuilt across the continent of North America, and on August the 21st 1959, in the same way Sir Christopher Wren's son had added the last stone to the Cupola of Saint Paul's Cathedral back in 1710, the final piece of the Architecture of the States was now being slid into place. This was again an illustration of the accuracy inherent in the building, this time for the benefit of the rest of the world, for one thing medieval stone masons had to get right was the appearance of the stones that faced outward for everyone else to see. So it was that a hundred and sixty nine years after the original thirteen had come together in a "Democratic Arch", the rest of the external aspect of the building was therefore completed, when Hawaii became the thirty-third border state of the United States of America.

33rd Month of the   *Thirteen State*

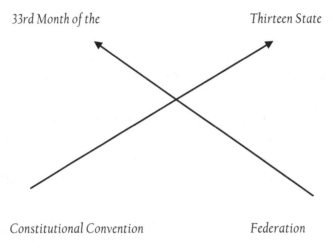

Constitutional Convention   *Federation*

Fig. 13: UNION. The Original thirteen States that made up the USA finally came together during the 33rd month of the constitutional convention. The last to join, Rhode Island, did so on a date — 29th May, 1790 — that adds up to the number thirty-three.

Figure 40. The thirty-three border states of the United States.

Fig.41. *COMPLETION*. The Fifty States of the Union form 1959 to the present

Chapter 13. "A Worke Unfinished"

> What Archimedes said of the mechanical powers may be applied to Reason and Liberty: "*Had we*," said he, "*a place to stand upon, we might raise the world.*"
>
> The revolution of America presented in politics what was only theory in mechanics. So deeply rooted were all the governments of the old world, and so effectually had the tyranny and the antiquity of habit established itself over the mind, that no beginning could be made in Asia, Africa, or Europe, to reform the political condition of man. Freedom had been hunted around the globe; reason was considered as rebellion; and the slavery of fear had made men afraid to think.
>
> —Thomas Paine, Introduction to *The Rights of Man*, 1792, part 2

I

As the Christmas of 1733 approached and winter tightened its grip on the new colony of Georgia, James Oglethorpe wound up the preamble of his letter to the enterprise's Trustees with the observation that '... providence itself seems visible in all things to prosper your Designs calculated for the Protection of the persecuted, the relief of the poor and the Benefit of mankind'. Of course, in accordance with the standards of the time, some literary license should have been expected of Oglethorpe, a Member of Parliament of ten years standing, and his attempt to 'sell' his philanthropic idea to anyone who would listen, especially people back in

England. Even so, it must also be borne in mind that he was, on this December day in 1733, only courting those already converted — the Trustees — who, involved in the whole dodgy venture up to their necks, must have shaken their heads in disbelief at their philanthropist-adventurers' fine words, especially his final, soaring exhortation, 'your Designs....for the Benefit of mankind'.

Well, without doubt, none of the Trustees or anybody else in England could deny that Georgia was certainly a good, if slightly eccentric, idea that was indeed delivering on its central thematic, rehabilitation and refuge, as the first year of its existence drew to a close. Former debtors, English Jews, and Bavarian Protestants were all to find a home in the new province, creating a momentum that would, in time, bring Georgia into line as a fully functioning British Colony and latterly an American State. Settlement on such a scale was a huge achievement in its own right, for it took guts to cross the Atlantic and set up shop in what was still referred to as a 'wilderness', though it stretches credulity to believe that the settlers shivering in their half-built villages amongst the Georgia pines during the December of 1733 shared their Leader's opinion that some kind of great leap forward had taken place. For anyone with eyes to see — be they American, English or any other tribe, knew that Georgia was merely another British colony, the last in a long line of New World schemes that had their origins in the culture, politics, and aspirations of Europe.

There is, of course, an alternative explanation behind Oglethorpe's florid bombast, namely that he was referring to Georgia's role within the greater architecture of British America. Six of the twenty trustees were proven Masons who could easily have recognized the hidden message in the MP's missive, even as their non-Masonic colleagues scratched their heads in wonderment. Such Masons, if they were in the know, would have recognized the coup Oglethorpe had pulled off and how it underpinned the overall structure. Even bearing this qualification in mind, it still left a question in the air: *why* were they laying America out in accordance with their idea of King Solomon's Temple? Was it simply to fall in line with Biblical prophecy, the idea of 'all nations' coming together under one roof, or did it have a secondary, more contemporary *rationale* too, a function that, recognized as absolutely vital for the 'benefit of man-

kind', only America could fulfill? Without doubt, many European thinkers, from the late 1500s on, had seen the potential inherent in the colonies
across the Atlantic, not just for mercenary reasons like the expansion of
British trade and Empire but for more enlightened social experiments
too. These ideas and the philosophy behind them varied greatly in both
size and influence, but there was one in particular, masquerading as a
half-finished novel, that actually placed great importance on the symbolism of King Solomon's Temple. This book, a blueprint in all but name,
had been in print for over a century by the year 1733. It was the work of
an individual who, it has been claimed, not only re-founded the Masons
as a 'speculative' Fraternity but edited the King James Bible and was the
real power behind the works of William Shakespeare: Sir Francis Bacon.

Death by frozen chicken must rank amongst one of the weirdest ways
to expire. Such an exit was, however, the way in which Bacon, one of the
great thinkers of the late Elizabethan and early Stuart era probably ended
his days. The date was sometime around the 6th April 1626, and London
was in the grip of an icy snowstorm. Taking advantage of the weather,
Sir Francis, a noted amateur scientist, was eager to test his notion that
cold slowed, or stopped, the decay of organic matter, and he used the
storm, as well as a chicken bought for the purpose from a shop-woman
on Highgate Hill, to further his investigations. The woman kindly gutted
the chicken's carcass for Bacon, who, heading up the street, stuffed it
with snow before making his way to the home of the Earl of Arundel to
see out the storm. There, Bacon became feverish, and after two or three
days in bed, passed away, either from pneumonia or infection brought on
by eating the raw chicken meat.

Suffering such an unlikely end doesn't, however, mean that Bacon was
a historical lightweight. Throughout the four hundred years since his
death, many of the world's finest minds have queued up to pay homage
to him and his contribution to civilization. Take, for example, Thomas
Jefferson, who, when writing to a certain Richard Price in January 1789,
had the following to say about the long dead Englishman:

> Dear Sir — I have duly received your favor of the 5'th. inst. With respect to
> the busts & pictures I will put off till my return from America all of them
> except Bacon, Locke and Newton, whose pictures I will trouble you to
> have copied for me: and as I consider them as the three greatest men that

have ever lived, without any exception, and as having laid the foundation of those superstructures which have been raised in the Physical & Moral sciences, I would wish to form them into a knot on the same canvas, that they may not be confounded at all with the herd of other great men. To do this I suppose we need only desire the copyist to draw the three busts in three ovals all contained in a larger oval in some such form as this each bust to be the size of life.

Jefferson had good cause to include Bacon alongside Newton and Locke in his pantheon of greatness. Born on 22 January 1561, near the Strand in London, Francis was the son of Sir Nicholas Bacon and his second wife, Anne. Sir Nicholas recognized the value of education and had his son home schooled during his early years, a policy that paid off handsomely when Francis entered Trinity College, Cambridge, at the age of twelve. Intellectual precocity on such a scale didn't go unnoticed, even by the monarch, and it so impressed Elizabeth I that on one occasion she described him as "the young Lord Keeper". What Elizabeth saw, others saw, for in 1576 at the grand old age of fifteen, Bacon began to train as a barrister, an occupation that would, in theory, keep the wolf from the door for the rest of his life.

Exposure to the 'Virgin Queen' had, however, turned the young man's head, and seeing where the power lay, Bacon realized that what he really desired was a place at Elizabeth I's Court. It hardly needs saying that teenage plotting rarely comes to much, in any age, and the usual fate befell the 'young Lord Keeper', for his great scheme came to nothing. To add to Bacon's woes, he was also suffering money troubles due to his father's death, and he was under pressure to get out and make a living, Francis quietly returned to the law. Nevertheless, late sixteenth century England still offered great opportunities for a young man well endowed with brains and aristocratic connections, and by 1584, now aged 23, the son of Sir Nicholas had not only succeeded in becoming a barrister but also Member of Parliament for the small hamlet of Melcombe Regis in the county of Dorset.

Like so many glittering careers, a period of relative stagnation then set in. A Queens Counsel fell into his lap easily enough, but the real prize of public office in those days, a highly lucrative position in the state structure, eluded him so completely he was even arrested for debt in

1598. After this low point, though, things started to improve, and as the sixteenth century became the seventeenth his standing with Elizabeth I started to rise. Doubtless, part of this was due to Bacon's adroit distancing of himself from the Earl of Essex, who had fallen into disfavor and paid the price by being executed for treason in 1601; though the real kick upstairs came with the ascent of the Scotsman James I to the throne of England in 1603. One of the new King's first acts was to knight Bacon, and from then on the Londoner worked assiduously to keep the favor of England's first Stuart monarch, a strategy that worked well, for by 1613 Bacon became attorney-general and five years later Lord Chancellor, and was created Baron Verulam.

At the peak of his powers, publicly at least, things were soon to go awry for the newly created Baron. A political system where blatant self-interest could be satisfied through public office might have seemed a good idea to those on the inside track, but in the hands of a hereditary head of state it could carry substantial risks. This must have gone though his mind many times, especially after he was found guilty of corruption. Opponents, delighted at the fall of the former prodigy, demanded he be stripped of his offices and parliamentary seat, and he avoided by a whisker the loss of his titles, too. Rejected by the establishment surrounding James I, and narrowly escaping a spell in the Tower of London, Bacon was left to contemplate the mistakes he had made and find something new to do.

Sir Francis reverted to writing to pass the time. This wasn't a particularly difficult change of direction for the former Attorney General, for even during his days as the honorable member for Melcombe he had been a prodigious man of letters. By 1597, he had already penned his *Essays;* followed up with *Advancement of Learning* (1605) and *Novum Organum* and *The Great Instauration* in 1620. Crucially for the future, in *The Great Instauration* he had argued for the transformation of mankind from the contemplative, faith bound individual characteristic of the Middle Ages towards a human experience based on reason and science, all underpinned with a more speculative nature than had been the case before. This theme of transformation was obviously important to Bacon; for it was one he would pursue, in his next—and final—work, *The New Atlantis.*

II

Francis Bacon didn't live to see *New Atlantis* in print, or even to complete it, for its title page also bore the sub-heading "a worke unfinished" when it first saw the light of day in 1627, a year after his unusual death. The half-book is written in the usual chronological style of the time, and the story centers around fifty-one (presumably) English sailors, who, whilst voyaging from Peru to China, are forced by prevailing winds towards a mysterious island to the north. There they discover the nation of Bensalem, a multicultural society which, although nominally Christian, also puts great faith in scientific research as a means of solving social problems. Although the Island keeps its existence a "secret" from the rest of the world, for fear that its great discoveries could be misused, the Bensalemites happily introduce the sailors to every aspect of their society, a plot device that enabled Bacon to disseminate his message to the reader with ease.

Of course, *Atlantis* wasn't the first time that anyone had attempted to paint a picture of an ideal, or even socially conscious, society. By the early seventeenth century, many such visions had been aired, and not simply ones that had been recycled from religions, such as Arcadia, Heaven, or the Garden of Eden. The philosopher Plato had got off to an early start with the concept around 400 BC, when he sketched out his version of an ideal society in his *Republic, which, a*ccording to him, was to be a society ruled over a sect of philosopher kings, an idea that had already permeated the thinking of Socrates too, who again saw the philosopher kings as the key to a successful society, so long as they maintained a disinterested and dispassionate view of the world.

Plato's Republic took place on an island to the west, so it is intriguing that this idea was again re-explored by Sir Thomas More in his *Utopia*, written in 1516. The first part of *Utopia* is a collection of discussions with the imaginary traveler Raphael Hythloday, who expounds on some of the shortcomings of the contemporary monarchies of the day, with More playing the part of his interlocutor. More tries to convince Raphael that he could find a good job in a royal court, as an advisor to monarchs, but the traveler explains that his views are too radical and would not be listened to, arguing — like Plato — that for good governance to take root, kings must act philosophically:

> Plato doubtless did well foresee, unless kings themselves would apply their minds to the study of philosophy, that else they would never thoroughly allow the council of philosophers, being themselves before, even from their tender age, infected and corrupt with perverse and evil opinions.[169]

The essential idea surrounding beneficial change within the societies outlined by Socrates, Plato and Sir Thomas More is that it is incremental, rather than swift and radical. Each new innovation is thought out carefully, to avoid misplaced implementation leading to poor governance or social instability. Looking specifically at More's *Utopia*, some of the ideas mooted, like a welfare state, divorce, religious tolerance and no lawyers would be considered rational — or at least acceptable — in today's world. Poverty and misery are generally absent, and the nation is not set on a warlike course, though, on the other hand, there are also prohibitions that would make Hitler or Stalin smile. Premarital sex is punished by a lifetime of enforced celibacy, and adultery by enslavement; food is eaten communally; women, second class citizens; and travel only permissible with an internal passport, the failure of holding which again leading to slavery.

The first quarter of the seventeenth century witnessed an increase in works devoted to the idea of something approaching an ideal society. These included Johann Valentin Andreae's *Christianopolis* (1619) a vision of a small Christian Democracy with a population of 400, and Tommaso Campanella's *The City of the Sun*[170] which like *Christianopolis* had a theocratic basis, albeit seasoned with a few Communistic ideas. In hindsight, however, this was too heavy a dose of Socialism for someone, because by the time *The City of the Sun* was originally published in 1602, Campanella was already imprisoned for heresy and sedition. Nevertheless, his work, originally written in Italian, survived to be translated into Latin a decade later. Like so much of the art, culture and literature that appeared in Italy during the Renaissance, works about improved societies like his had a particular Latin flavor, especially noticeable in the emphasis on the pre-

---

169 More, *Utopia*
170 Italian: *La città del Sole*; Latin: *Civitas Solis*.

eminence of Christianity, an absolute essential in countries still under the heel of an unreformed Catholic Church.

Like the earlier writers who had explored the idea of a society based on reason, Sir Francis Bacon placed the government of Bensalem in the hands of philosopher kings: the fellows or brethren of Salomons House, or the 'College of the Six-Day Works' as the ex-MP alternatively named it. Bacon clearly based Salomon on Solomon, and the "House", which he saw as some kind of university or scientific institute, on the Old Testament monarch's Temple. This isn't to mean the story of the building was the sole Bible tale mined by Bacon, because in addition to the allusions to this specific construction, *Atlantis* is peppered with other imagery drawn from this particular religious book. The "College of the Six Day Works" is an obvious example of this, being lifted from *Genesis*, and the story that God took six days to create the world. Another case in point is the name of Bensalem itself, for this, when translated into English, is the child of Salem: i.e., the New Jerusalem, the ideal city.

By doing things this way, Sir Francis was, apart from avoiding the fate of the unfortunate Campanella, falling into line with contemporary thinking regarding Bible stories as symbols of the "ideal", and the Temple as the architectural aspect of that ideal. It is noteworthy that Bacon also makes it clear that the fellows of Salomon's House are a sect, or semi-secret society, devoted to mastering scientific principles, and who spend their time conducting research into all areas of the natural world:

> Ye shall understand (my dear friends) that amongst the excellent acts of that king, one above all hath the pre-eminence. It was the erection and institution of an Order or Society, which we call *Salomon's House*; the noblest foundation (as we think) that ever was upon the earth; and the lanthorn of this kingdom. It is dedicated to the study of the works and creatures of God. Some think it beareth the founder's name a little corrupted, as if it should be Solamon"s House. But the records write it as it is spoken. So as I take it to be denominate of the king of the Hebrews, which is famous with you, and no stranger to us[171].

Significantly, membership of this august body wasn't open to anybody, for Bacon makes it plain that only the most eminent intellectuals in Bensalem society are eligible to become fellows. Once initiated, the leaders of the "House" divide them up into smaller groups, much like any

---

171 Bacon, *The New Atlantis*

modern institute, to conduct research and scientific experiments into all aspects of science and the natural world, so that, with time and application, their findings may be used for the improvement of society:

> For the several employments and offices of our fellows, we have twelve that sail into foreign countries under the names of other nations (for our own we conceal), who bring us the books and abstracts, and patterns of experiments of all other parts. These we call merchants of light.
>
> We have three that collect the experiments which are in all books. These we call depredators.
>
> We have three that collect the experiments of all mechanical arts, and also of liberal sciences, and also of practices which are not brought into arts. These we call mystery-men.
>
> We have three that try new experiments, such as themselves think good. These we call pioneers or miners.
>
> We have three that draw the experiments of the former four into titles and tables, to give the better light for the drawing of observations and axioms out of them. These we call compilers.
>
> We have three that bend themselves, looking into the experiments of their fellows, and cast about how to draw out of them things of use and practice for man's life and knowledge, as well for works as for plain demonstration of causes, means of natural divinations, and the easy and clear discovery of the virtues and parts of bodies. These we call dowry-men or benefactors.
>
> Then after divers meetings and consults of our whole number, to consider of the former labors and collections, we have three that take care out of them to direct new experiments, of a higher light, more penetrating into nature than the former. These we call lamps.
>
> We have three others that do execute the experiments so directed, and report them. These we call inoculators.Lastly, we have three that raise the former discoveries by experiments into greater observations, axioms, and aphorisms. These we call interpreters of nature.[172]

At one stage in *Atlantis*, the Fellows' leader reveals to the Englishmen that the brethren may occasionally guard their discoveries from the eyes of anyone else, "And this we do also: we have consultations, which of the inventions and experiences which we have discovered shall be published, and which not; and take all an oath of secrecy for the concealing of those which we think fit to keep secret; though some of those we do reveal sometime to the State, and some not." The implication of the fel-

---

172 Bacon, *The New Atlantis*

low's secrecy is that Salomon's House is not only independent of the civil government, but that it is also willing, on occasion, to ignore it. Even with this slightly sinister qualification, the central message of the book ends on a positive note, and that is a scientific and speculative approach to the natural world will, given time, lead to an advanced and rational, if not ideal, society.

III

Although Bacon wasn't around to see *Atlantis* in print, the ideas contained within — and indeed his general beliefs about the nature of scientific inquiry — would live on. In the English-speaking world, the seed Bacon had planted first started to bear fruit a mere twenty-two years after his death, when, during the civil war, a club devoted to experimental science first met in the Oxford lodgings of the economist, Doctor William Petty. The principal members at the time were Seth Ward, the Savilian professor of astronomy and author of *Astronomia geometrica;* Lawrence Rooke, who wrote papers on longitude and the moons of Jupiter; John Wilkins, author of *An Essay towards a Real Character and a Philosophical Language*, in which he proposed a universal language and the decimal system; the mathematician and cryptographer John Wallis; Robert Hooke: polymath, architect, and professor of Geometry; the Anglo-Irishman Robert Boyle, best known for Boyle's law and *The Sceptical Chymist*, an important contribution to Chemistry; Christopher Wren and his cousin Matthew; Petty, and the physicians Ralph Bathurst, Thomas Willis, and Jonathan Goddard, all three of whom would be present ten years later when the Protector, Oliver Cromwell, passed on. The purpose of the society Sprat wrote:

> Was no more than onely the satisfaction of breathing a freer air, and of conversing in quiet one with another without being ingag'd in the passions and madness of that Dismal age [and] the club was frequented by some Gentlemen, of Philosophical Minds whom the misfortunes of the kingdom and the security and ease of a retirement amongst Gown-men, had drawn thither...a race of young Men...invincibly armed against all the inchantments of Enthusiasm.[173]

---

173 Doctor Thomas Sprat *History of the Royal Society*

And it was a "dismal age" indeed. England was in the middle of its civil war, a conflict that would soon be defined by the execution of King Charles I; and, in the following decade, the rise and fall of Oliver Cromwell's dour Commonwealth. The average Englishman's troubles weren't confined to who — or what — should rule the country. He — and especially his wife — also had to take care not to cross Matthew Hopkins, the self-styled Witch-finder General, who, until a year earlier had spent his hours scouring the East Anglian countryside for witches to burn. England was illustrating an aversion to religious toleration as well, for Roman Catholics still had to keep their faith to themselves, Jewry was banned, and dissidents, despairing of ever finding security or safety in their homeland, were leaving in droves to chance their luck in the "wastes" of New England.

Europe — and the rest of the world — couldn't claim to be in any better shape. Rule by the "divine right" of kings or popes was almost universal, and Christianity, for a thousand years a symbol of unity across Western Europe, was gradually becoming a source of greater and greater friction as different interpretations of Biblical truth started to be aired, which in turn split like amoeba into more and more extreme forms as the century unraveled. The times were out of joint, and Petty's Oxford lodgings formed a refuge for thinkers and experimenters who refused to be fanatics in party and religious warfare. Meetings were as frequent as possible, and rather than debate and discussion there were "particular Trials in Chymistry or Mechanicks" and a sharing of discoveries.

Averse to coffee and its consumption, Charles II was, however, enthusiastic about this little gang of Oxford experimenters. Like the architectural styles brought back by other royalist exiles, Charles had been exposed to science whilst spending his time abroad in the Dutch Republic, which was one of the more progressive nations in Europe. The King's involvement and the creation of a more straightforward organization took place in less than a week: on 28 November 1660 after one of Wren's lectures, the architect and a dozen old friends withdrew to Laurence Rooke's old quarters and there took the first steps towards formally constituting a new society — "a designe of founding a College for the promotion of Physico-Mathematicall Experimental learning" as they described it. The Society was to meet regularly on Wednesdays at three in the afternoon, and on 5 December, one of the Groups, Sir Robert Moray, who was now the King's chief advisor on Scottish affairs, brought the good news that Charles II himself was interested in the project and was even prepared to grant it a royal charter. Backed by this all-powerful royal imprimatur, the experimenters signed a covenant that bound them "to consult and debate concerning the promotion of Experimental learning", and that "each will allowe one shilling weekly towards the defraying of occasional charges". What was soon to become the Royal Society was thus constituted, and on 3 December 1661, John Evelyn, confident for the future of the new institution, wrote in his diary:

> By universal suffrage of our Philosophic Assembly, an order was made & registered that I should receive their Publique Thanks for the honorable mention I made of them by the name of *Royal Society*, in my Epistle Dedicatory to the Lord Chancellor, before my Traduction of Naudens. Too greate an honor for a trifel.

Like Salomon's House, the Royal Society was duty bound to emphasize the social usefulness of its existence. Christopher Wren drew up a rough draft for the preamble of the Royal Charter, which, whilst enthusing about the role of His Majesty King Charles, did indeed drive home the message that the aim of the Society was the good of society as a whole. In September 1661, the new society received its first royal warrant, and on 15 July 1662 it received its final royal charter—the official date for the founding of the *Royal Society of London for Improving Natural Knowledge*[174].

Although Charles II had given his blessing, the Royal Society was not destined to become the creature of the monarchy or the British government. Its rules forbade the exploration of political and religious issues within its meetings, and membership was open, in theory, to men of any faith, nationality or occupation. Inevitably, because of the conditions prevailing at the time, it did however attract those with enough money and time to spare: the "English Gentlemen" of the age. Even these had their uses, for science requires cash to make it happen; such people

---

174   The RS was not the earliest scientific society. As early as 1560, there had been an Academia Secretorum Naturae at Naples; from 1603 to 1630, an Accademia dei Lincei in Rome; and in 1651, an Accademia del Cimento in Florence.

played a major role, for the Royal Society remained a self contained, and self regulated institution, devoted to experimentalism, and the betterment of society in general.

The idea of small twelve- or thirteen-member societies working towards scientific or social improvement wasn't peculiar to England, France or Italy, for it took root across the Atlantic too. The catalyst for this was again Desaguliers' fellow Mason, Benjamin Franklin, who, along with others, began to campaign from 1727 onwards for proper lighting, cleaning and policing of Philadelphia's streets. A fire service and the first subscription library in America were also created in Philadelphia due to his, and his friends', efforts, ideas which occasionally came about due to individual initiative but other times were the result of formal meetings of small groups. These small bodies, or 'Junto' as Franklin named them, again first appeared around 1727, with the civic improvement of Philadelphia in mind. Usually with a total membership of twelve, they met on Friday nights, and their purpose was outlined in Franklin's *Autobiography* as:

> My ideas at the time were, that the sect should be begun and spread at first among young and single men only; that each person to be initiated should not only declare his assent to such creed, but should have exercised himself with the thirteen weeks' examination and practice of the virtues, as in the before-mention'd model; that the existence of such a society should be kept a secret, till it was to become considerable, to prevent solicitations for the admission of improper persons, but that the members should each search among his acquaintance for ingenuous, well-disposed youths, to whom, with prudent caution, the scheme should be gradually communicated... 'tho' I am of the still of opinion that it was a practicable scheme, and might have been very useful, by forming a great number of good citizens; and I was not discourag'd by the seeming magnitude of the undertaking, as I have always thought that one man of tolerable abilities may work great changes, and accomplish great affairs among mankind, if he first forms a good plan, and, cutting off all amusements or other employments that would divert his attention, makes the execution of that same plan his sole study and business.

On a grander scale, Franklin was also instrumental in founding the American Philosophical Society, again modelled on England's Royal Society, during 1743. The APS was, in some respects, the apogee of Franklin's "Junto" efforts, and alongside its old world progenitor, another link in the chain stretching back to Bacon's College of the Six Day's Works. Each of these — alongside the Masonic fraternity — had declared its interest in the improvement of society; and their desire to employ secrecy on occasion to carry this out; so there was again a question, and this was, were they — or elements within each, or all — prepared to work towards the ultimate scientific experiment, what Franklin called a 'great and extensive plan'?

IV

Certainly, from the standpoint of the time, such an approach was desperately needed for even as the eighteenth century reached its third-way mark, despotism, backwardness and stupidity still ruled, across every continent and country. Of course there was some light, such as that found in England's Royal Society. But even they must have realized how close the darkness was, and as they left Crane Court following Desaguliers' exhibition of his Planetarium that cold February night in 1733, some members may well have stood under the flickering lamp marking their meeting before heading home, and mused over the state of the world. All around there was the same superstition, chaos and ignorance that had existed when the experimenters had first met in Oxford back in 1648. Down the alleyway they may have heard the drunken shouting and laughter of the prostitutes and their clients in Fleet Street, whilst the city choked, as John Evelyn noted, on "Clouds of Smoake and Sulphur, so full of stinke and Darkness"[175] to turn a man's coat black with soot in a single day. Far from inheriting the role of Salomon's House as the "Lanthorne[176] of the Kingdom", the fellows of the Royal Society must have often pondered the hard and painful fact that, for all their genius, they still only operated on the fringes of the British consciousness.

What the scientists of the early eighteenth century really needed were facilities within which they could explore every aspect of the natural world. This didn't necessarily mean laboratories with benches and test-tubes; but rather a *space*, a refuge, a place where the scientific method—and its cousins reason and tolerance—could flourish free from all the encumbrances of the age. Certainly, the Old World couldn't provide such a location, and indeed was the cause of many of the evils plaguing

---

175 Quoted in Christopher Hibbert: *London, A Biography*, p.147
176 An archaic word for lantern.

scientific research in the first place, so the only place such an institute, temple, or "college of the six day works" could conceivably be founded was in the New World. Again, even here there was a catch, because by 1733 all of the Americas were being claimed by one or another of the European imperial powers, so theoretically at least one of them had to, in the short run at least, act as host for science's great leap forward. What this meant was that over time the Temple of Science would also have to become independent of Europe, too, and this was not simply to embed the idea of rationalism but to lay the basis of a further experiment: that provinces and colonies could go it alone, thus driving the first of many nails into one of the Old World's poorer ideas, imperialism.

Staying clear of the Europeans would also dictate that the building would have to grow quickly to a point where it couldn't be intimidated by outsiders. Undoubtedly, on occasion the fellows of the Royal Society were pestered by the noise and bustle of the streets outside, regardless of whether they were at Petty's lodgings in Oxford or Crane Court in the West end of London. Now, on a far greater scale, the same idea had to be applied to the potential nuisance that might spring from the hooligans of the old world, and the only way to do this would be to grow to a point where such interference would be foolhardy. Size also had another advantage not applicable to Britain and France: the ability to supply any raw material from within the national border. Unlike Hooke and Boyle in their Oxford Laboratory, this time the Temple of Science would draw on its own resources, without having to butter up benefactors.

Of course, the whole idea was pointless without considering social improvement. Both Bacon's imaginary institute and the Royal Society had been duty bound by Kings Salomon and Charles II to work for the benefit of society as a whole, and whilst this was fairly straightforward with regards to the application of physical innovations — like paved roads or street lighting for example — it was far trickier being applied to human beings. The institute was only going to move forward if its underlying idea carried the public with it, thus the chance to carry out another great experiment: where the people, rather the government or a monarch were sovereign. Again, the catch here was that it was implied that humanity, when free to make their own decisions, would make the right ones, and nobody needs telling this isn't always the case.

When it came to the actual work of construction, science was in far calmer waters, for the symbolism, imagery, fraternal spirit and general air of secrecy that surrounded the Freemasons were also ideal for the purposes of creating a scientific nation. Back in the days of William of Sens, the raising of the cathedrals represented the cutting edge of science and indeed in some ways was the main contribution to progress during that era. The reuse of architectural imagery through political and physical cartography therefore had the effect of reinforcing America's role as a beacon of science, with specific attention to two areas in particular: mathematics and geometry.

Another area where architecture worked well was as a symbol of unity. Due to its vast size, federalism was the only viable option for the country's political units, and a concept that could hold them together in a single whole was infinitely better than nothing at all; and it was something that found an echo within collective humanity too, for it stressed cohesion, linking the dispirit peoples who would make up the nation. For the Reverend Desaguliers and the rest of his fellows and brothers, it was therefore not too much of a task to alter the layout and ritual of the Masons Lodge so that it harmonized neatly with the physical geography of North America, becoming, in effect, a *blueprint* for the intended structure.

As a fraternity that allowed membership from such a wide section of (male) society, the Masons could also be relied on to provide the human raw material for such an enormous enterprise. For all their genius, the likes of Stukeley, Senex and Desaguliers weren't cut out for the mental and physical demands of building this specific structure, and though they could provide much, if not all of the theory, construction needed men of a more practical nature to complete the design. Thus the merging of so many different men into the Masonic Order in the 1720s and 30s: with contemplative scientists like Stukeley and Desauliers rubbing shoulders with men of action, such as James Oglethorpe, George Shelvocke and James Figg.

At the end of the day, the architecture behind America's states has, since 1733, been simply the outward manifestation of Bacon's *Atlantis*: the bit that talks. Like Saloman's House, the United States was never designed to be a vision of perfection but rather another country in the Western tradition, albeit one where progressive concepts built around the idea of social improvement, long struggling to breathe in the fetid atmosphere of seventeenth and eighteenth century Europe, could be tested to the full. Certainly, the proof of the pudding is in the eating, because one truth that is incontrovertible is the notion that the United States has contributed an enormous number of innovations and ideas into the mix that is the global human condition during the last two hundred and eighty years. Whether these be human concepts, like popular democracy, the separation of church and state, even anti-imperialism, or physical inventions such as vulcanized rubber, the Saturn V rocket, or the personal computer aren't as important as the notion that the experience of humanity has undergone a complete overhaul since 1733. How much of this is due to the former colonies in isolation will, of course, remain the subject of conjecture; though to play the game of alternative history for a moment, *à la* the Reverend Samuel Madden, it is difficult to believe the pace of progress could have been maintained had America not existed, or matured in an entirely different way.

So it is incontestable is that the creation and subsequent rise of the USA has definitely led to *acceleration* in the development of humanity, something that began nearly four hundred years ago when Sir Francis Bacon outlined the island kingdom Bensalem, its leading civic institution, Salomon's House, and the scientific processes used therein to forward social development. The parallels between the novel and modern America are close indeed, suggesting that far from allegory Bacon's work was actually a blueprint for society. Can it be, therefore, that Bacon's Bensalem, far from being an island in a conventional sense, was actually an image of a world freed from superstition and subjectivity, an island in space rather than the sea? Certainly, any successful experiment, regardless of how trivial or obscure it might be, will in time become universally accepted and applied. Can it be that the whole idea of America, and its place as the Temple of Science within this particular experiment — the creation of the New Jer-(USA)-lem that is the modern world — was never accidental, but designed deliberately, in line with the demands of the times?

The answer will remain obscure, because credit for this revolution lies with millions of people, Masons and non-masons, and citizens of 'all nations'. However, when it comes to the laying out of the United States, its underlying design, members of one particular fraternity come to the fore, and the achievement of these men is best summed up in words written about another architect, a non-Mason, Sir Christopher Wren. Born in 1632, Wren actually lived long enough to see the foundation of the Grand Lodge of England in the City dotted with his churches and cathedral, within whose precincts he was laid to rest at the end of February, 1723. Today, as then, his memorial consists of a simple epitaph, written in Latin, but with a meaning quite universal, regardless of language, in that it also sums up the achievement of Sir Francis Bacon, the Fraternity he influenced so comprehensively, and the men who built America:

Reader, if you seek his monument, look about you.

Fig.42 Sir Francis Bacon

BIBLIOGRAPHY

Alden, John R: *History of the American Revolution*, Macdonald, 1969

Allen, H.C: *The United States of America*, Ernest Benn, 1964

Allen, Robert J: *The Clubs of Augustan London*, London, 1933

Allsop, Bruce: *The Study of Architectural History*, November Books Limited, 1970

Aligh, Josten, *Elias Ashmole*, Oxford, 1966

Anderson, Dr James: *The Constitutions of the Free-Masons*, London, 1738

Anderson, Dr James: *Royal Genealogies or the Genealogical Tables of Emperors, Kings and Princes, from Adam to These Times*, London, 1732

Anderson, Fred: *Crucible of War: The Seven Years' War and the fate of the Empire in British North America, 1754–1766*, Faber and Faber, 2000

Andrews, C.L: *The Story of Alaska:* The Caxton Printers Limited, Caldwell, Ohio, 1944

Angle, Paul M: *The American Reader — from Columbus to Today:* Rand McNally and Company, New York, 1958

Anonymous: *Perfect Ceremonies of the Supreme Order of the Holy Royal Arch, 1907,* Kessinger Publishing, New York, 2002

Ariel, Abraham & Ariel, Nora Berger: *Plotting the Globe: Stories of Meridians, Parallels, and the International Date Line*, Praeger Publishers, 2005

Atack, Jeremy and Passell, Peter: *A New Economic View of American History from Colonial Times to 1940:* W.W.Norton and Company, 1994

Baigent, Michael & Leigh, Richard: *The Temple and the Lodge*, Arrow, 1989

Ball, Pamela: *Spells, Charms, Talismans and Amulets*, Arcturus, 2001

Barbon, Nicholas: *An Apology for the Builder or a discourse Shewing the Cause and Effects of the Increase of Building*, London, 1685

Barker Cryer, Neville: *What Do You Know about the Royal Arch*, Lewis Masonic, 2002

Beier, A.L. and Finlay, Roger, eds.: *London, 1500–1700: The Making of the Metropolis*, London, 1986

Bible, The, *King James Version*

Bishop, Morris: *The Penguin Book of the Middle Ages*, Penguin, London, 1971

Black, Jeremy and Green, Anthony: *Gods, Demons and Symbols of Ancient Mesopotamia*, British Museum Press, 1998

Black, Lydia T: *Russians in Alaska, 1732–1867*, University of Alaska Press, Fairbanks, 2004

Blacker, Irwin (Ed): *The Principal Navigations, Voyages, Traffiques and Discoveries of the English Nation Made by Sea or Over-land to the Remote and Furthest Distant Quarters of the Earth at any time within the compasse of these 1600 Yeeres By Richard Hakluyt Preacher, and sometime Student of Christ-Church in Oxford*, Viking Press, New York, 1965

Boorstin, Daniel J. *The Americans: The Colonial Experience*, Cardinal, 1988

Boorstin, Daniel J. *The Americans: The National Experience*, Cardinal, 1988

Boorstin, Daniel J. *The Americans: The Democratic Experience*, Cardinal, 1988

Borneman, Walter R: *Alaska: A Narrative History*, Harper Collins, New York, 2003

Breckon, Bill & Parker, Jeffrey: *Tracing the History of Houses*, Countryside Books, 1991

Brock, William R, (Introduction by): *The Federalist Or, The New Constitution* Alexander Hamilton, James Madison and John Jay, Everyman, 1992

Brock, William R, *Conflict and Transformation: The United States, 1844–1877*, Penguin, 1978

Brogan, Hugh: *The Penguin History of the United States of America*, Longman, 1985

Bullock, Steven J.: *Revolutionary Brotherhood: Freemasonry and the Transformation of the American Social Order, 1730–1840*, University of North Carolina Press, 1996

Calder, Angus: *Revolutionary Empire: The Rise of the English Speaking Empires from the Fifteenth Century to the 1780s*, E.P.Dutton, New York, 1981

Carr, Harry: *Three Distinct Knocks and Jachin and Boaz*: Masonic Book Club, 1981

Christie, I.R: *Crisis of Empire: Great Britain and the American Colonies, 1754–1783*, Edward Arnold Limited, London, 1974

Churton, Tobias: *The Golden Builders — Alchemists, Rosicrucians and the first Freemasons*, Signal Press, 2002

Clarke, Peter: *The English Alehouse, A Social History 1200–1830*, London, 1983

Coil, Henry Wilson, *Coil's Masonic Encyclopaedia*, Macoy Publishing and Masonic Supply Co. Inc, New York, 1961

Coil, Henry Wilson: *A Comprehensive View of Freemasonry*, Macoy Publishing and Masonic Supply Co. Inc., New York, 1954

Cole, Emily (ed): *A Concise History of Architectural Styles*, A & C Black, London, 2003

Coleman, Kenneth: *A History of Georgia*: University of Georgia Press, 1991

Coulter, E. Merton (ed): *The Journal of Peter Gordon, 1732–1735*: Wormsloe Foundation Publications, Number 6, Athens, University of Georgia Press, 1963

Cushing, Sumner W: *The Boundaries of the New England States* in the *Annals of the Association of American Geographers* 10, 1920

Dawkins, Peter: *Building Paradise — the Freemasonic and Rosicrucian Six Days' Work.* The Francis Bacon Research Trust, 2001

Daws, Gavan: *Shoal of Time: A History of the Hawaiian Islands,* MacMillan, New York, 1968

De Bolla, Peter: *The Fourth of July and the Founding of America,* Profile Books, London, 2007

Degler, Carl N.: *Out of our Past: The Forces that Shaped Modern America* (Third Edition) Harper & Row, 1984

Denslow, William R: *10,000 Famous Freemasons,* Transactions of the Missouri Lodge of Research, 1959

Dictionary of National Biography, Oxford University Press, 1964

Dugard, Martin: *Farther Than Any Man: The Rise and Fall of Captain James Cook,* Pocket Books, 2001

Dyer, Colin: *Symbolism in Craft Freemasonry,* Lewis Masonic, London, 2003

Earle, Peter: *The Making of the English Middle Class, Business, Society and Family Life in London, 1660–1730,* London, 1989

Ellis, Aytoun: *The Penny Universities. A History of the Coffee-Houses,* London, 1956

Fardell, Micheal and Phillips, Nigel (eds) 'A Demonstration of the Use of the Diving Engine in Searching a Ships Bottom and Stopping any Leake at Sea...' (Jacob Rowe) National Maritime Museum and the Historical Diving Society, London, 2000

Ferguson, Niall: *Empire,* Basic Books, 2004

Ferrell, Robert H & Natkiel, Richard: *Atlas of American History:* Brompton Books, 1993

Franklin, Benjamin: *The Autobiography of Benjamin Franklin* Wordsworth American Library 1996

Gilbert, Adrian: *The New Jerusalem* Bantam Press, London 2002

Gittins, Ian: *Unlocking the Masonic Code: Secrets of the Solomon Key,* Collins, London, 2007

Gooch, Stan: *Guardians of the Ancient Wisdom,* Fontana, London, 1980

Gould, Robert F: *History and Antiquities of Freemasonry,* (Third Edition, revised by H Poole) London, 1951

Griffith, Samuel B: *The War for American Independence,* University of Illinois Press, 2002

Griswold, Wesley S: *The Boston Tea Party* Abacus Press, 1973

Gruening, Ernest: *An Alaska Reader, 1867–1967* New Amsterdam Books, New York, 1966

Gruening, Ernest: *The Battle for Alaska Statehood,* University of Alaska Press, Fairbanks, 1967

Gruening, Ernest: *The State of Alaska,* Random House, New York, 1954

Haley, Alex: *Roots,* Hutchinson, London, 1977

Hamill, John: *The Craft: A History of English Freemasonry,* Wellingborough, 1986

Hamill, John and Gilbert, Robert: *Freemasonry: A Celebration of the Craft,* Angus Books, London, 2004

Hamill, John and Gilbert, Robert: *World Freemasonry, An Illustrated History,* London, 1991

Hampson, Norman: *The Enlightenment,* Penguin, 1990

Hancock, Graham and Bauval, Robert: *Talisman: Sacred Cities, Secret Faith*, Michael Joseph, London, 2004

Harding, Nick: *Secret Societies* Pocket Essentials, 2005

Haydock, David Boyd: *William Stukeley: science, religion and archaeology in eighteenth-century England*, 2002

Hibbert, Christopher, *London: The Biography of a City*, Longmans, 1969

Hieronimus, Robert R, *America's Secret Destiny: Spiritual Vision and the Founding of a Nation* Destiny Books, 1989

Hislop, Malcolm: *Medieval Masons*, Shire Publications Limited, 2000

Holms, John Pynchon: *The American Presidents: from Washington to Clinton*, Pinnacle, 1996

Horne, Alex: *King Solomon's Temple in the Masonic Tradition*, The Aquarian Press, London, 1972

Horne, Alex: *Sources of Masonic Symbolism*, Macoy Publishing and Masonic Supply Co. Inc., New York, 1981

Hughes, Robert: *The Fatal Shore*, Pan, London, 1988

Hutchinson, Harold H: *Sir Christopher Wren — A Biography* Readers Union, 1976

Jacob, Margaret C: *Living the Enlightenment: Freemasonry and Politics in Eighteenth Century Europe*, Oxford University Press, 1991

James, Lawrence: *The Rise and Fall of the British Empire*, Abacus, 2001

Jenkins, Phillip: *A History of the United States*, Macmillan, London, 1997

Jenkins, Roy: *Truman*, Harper Collins,1987

Jones, Bernard E: *Freemasons' Guide and Compendium*, George C. Harrap and Company Limited, London, 1952

Jones, Bernard E: *Freemason's Book of the Royal Arch*, Harrap, London, 1975

Kennedy, Roger. G (ed.): *The Smithsonian Guide To Historic America: The Rocky Mountain States*, Stewart, Tabori & Chang, New York, 1989

Kinzer, Stephen: *Overthrow: America's century of Regime Change from Hawaii to Iraq*, University of Hawaii Press, 2006

Knoop, Douglas & Jones. G.P: *The Genesis of Freemasonry*: London, 1947 (Reprinted 1978)

Knoop, Douglas & Jones, G.P: *The Medieval Mason*, Third revised edition, Manchester, 1967

Krakow, Kenneth: *Georgia Place Names*, Winship Press, 1994.

Landay, Jerry M: *The House of David*: Weidenfeld and Nicholson, London, 1973

Lane, John: *Masonic Records 1717–1894*, London 1895

Lawrence, Rev. J.T: *The Perfect Ashlar and Other Masonic Symbols*, A. Lewis Limited, London, 1937

Lawrence, Rev. J.T: *The Keystone and other Essays on Freemasonry*, A Lewis (Masonic Publishers) Limited, London, 1947

Lawrence, Shirley Blackwell: *The Secret Science of Numerology — The Hidden Meaning of Numbers and Letters*, The Career Press, Franklin Lakes, New Jersey, 2001

Lewis, A: *The Perfect Ceremonies of Craft Masonry*, A. Lewis, London, 1926

Lillywhite, Bryant: *London Coffee Houses*, London, 1963

Lincoln, Henry, *Key to the Sacred Pattern*, Windrush, 1997

Linklater, Andro: *Measuring America*, Harper Collins, 2003

Lomas, Robert: *The Invisible College: The Royal Society, Freemasonry and the Birth of Modern Science*, Headline Book Publishing, London, 2002

Lomas, Robert: *Turning the Hiram Key*, Lewis Masonic, 2005

March, the Earl of: *A Duke and his Friends: The Life and Letters of the Second Duke of Richmond*, London, Hutchinson, 1911

Martin, Sean: *The Knights Templar*, Pocket Essentials, 2004

McCullough, David: *John Adams*, Simon and Schuster, 2001

McLynn, Frank: *1759: The Year Britain Became Master of the World* Book Club Associates 2004

McNulty, W. Kirk: *Freemasonry: A Journey through Ritual and Symbol*, London, 1991

McPherson, James M (ed.): *The American Presidents*, DK Publishing, Inc. 2004

Meinig, D.W: *The Shaping of America: A Geographical Perspective on 500 Years of History, Volume 2: Continental America, 1800–1867* New Haven, Yale University Press, 1993

Middleton, Richard: *Colonial America, A History, 1607–1760*, Blackwell, 1992

Minot, George (ed.): *Public Laws of the United States of America, Passed at the First Session of the Thirty-third Congress, 1853–1854* Little, Brown & Co., Boston, 1854–1855

Mitchener, James A: *Texas*, Corgi, 1992

Morgan, William: *Illustrations of Masonry*, New York, 1827 (C.T.Powner, 1986)

Morison *John Paul Jones*, Naval Institute Press, 1999

Mumford, Lewis: *The City in History*, Penguin, 1966

Murray, Peter: *The Architecture of the Italian Renaissance*, Thames and Hudson, 1996

Naske, Claus M & Herman E Slotnick: *Alaska: A History of the 49th State*, University of Oklahoma Press, Norman, Oklahoma, 2003

National Geographic Society: *Atlas of the World* (Sixth Edition), National Geographic Society, 1996

Nash, Roderick: *Wilderness and the American Mind*, Yale University Press, 1982

Noordlander, David J: *For God and Tsar: A Brief History of Russian America, 1741–1867*, Alaska Natural History Association, Anchorage, Alaska, 1994

North, Douglass C: *The Economic Growth of the United States, 1790–1860* W.W. Norton & Company Inc., New York, 1966

Oglethorpe, James Edward: *New and Accurate Account of the Provinces of South Carolina and Georgia*, London, 1733

Oken, Alan: *Numerology Demystified*, The Crossing Press, 1996

Ovason, David: *The Secret Zodiacs of Washington D.C.*, Arrow, London, 2000

Palmer Hall, Manly: *The Secret Destiny of America* Penguin 2008

Parry, Dick: *Engineering the Pyramids*, Sutton Publishing, 2004

Partner, Peter: *The Murdered Magicians, The Templars and their Myth*, Oxford, 1982

Peltzer, J. and Peltzer, L.: 'The Coffee Houses of Augustan London' in *History Today*, October, 1982

Pennick, Nigel: *Sacred Geometry Symbolism and Purpose in Religious Structures*, Capall Bann Publishing, 1994

Piggott, Stuart: *William Stukeley: An Eighteenth Century Antiquary*, Clarendon Press, 1950

Plumb, J H: *Sir Robert Walpole — The Making of a Statesman*, London: The Cresset Press, 1956

Plumb, J H: *Sir Robert Walpole — The King's Minister*, London, The Cresset Press, 1956

Pomeroy, Earl: *The Pacific Slope: A History of California, Oregon, Washington, Idaho, Utah and Nevada*, University of Washington Press, 1973

Porter, Roy: *Enlightenment, Britain and the Creation of the modern World*, Penguin, 2002

Pritchard, Samuel: *Masonry Dissected*, Poemandres Press, Boston and New York, 1996

Rau, Weldon Willis: *Surviving the Oregon Trail, 1852: As Told by Mary Ann and Willis Boatman and Augmented with Accounts by other Overland Travellers*, Washington State University Press, 2001

Read, Piers Paul: *The Templars*, Phoenix Press, 2001

Reddaway, Thomas Fiddian: *The Rebuilding of London after the Great Fire*, London, 1940

Reese, Trevor R (ed.): *Our First Visit in America: Early Reports from the Colony of Georgia, 1732–1740*, Beehive Press, Savannah, 1974

Ricks, Christopher and Vance, William L, (eds.) *The Faber Book of America*, Faber and Faber, London and Boston, 1992

Roberts, Allen E., *George Washington, Master Mason*, McCoy Publishing and Masonic Supply Co. Inc., 1976

Roberts, Allen E: *House Undivided: The Story of Freemasonry and the Civil War*, Missouri Lodge of Research, 1961

Rollins, Phillip Ashton (ed): *The Discovery of the Oregon Trail: Robert Stuart's Narratives of His Overland Trip Eastward from Astoria in 1812–13*, University of Nebraska, 1995

Russ, William Adam: *The Hawaiian Revolution, (1893–94)*, Associated University Presses, 1992

Saussure, Cesar de: *A Foreign View of England in the Reigns of George I and George II. The Letters of Monsieur Cesar de Saussure to his Family*. Translated and Edited by Madame van Myden, London, 1902

Schwartz, Stephan A., *Dr. Franklin's Plan*, Smithsonian, June 2001

Shearer, B.F and Shearer, B.S: *State Names, Seals, Flags and Symbols*, Greenwood Press Westport, Connecticut, 2001

Short, Martin: *Inside the Brotherhood*, Grafton 1990

Sitwell, Sacheverell: *British Architects and Craftsmen*, Pan Books Limited, London, 1960

Smith, T. Roger (ed.): *An Illustrated History of Architectural Styles*, Omega Books Limited, London, 1987

Sobel, Dava: *Longitude*, Fourth Estate, 1998

Steblecki, Edith J: *Paul Revere and Freemasonry*, Paul Revere Memorial Association, Boston, 1985

Stevenson, David: *The Origins of Freemasonry*: Cambridge University Press, 2004

Stoker, Bram: *The Jewel of Seven Stars*, Oxford University Press, 1996

Stokes, Anthony: *A View of the Constitution of the British Colonies in North-America and the West Indies*, London, 1783

Tailfer, Patrick, Hugh Anderson, David Douglass (and Others): *A True and Historical Narrative of the Colony of Georgia*, Charleston and London, 1740

Taylor, Alan: *American Colonies: The Settlement of North America to 1800*, The Penguin Press, 2002

Thomas, Emory M: *The Confederate Nation: 1861–1865*, Harper & Row, 1979

Thornton, P.: *Seventeenth Century Interior Decoration in England, France and Holland*, London, Yale University Press, 1981

Timbs, John: *Clubs and Club Life in London*, London, Chatto and Windus, 1908

Trevelyan, G.M, *English Social History*, Longmans, 1948

The Concise Oxford Dictionary, Oxford University Press, Eighth Edition, 1991

Waller, Maureen: *1700: Scenes from London Life*, Hodder and Stoughton, London, 2000

Ward, J.S.M: *An Interpretation of Our Masonic Symbols*, London, 1956

Ward, J.S.M: *The Higher Degrees Handbook* Kessinger Publishing, 2010

Ward, J.S.M: *The EA's Handbook*, The Warrington Publishing Co., London, 1923

Ward, J.S.M: *The FC's Handbook*, A. Lewis (Masonic Publishers) Limited, London, 1974

Weinberger, Jerry (ed.) *New Atlantis and the great Instauration: Bacon* H.Davidson, 1989

White, Michael: *Isaac Newton: The Last Sorcerer* Basic Books, 1999

Wilford, John Noble: *The Mapmakers*, Pimlico, 2002

INDEX